THE ROUGH GUIDE TO
Jimi Hendrix

11/2009

by
Richie Unterberger

ROUGH
GUIDES

www.roughguides.com

Credits

The Rough Guide to Jimi Hendrix

Text editing: Neil Foxlee
Picture editing/layout/index: Tom Cabot/ketchup
Proofreading: Jason Freeman
Production: Rebecca Short

Rough Guides Reference

Director: Andrew Lockett
Editors: Kate Berens, Peter Buckley, Tracy Hopkins, Matthew Milton, Joe Staines, Ruth Tidball

Picture Credits

Corbis 29, 53 (Hulton-Deutsch Collection), 56, 63 (Henry Diltz), 105 (Douglas Kent Hall/ZUMA), 110 (Bettmann), 127 (Scott T. Smith); **Getty Images** 58, 86, 94, 101, 111, 120, 130 (Bob Peterson), 131, 182, 189, 204, 217; **Mirrorpix** 65, 71, 125; **Redferns** 15, 23, 31 (K&K ULF KRUGER OHG), 41, 43 (Chris Morphet), 47 (K&K ULF KRUGER OHG), 50 (Ron Howard), 61 (GAB Archives), 72 (Elliott Landy), 75 (Robert Knight), 77 (Gilles Petard Collection), 83 (GAB Archives), 84 (Petra Niemeier), 90 (Ron Howard), 92 (David Redfern), 97 (Robert Knight), 106 (Elliott Landy), 114 (Robert Knight), 213 (Alain Dister), 214 (Bob Baker), 229 (David Redfern), 235 (Cummings Archives); **Seattle Public Schools** 3, 7; **Seattle Times/Mark Harrison** 8

Publishing Information

This first edition published June 2009 by
Rough Guides Ltd, 80 Strand, London WC2R 0RL
375 Hudson Street, New York 10014, USA
Email: mail@roughguides.com

Distributed by the Penguin Group:
Penguin Books Ltd, 80 Strand, London WC2R 0RL
Penguin Putnam, Inc., 375 Hudson Street, New York 10014, USA
Penguin Group (Australia), 250 Camberwell Road, Camberwell, Victoria 3124, Australia
Penguin Books Canada Ltd, 90 Eglinton Avenue East, Suite 700, Toronto, Ontario M4P 2Y3, Canada
Penguin Group (New Zealand), Cnr Rosedale and Airborne Roads, Albany, Auckland, New Zealand

Printed in Singapore by SNP Security Printing Pte Ltd

A catalogue record for this book is available from the British Library

ISBN 13: 978-1-84836-002-0
ISBN 10: 1-84836-002-9

1 3 5 7 9 8 6 4 2

Contents

Contents

Introduction: A Life Experienced

When Jimi Hendrix died in 1970 at the age of 27, his career as a bandleader and featured solo artist had lasted just four years. He had released only four albums, one of them a live recording. Yet nearly forty years after his death, he remains one of the giants of rock. Universally recognized as its greatest guitar virtuoso, he continues to inspire musicians in fields as diverse as hard rock, post-punk, soul and jazz. There may be no other figure in rock music with such a short lifespan who has generated such wide and enduring fascination and admiration.

When he arrived in London from his native US in September 1966, Jimmy Hendrix – as he then spelled his name – was entirely unknown to the international rock audience, and indeed barely known on the New York club circuit he'd scuffled around for the previous couple of years. It's a measure of both how astonishingly quickly his skills developed, and how innovative his playing was, that by the end of the year he had already established himself as the premier guitarist on the intensely competitive British rock scene. It's also a measure of his universal appeal that within months, he was one of the hottest recording artists in the UK, and within a year, one of the biggest music stars in the world. His fame and influence would grow to huge proportions before his sudden death, just under four years after he had moved to London to begin his meteoric rise.

In many ways, Hendrix was very much a product and symbol of the psychedelic age. It was Jimi, more than any other musician, who took psychedelia to its extremes through the mind-bending fuzz tones, distortion and miscellaneous arsenal of effects unleashed by his guitar; the frankly trippy nature of many of his songs; his garish wardrobes and the flamboyant, often blatantly sexual nature of his onstage performances; and the sheer outrageous volume of his concerts. Combined with his enigmatic, whimsical manner of speech and his reputation for living the sex'n'drugs lifestyle to the hilt, he was and continues to be seen by many as the ultimate exponent of the hippie ethic – one determined, as he sang in one of his songs, to "wave [his] freak flag high" ("If Six Was Nine").

Yet in many ways Hendrix, more than many of his fellow psychedelic stars, transcended the age that made his music possible and which he helped to define. In the four decades since his death, his work is, if anything, even more popular than it was in his heyday, his annual album sales greater than in any year during his lifetime. Countless guitarists have tried – and, almost without exception, failed – to match the inventiveness of his playing and his pioneering use of amplification and sonic magicianship, even in an age in which technology makes such trickery far easier and more affordable than it was when Hendrix was alive. His influence has been most easily (and all too often unimpressively) audible on legions of subsequent hard rock and heavy metal acts. But it's also evident, if more subtly, in the work of many musicians inspired, largely or at least in part, by Hendrix's example to reach for sounds that haven't yet been created.

In part it's because Hendrix, though still too often remembered primarily for his flashy guitar pyrotechnics and stunning visual image, had more artistic depth and sensitivity than is often acknowledged. His instrumental virtuosity was such that his substantial gifts as a songwriter are sometimes overlooked, as is the sensitivity he often displayed alongside the blustering swagger of his more aggressive numbers. Though not as great a singer as a guitarist or songwriter (and one who almost bashfully deprecated his own singing), Jimi nonetheless cultivated a highly likeable, effective vocal style which superbly complemented his often cosmically playful, sometimes deeply personal lyrics. He was also a master of the studio, his

innovations as a multi-track recording artist being nearly as ground-breaking and widely influential as the ones he made as an instrumentalist and concert performer. Additionally he, more than any other African-American musician of his age, had crossover appeal to a white rock audience without compromising his ethnic heritage in the least, helping lay a path that would be explored, both soon after his emergence and in subsequent decades, by legends like Sly and the Family Stone, Stevie Wonder and Prince.

It's also often not fully appreciated how, for all his futuristic endeavours, Hendrix's music was usually very much both grounded in earlier forms of black music and influenced by his contemporaries. Even his onstage showmanship was in many respects a direct offshoot of gimmicks perfected by earlier R&B performers, some of whom he'd actually backed in the shadowy years before his rise to fame, although few fans were aware of that background at the time. For all the astral planes navigated by some of his most famous songs, his work was very often based in the blues and soul on which he'd cut his teeth as a player, even if it sometimes took an almost unrecognizably avant-garde form. At a time when many African-American musicians were largely uninfluenced by happenings in the white rock world, on the other hand, he was unashamed of drawing inspiration from Bob Dylan, The Beatles, and British rock guitarists like Jeff Beck, Eric Clapton and Pete Townshend, who were generating cultural and musical earthquakes of their own. Hendrix's genius was to synthesize all these influences – black and white, old and new, rock, soul, blues and even some jazz – into something wholly new, the most crucial common ingredient being his phenomenal abilities as a guitarist.

There is a final, less glamorous element that cannot be discounted in explaining the public's enduring fascination with Jimi Hendrix. This is the drama of his sordid death at the peak of his powers, as well as the mysteries surrounding the impossibly tangled controversies that swirled around his personal and business affairs. Bob Marley apart, there's probably no other twentieth-century musician whose estate has been so hotly and publicly contested, in ugly struggles which, sadly, continue unabated to this day. In this sense, Jimi Hendrix is very much alive, if only as a financial asset to be endlessly fought over and exploited by family, business associates and lawyers.

Even among those who have no financial stake in the matter, there are passionate and occasionally bilious arguments over how his considerable recorded catalogue should be packaged; how his life should be honoured, documented, and commemorated; how true

he was to his African-American heritage; and what trajectories his life and music would have taken had his life not been cut so tragically short. Even sadder, it was precisely these kind of conflicts – over preserving his art versus exploiting his reputation, and pleasing one faction of his fans at the expense of alienating others – that led to the kind of personal stress and confusion that may well have indirectly caused his death in the first place.

No matter what their stance, one thing that everyone can agree on is that Jimi Hendrix didn't have enough time to fully explore his prodigious musical gifts. Fortunately, he *did* have enough time to record a great deal of music between 1966 and 1970 – far more, in fact, than the four official albums that came out during his lifetime. Even much of that music has been subject to post-production carried out without his approval, and legal wrangling that's led to numerous sub-par compilations. A lot, though, remains readily available and untarnished by posthumous overdubs. It is the best of this music, more than any other aspect of Jimi Hendrix, which is responsible for the timelessness of his work. And it is this music that this book aims to celebrate.

Acknowledgements

The author would like to thank Andrew Lockett of Rough Guides for initiating this book project; Neil Foxlee for his work as editor of the text; Ruth Tidball and Matthew Milton of Rough Guides for their feedback on the manuscript; and Robert Shepard, agent and friend. Also thanks to all of the following for their help in research and generosity in helping me to acquire Jimi Hendrix recordings and video footage: Sujata Murthy of Universal Music Enterprises; John Hagelston of Rhino Entertainment; Jon Arnold; Don Rogers; Stuart Kremsky; Pat Thomas; Diane Wallis; Jonathan Hess; Jack Thompson; and Charlie Milgrim.

About the Author

Rock historian Richie Unterberger's books include *Unknown Legends of Rock'n'Roll*; *The Unreleased Beatles: Music and Film*; *The Rough Guide to Music USA*; and a two-part history of 1960s folk-rock, *Turn! Turn! Turn!/Eight Miles High*. He is a contributor to the All Music Guide, *MOJO* and *Record Collector*. He lives in San Francisco.

Part 1:
The Story

The Early Years
1942–1961

"I remember saying to him, son, you really aren't interested in this class. Why don't you just leave this place called Garfield High School, get your guitar, and just make music? It's something that you thoroughly enjoy."

Ralph Hayes, Jimi Hendrix's high-school history teacher, from an interview with Mary Willix in *Jimi Hendrix: Voices from Home*

The Early Years
1942–1961

In some ways, Hendrix's upbringing was as mundane as his adulthood would be extraordinary. Born far away from the cities of New York and London where he would make his home as a superstar, there were few indications of his artistic brilliance. Indeed, there were few hints that he was destined for anything other than struggling to make the most of the very limited opportunities available to African-Americans of modest means and education in the mid-twentieth century. With hindsight, however, it is evident that his childhood and adolescence brought exposure to key influences that would inform his eclectic music, as well as helping to set the pattern for the nomadic and insecure existence that he would lead even after becoming rich and famous.

Family Roots

Like many African-Americans, Hendrix came from mixed blood. His paternal grandfather was born to a black slave and a white slave-owner, while his paternal grandmother was the granddaughter of a full-blooded Cherokee. Hendrix himself would seemingly acknowledge his Native American ancestry by giving the title "Cherokee Mist" to a haunting instrumental recorded shortly before his death. He would also sometimes make onstage dedications of one of the songs on his debut album, "I Don't Live Today", to the plight of the American Indian, far from a common lyrical subject in pop music then or now.

Jimi's father, James Allen Hendrix, better known as **Al Hendrix**, was born in 1919 in Vancouver, Canada. In the early 1940s, Al moved to Seattle, a few hours' drive away, where he met **Lucille Jeter**, who had been born there in 1925. After a brief courtship, the pair married – an event necessitated, according to the morals of the day, by Lucille's pregnancy. Al and Lucille barely had time to tie the knot, however, before he was drafted, joining the army just three days after their wedding on 31 March 1942. The US had just entered World War II, and like many other young couples of the time, they hardly knew each other when Al left to serve – and would barely have time to know each other better in the next few years, as Al, like millions of other soldiers, would be stationed far away from his home town for longer than anyone anticipated. Their son was born **Johnny Allen Hendrix** in Seattle on 27 November 1942, while Al was stationed at Camp Rucker in Alabama.

Lucille, who was still a teenager, was ill-equipped to raise a small child on her own. Compounding the uneasy situation, apparently, was a wandering eye which led her to take up with other men in Al's prolonged, indefinite absence. The result was that Johnny (or Buster, as he was nicknamed early on) was passed around to relatives and other foster parents of sorts during the first three years of his life. By the time Al was discharged in September 1945, Johnny had ended up living in Berkeley, California, with a Mrs Champ. Although she apparently intended to adopt Johnny and raise him as one of her own family, Al decided to travel to Berkeley, reclaim the small boy as his own son, and return with him to Seattle.

It's tempting to speculate what would have become of young Johnny Hendrix if Al had let events take their course and allowed his son to be adopted. Quite possibly, the boy would have grown up in a far more secure, loving and stable environment than he did. Perhaps some of the tensions, uncertainty, and burning desire to prove himself that would fuel his music would have been absent, and Johnny Hendrix would have led a far more ordinary and, in some respects, far happier life. Al Hendrix,

however, had other plans, resettling with the boy in Seattle and giving him a new name – **James Marshall Hendrix.**

As much as Al was committed to claiming Jimmy (as he was known then, although this book will refer to him as Jimi from this point on) as his own, he was far from being a reliable father. In part this was due to the uncertain state of his marriage when he returned to Seattle. He had almost finalized a divorce from Lucille when the couple decided to give their relationship another chance, but he soon went off to work as a merchant seaman. The couple's fighting meant that Jimi was once again farmed out to various relatives from time to time, while Lucille complicated the situation still further by taking up with other men and giving birth to two more boys, Leon and Joey. According to some sources, they were not full brothers but half-brothers, fathered outside the marriage. Al would later deny that he was the blood father of any of Lucille's other children (who also included two girls and another boy), and in 1955, the pair gave up their parental rights to all but Jimi and Leon in court.

When Al finally divorced Lucille, it was with the intention of raising Jimi and Leon on his own, but he found steady and lucrative employment elusive, working mostly as a gardener. Jimi still stayed with other families sometimes, and Leon was eventually placed in a foster home. Al's problems with drinking, gambling and keeping up with his conventional parental responsibilities almost caused him to lose Jimi as well on a few occasions. Jimi was even briefly sent back to Vancouver to live with

Jimi (third from left, second row from front) with his classmates from Leschi Elementary School (image courtesy of Seattle Public Schools, 244-089)

his grandmother when he began his term as a first-grade elementary school student.

Although Al Hendrix is far from being the most controversial figure in Jimi's life, doubts have been raised as to how good a father he was for any of his children, let alone for a young, sensitive and artistic boy such as Jimi growing up in post-war America. Some biographers have portrayed him as a rather gruff,

callous and penny-pinching man who didn't give Jimi much emotional or material support during a difficult adolescence. Others intimate that he never fully appreciated his son's artistic gifts, reacting to his success many years later with befuddlement as well as belated pride. Some also feel that he made an inappropriate heir to (or at least an inadequate manager of) his son's considerable estate, considering that

The Story

Jimi Hendrix Landmarks in Seattle

Although he was born and for the most part raised in Seattle, Hendrix seemed to have relatively little affection for his home town, considering that he didn't return for many years after joining the army, and only passed through briefly on a few occasions after he became famous. Some locals have claimed that his formative years in the city were a substantial influence on his subsequent achievements. In truth, however, the key elements of his musical vision were conceived elsewhere, whether grinding it out on the "chitlin' circuit" of black-oriented venues in the South in the early to mid-1960s, ascending to front man after moving to Greenwich Village, or finally developing into a star recording artist and concert attraction after moving to London. Seattle for Hendrix was not a home town to return to as much as it was somewhere to escape from.

Still, Hendrix *is* arguably Seattle's most famous son, and since his death, the city has tried to honour him in various ways. Sadly, the oft-faltering attempts to do so have often not so much signalled a rapprochement between Hendrix and Seattle as seemed like a continuation of their uneasy relationship.

For many years, you had to be quite dedicated or clued-up to find the only Hendrix memorials of sorts in Seattle. One was a large **black-and-white mural** above a downtown shop (on 1208 1st Avenue) where one of his first guitars was purchased. Another was the life-sized, unlabelled **statue** of Hendrix, caught in his famous kneeling-to-burn-the-guitar-at-Monterey pose. It was erected across the street from the Seattle Central Community College on Broadway near Pine, on the sidewalk in front of the **AEI Music Building** – not exactly a tourist hotspot, despite being a convenient enough stroll

1208 1st Avenue, Seattle – muralist Dan Hitchcock at work (*Seattle Times*/Mark Harrison)

from the lively and youthful/artsy Capitol Hill district. In 2006, the statue was offered to the city for a proposed **Jimi Hendrix Park** in the Central district (at 2400 S. Massachusetts Street), just over a mile from where Jimi went to **Garfield High School** at 400 23rd Avenue. A bronze bust is on display in the school's library, and there's also a mural with different images of Hendrix, his failure to graduate notwithstanding.

Not so much obscure as ill-conceived is the small **plaque** in the African Savannah exhibit at the Woodland Park Zoo. Shaped like a gold, bursting sun, and perched on top of a rock overlooking the field where giraffes and other African creatures run free, the inscription reads: "This viewpoint was funded by worldwide donations to KZOK Radio in the memory of Jimi Hendrix and his music." Considering how tiny and inconspicuous the memorial is – if a bird lands on it, you'll miss it entirely – you could be forgiven for wondering whether the donations amounted to much or what they were spent on. The original, more appropriate idea had been for a statue of Hendrix to be erected in one of Seattle's parks, which apparently met with opposition from civic organizations when the fund-raising drive took place in the early 1980s.

In 2000, the **Experience Music Project**, largely funded by billionaire Microsoft co-founder and huge Hendrix/rock fan Paul Allen, opened near Seattle's Space Needle. Originally it was intended as a Jimi Hendrix Museum, but it changed its focus to rock and pop music in general after Allen and the Hendrix estate fell out. The EMP collection still has a lot of interesting Hendrix memorabilia, although what you see will depend on what's being exhibited when you visit. At the time of writing, an exhibition titled **"Jimi Hendrix: An Evolution of Sound"**, centring on "Hendrix's guitar sound and its continued resonance with music listeners", will be running until 11 April 2010. The EMP has had some financial problems, however, and mystified some observers with its decision to convert some of its space into a Science Fiction Museum and Hall of Fame, although at least it's cut its admission fee to $15 ($12 for children and seniors).

Hendrix's grave can be found in **Greenwood Memorial Cemetery** at 350 Monroe Avenue NE in Renton, a suburb about fifteen miles south of downtown Seattle. In contrast to the high-profile markers and stream of visitors common to many celebrity graves, visiting Hendrix's place of rest was for many years a surprisingly simple, even mundane experience. Marked by a flat marble stone inscribed with a guitar and Hendrix's name, visitors were sparse enough that they often had to ask cemetery staff for directions (though now, according to *jimihendrixmemorial.com*, more than 14,000 visitors come every year). And although, as even many casual Hendrix fans know, Jimi played the guitar left-handed, the instrument on the grave clearly belongs to a right-handed player.

In 1999, however, plans were announced for a far more elaborate **Jimi Hendrix Memorial** to include 54 family plots and a large brass statue. To date, however, it remains incomplete, although work has been done on granite pillars and a dome, and Jimi's original gravestone is incorporated into its granite base. If its construction continues to languish, it will be entirely too typical of the mostly half-baked projects intended to immortalize Hendrix's legacy in the Seattle area.

they were hardly close during the last decade of Jimi's life. Certainly the relationship seemed distant even before the 1960s, with Al leaving Jimi pretty much to fend for himself in many respects.

Still, in some ways Al Hendrix was doing the best he could for his sons with what limited assets he had. Al's struggles to make ends meet, however, did often leave Jimi to his own devices, and few options other than to create his own entertainment. Against this background, it's unsurprising that he not only drifted toward music, like so many other millions of teenagers in the rock'n'roll explosion of the mid-1950s, but also became determined to make some of his own.

First Guitars and Rock Groups

As he entered his teens, Jimi had already begun to develop an enthusiasm for blues artists such as Muddy Waters, B.B. King, Howlin' Wolf and Lightnin' Hopkins after listening to some singles of his father's and a boarder at the Hendrix home, Ernestine Benson. In the absence of spare cash to buy a guitar, however, the best he could do was pretend to play along with a broom; a one-string ukulele his father found while cleaning out the garage made for hardly any better a substitute. His first "real" instrument, bought when he was fifteen years old, wasn't much of an improvement either, being a used $5 acoustic guitar with one string. Money was so short that when Elvis Presley came to Seattle for a concert at Sicks's Stadium in 1957, Jimi couldn't afford the $1.50 ticket to get in, watching from a nearby hill instead. Perhaps precisely because of his dire material circumstances, however, Jimi clung to his guitar, carrying it around with him everywhere and even sleeping with it – a habit he would keep until his death, when his guitars were the fanciest in the world.

In his ninth grade at school, Jimi finally managed to get hold of some strings and began to play his guitar properly. Although the death of his mother Lucille in early 1958 made an already shy boy even more introverted, Jimi continued to bang away at his instrument, to the increasing neglect of his already indifferent schoolwork. By 1959, his father, finally sensing which way the wind was blowing, bought his son an electric guitar on hire purchase, although Jimi still didn't have an amplifier. He would plug into other musicians' amps when he could, with the goal of somehow forming a band.

Like most models, the electric guitar was designed for right-handers, but Hendrix was naturally left-handed, so in order to play it, he had to restring the instrument and play it upside down from its natural position. From one viewpoint, Jimi was already having enough problems without needing to cope with another inconvenience which might have discouraged many budding guitarists from going any further. It's often been wondered, however, whether this apparent handicap might not ultimately have worked to his advantage, forcing him to work harder at

The Real Spanish Castle Magic

Such is the spaced-out, or at least spacey, nature of many of Hendrix's songs that it's often assumed that many of them were written under the influence of drugs, or at least with matters far more celestial than earthly in mind. It often turns out, however, that many of those songs were grounded in very basic real-life experiences, albeit ones that very few people outside of his closest acquaintances would have known about at the time they were recorded.

The Spanish Castle, c. 1960

Hendrix made his most specific reference to his Seattle boyhood in **Spanish Castle Magic**, a highlight of The Jimi Hendrix Experience's second album, *Axis: Bold as Love*. The subject of this tune wasn't some imaginary castle in Spain – as he made clear in one of its very first lines – or some mystical vision conjured by an acid trip. Instead, it was "a really groovy place" of the same name about twenty miles south of Seattle. Actually designed to look like a Spanish castle, the venue hosted many of the Northwest's biggest rock'n'roll shows for years after opening on Thanksgiving Day in 1959.

It's sometimes reported, or at least assumed, that Hendrix must often have played with and grooved to bands at the Spanish Castle if he was inspired to commemorate it in song. Seattle radio DJ Pat O'Day, who booked many shows at the venue, would later say that Jimi came down to shows with his guitar and amplifier at the ready, in the hope that he could fill in should something go wrong with the onstage act's equipment. However, there's probably some poetic licence here, as Hendrix didn't have a car, much money or even a very good amp, and transporting it back and forth on a regular basis was probably beyond his means.

The Spanish Castle *did* host many big names while, and after, Hendrix was in Seattle, including not just major Northwestern groups like The Wailers and The Ventures, but also national stars like Conway Twitty, Jerry Lee Lewis and Roy Orbison. It closed, however, in 1964 after some major accidents on Highway 99 right outside the club. Eventually the place that remained a paradise in Jimi's memory was turned into a parking lot.

mastering his instrument than most novices and leaving him more open to unconventional ways of doing things right from the start. Guitar lessons were certainly out of the question, and Jimi ended up teaching himself how to play by listening to records and the radio, as well as picking up hints here and there from other more experienced guitarists. One advantage he did have, however, was huge hands, which would enable him to pull off riffs and fingerings that many other players would have found far more difficult.

The Story

In some ways, the Seattle of the late 1950s might seem like one of the least promising American cities for a future rock legend to grow up in. A far less cosmopolitan metropolis then than it is today, it also had a fairly small African-American population, and was quite isolated from the major US media and recording centres, even on the West Coast. Yet it was a more promising breeding-ground than it might appear on first glance. It had a small but very active, black-dominated jazz and R&B scene in which two other major musicians, **Ray Charles** and **Quincy Jones**, had launched their early careers in the late 1940s. **Garfield High School,** where Hendrix was a nominal student (and which Jones himself had attended), was remarkably integrated by late-1950s standards, its student body being fifty percent white, thirty percent black, and twenty percent Asian. Although Jimi's ease at moving in the white musical and social worlds has generated some isolated but vociferous criticism for his supposed failure to be as true to his black roots as he should have been, his early exposure to a multiracial environment may well have opened him up to a variety of musical influences, regardless of colour.

Remote as they were from the major American recording studios, Seattle and the whole of the Pacific Northwest were also home to a host of young rock'n'roll bands. Even when they were white, these often played in a raunchy, heavily R&B-influenced style, often including or even favouring instrumentals. Some of these bands got to make records, and once in a blue moon, gained national as well as regional airplay. One such record, **The Wailers'** 1959 top-forty instrumental hit "Tall Cool One", was the first song Hendrix learned to play from beginning to end. Material such as this was heavily featured in Jimi's first real band, **The Velvetones,** who also played instrumentals by the likes of **Duane Eddy** – one of the first true American rock'n'roll guitar heroes, noted for his low, echoing twang – and **Bill Doggett,** who had scored one of the biggest hits of the 1950s with the sensuous-yet-gritty shuffle "Honky Tonk".

Leaving School and Joining the Army

As much as finally launching a musical career of sorts did to lift Jimi's spirits, he was still hounded by family and school problems. Although his subsequent lyrics and interviews revealed him to be a highly (if quirkily) intelligent man, his lack of interest in his studies meant that he was on the verge of being thrown out of Garfield. Of more immediate concern were continuing tensions with his father, who refused to pay for a new guitar after Jimi lost his backstage at one of his early gigs. The level of his skill was already such, however, that several members of another high-school band with whom he'd started to play, **The Rocking Kings,** rallied round to buy Jimi a $49.95 Danelectro Silvertone so that he could continue playing with their group.

Hendrix's grades, however, fell from borderline to abysmal. Having already been forced to

Lucille Hendrix: Gypsy Eyes

Al Hendrix was far from a model father, but **Lucille Hendrix** was even less of a model mother to Jimi and her other children. In part, this is understandable, given that she had been thrust into a situation for which she was wholly unprepared, after becoming pregnant by a man she hardly knew at the age of sixteen. However, she didn't prove a stable parent when more children followed and she grew into adulthood. Not only did she have flings outside the marriage, but she also apparently continued to be more preoccupied with going out and having fun sometimes than with making sure her children were properly looked after. Lucille's heavy drinking led to cirrhosis of the liver by her early thirties, and shortly after marrying again, she died under mysterious circumstances after being found unconscious in an alley by a tavern.

According to some accounts, Al did not allow Jimi to attend her funeral.

Hendrix nonetheless seems to have had happy memories of the sporadic good times he had shared with his mother, and several of his songs are believed to have been inspired by her. Not all of these idolized Lucille: **Castles Made of Sand**, in addition to alluding to fights between her and Al, also depicts both her sadness and an illness in her final months that put her in a wheelchair for a time. The posthumously released **Angel**, however, has been interpreted as expressing hope for a reunion between mother and son in the afterlife. **Gypsy Eyes** is also thought to be about Lucille, reflecting the free-spirited ways that she might have passed on to her son, who would die even younger than she had.

repeat the ninth grade owing to his poor performance, he finally flunked out of Garfield High in October 1960. Later, when Hendrix played his first show in Seattle as a star in February 1968, the school was happy to claim Jimi as one of its own, inviting him to speak at an assembly held in his honour. At the time, however, the future looked pretty bleak for an eighteen-year-old African-American with no qualifications or marketable skills other than his guitar-playing. He continued to gig with The Rocking Kings at progressively more impressive venues in and around Seattle, most notably **The Spanish Castle** in nearby Kent (see box on page 11). Already Hendrix was getting noticed for his uninhibited style of playing and an onstage showmanship quite at odds with his habitually reserved offstage manner, although his in-concert exhibitionism would sometimes make it difficult to fit into bands who valued team players above individualistic expression.

The Rocking Kings changed their name to **Thomas and the Tomcats** after manager James Thomas took on the lead vocal duties, but any road to greater success looked bumpy at best. Jimi had to help his father with gardening to support himself and he was still using equipment that wasn't up to the standard he needed to make his way as a professional musician. On top of that, relations between Jimi and his father were sufficiently strained to make it unlikely that they could continue living under the same roof for much longer.

As it turned out, it wouldn't be long before Jimi left Seattle altogether. Matters came to a head in May 1961, when he was arrested on two separate occasions for riding in a stolen car. According to one of the most recent and thorough Hendrix biographies, Charles R. Cross's *Room Full of Mirrors*, a juvenile court gave Jimi a two-year suspended sentence on the condition that he joined the army, and the very next day he enlisted for a three-year stint in the military, hoping to join the 101st Airborne Division. Hendrix himself would later claim that he figured he was going to get drafted soon anyway, and thought he might as well get his commitment out of the way as soon as possible. In fact, he had already tried to join the air force and been turned down, and although music was his true calling, there certainly seemed little reason to stay in Seattle, where work and money for what he really wanted to do were scarce.

On 29 May 1961, the day after his final show with the Tomcats, Jimi took a train to Fort Ord, California, to begin his basic training. With the exception of a week's leave in September, it would be almost seven years before he returned to Seattle.

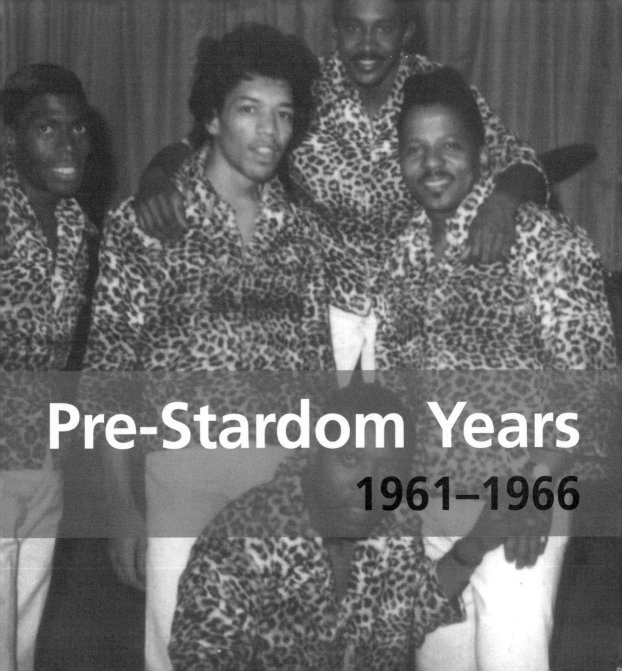

Pre-Stardom Years

1961–1966

"I can't tell you the sounds he was getting out of his instrument ... I didn't want to pick up a guitar for the next year."

Mike Bloomfield, on seeing Jimi Hendrix in mid-1966

Pre-Stardom Years 1961–1966

When Jimi Hendrix exploded onto the British rock scene at the end of 1966 and then in the US around mid-1967, such was the exotic brilliance of his music and image that it must have seemed to many as if he had arrived from an entirely different planet. In fact, however, his journey to stardom was far from an overnight success, while the otherworldly sounds he created had a down-to-earth origin. They were the product of a good five years or so of struggle at perfecting his craft, under circumstances that were often so murky that they may never be properly documented.

Army Days

The first, arduous steps in Hendrix's transition from Seattle high-school dropout a whisker away from being sent to prison to a full-time professional musician were taken when he went for basic training at Fort Ord, California, after enlisting in the army. Even in the late 1960s, it seemed inconceivable that such a free spirit as Hendrix could have ever been in the US military, especially when songs like "Machine Gun" and his interpretation of "The Star Spangled Banner" offered what some took as implicit criticism of US intervention in Vietnam. But then (as, unfortunately, now) many African-Americans joined the forces, not because they had a burning desire to serve their country, but because of the absence of any other meaningful opportunities as they reached adulthood. Hendrix was one such young man

and might have volunteered for service anyway, even if he possibly did so to evade a jail sentence.

The idea of floating down from the skies as a paratrooper may have also played a part in Hendrix's decision, but any romantic preconceptions he might have had were dashed by his eight weeks of basic training. Although he completed them without major incident, Hendrix proved less suited than the average young recruit for the spartan conditions and rigorous discipline of army life. In part this was because he was separated from the one thing that meant the most to him: not a girlfriend, his family or friends, but his guitar. Although he had left it with girlfriend Betty Jean Morgan for safekeeping, not two months had gone by before he wrote to his father asking him to send it.

The Story

Assigned to the **101st Airborne Division** in Fort Campbell, Kentucky, Hendrix did soon fulfil his goal of getting trained as a parachutist, in part because it qualified him for an extra $55 a month. Some later accounts even indicate that the sounds of the wind and aircraft that he heard on his jumps would inform his own wilder experiments with sound effects in his recordings and stage performances. Of far more immediate musical value, however, were the instruments and amplifiers available for his use at Fort Campbell's service club. It was there that he met bassist and fellow soldier **Billy Cox**, who would become an important member not only of his early groups, but also of the bands Hendrix would lead during the final year or so of his life.

By late 1961, Hendrix and Cox had formed a band with other soldiers, playing clubs on their base with shifting personnel as the opportunity arose. Although Jimi had seemed to take some pride in his uniform and accomplishments in the military early on in his stint, this soon withered as the band (now called either **The Kasuals** or **The King Kasuals**, according to various biographies) began to pick up more gigs, sometimes in Nashville and out-of-state army bases as far away as North Carolina. Cox had almost finished his service, but Hendrix, already counting the days until he could leave the army, was impatient to pursue a musical career. Having signed up for a three-year term, however, he was more than a couple of years away from fulfilling his obligations.

In spring 1962, Hendrix succeeded in obtaining a discharge, although the exact circumstances are difficult to determine with any certainty. Jimi himself would claim that he broke his ankle and injured his back on his twenty-sixth parachute jump. Drawing on evidence from army medical records, however, Charles R. Cross's biography *Room Full of Mirrors* concludes that he was in fact dismissed for feigning homosexual tendencies and psychological disorders. In *Hendrix: An Illustrated Experience*, on the other hand, stepsister Janie L. Hendrix and John McDermott contend that it's "clear the issues were based on Hendrix's abysmal performance as a soldier", quoting this statement from his official military records: "Private Hendrix plays a musical instrument in a band off duty and has let this interfere with his military duties in so much as missing bed check and not getting enough sleep. He has no interest whatsoever in the army."

That final sentence was certainly true enough by mid-1962, and whatever the sequence of events that led to his discharge, Hendrix was undoubtedly relieved to be out of the army and free to become a full-time musician. He still had a few months to wait until Billy Cox was able to join him, though, and he had to scuffle around to keep on his feet in the meantime – having blown much of his bonus for unused leave the day he got out, he didn't even have enough money to take a bus back to Seattle. At least he was accustomed to living from hand to mouth, having had to do much the same thing even when he was living with his family back home. But it did reinforce a pattern of instability in his finances and living arrangements that would remain for the next four years.

Early 1960s Bands

Over the next year or so, Hendrix and Cox led various bands that slowly built up a steadier work schedule, concentrating first on Clarksville, Tennessee, just across the state border where the pair had served in Kentucky. Among the musicians they played with was guitarist **Larry Lee**, who like Cox would unexpectedly resurface to play a part in Jimi's late-1960s projects. More work was available in Nashville, then as now known as the capital of country music, but also home to a substantial African-American population who wanted to hear blues, R&B and the mixture that was developing into soul music.

A two-month visit in late 1962 to stay with his grandmother in Vancouver (during which, tellingly, he did not call in to nearby Seattle to see his father) saw him playing rhythm guitar with local R&B band **Bobby Taylor and the Vancouvers**, doing a brief residency with them at a nightclub called Dante's Inferno. But then he went back to the South, a courageous decision in some ways for a black man in the early 1960s. Probably it was because there was not only more interesting work there, but also because Hendrix was far more likely to be able to see and learn from blues guitarists like fellow left-hander **Albert King** – whom he was bold enough to ask for string-bending and fingering tips – and **B.B. King** on the southern circuit than in the Northwest. Licks and technique weren't all he was digesting: he also observed and began incorporating some crowd-pleasing showboating into his own act, such as playing his guitar behind his back and with his teeth. While these tricks wowed white rock crowds when they first saw Hendrix in 1966 and 1967, in fact they had been used by other blues and R&B performers for quite some time, including legends like bluesman **T-Bone Walker** and seminal early rocker **Bo Diddley**. Less exotically, Jimi would also use a 75-foot cord so that he could play in the audience and roam as far offstage as the sidewalk outside.

Hendrix's appetite for both practising and performing was insatiable, reflecting his eagerness to make a name for himself beyond the local scene in Nashville or anywhere else. Since he wasn't a singer or front man, however, the only way to advance his prospects was to pick up jobs backing more established artists, as he began to do by 1963. The full list of stars he toured with temporarily, or at least played with while they passed through town, will never be known, so extensive are the references that have been tossed around in numerous interviews and bios. It's certainly an impressive roll call, though, almost amounting to a who's who of early-1960s soul and R&B, including Hank Ballard, Jerry Butler, Solomon Burke, **Sam Cooke**, Slim Harpo, Chuck Jackson, B.B. King, The Marvelettes, **Otis Redding**, Carla Thomas, Tommy Tucker, Jackie Wilson and **Bobby Womack**.

But as much of an education as artists of this calibre offered in both musicianship and showmanship, Hendrix was also learning a harsh lesson: that the headliners didn't like being upstaged by a mere sideman. Although

The Story

his playing was already developing into something notably flashy and distinctive, the stars of the show often resented any attention being directed elsewhere. And Jimi's wilder soloing was often felt unsuitable, ill-fitting, excessive or otherwise unbecoming for the song-oriented R&B/soul arrangements in which most of them specialized. "I learned how not to get an R&B group together", he told *Melody Maker* in 1969. "The trouble was, too many leaders didn't seem to want to pay anybody. Guys would get fired in the middle of the highway because they were talking too loud on the bus or the leader owed them too much money."

On the Chitlin' Circuit

Around the beginning of 1964, Hendrix set his sights a little higher, moving to **New York** in the hope of finding something with better prospects. He probably also had an eye on the possibility of picking up session work, as many more R&B records were made in the Big Apple than in Nashville. Like many a young gun arriving in the city without the means to support himself, he took some rough knocks in his first months, living hand-to-mouth in Harlem and finding work scarce, despite winning a $25 first-place prize at the Wednesday amateur night in Harlem's legendary **Apollo Theater**.

Were it not for the generosity of his first truly serious post-high-school girlfriend, **Fayne Pridgeon,** Hendrix might not have been able to keep his head above water. Sometimes portrayed as a sort of groupie who, like Jimi, was close to living on the streets, Pridgeon hasn't been treated particularly kindly by biographers and came across as something of a goofball in the first major Hendrix film documentary (*Jimi Hendrix*). However, she not only looked after Jimi at a crucial time in his life – the pair even lived with her mother for a while – but also undoubtedly gave him something even more important than food, shelter and sex: a sense, perhaps for the first time, that his musical talent was unique and worthy of a spotlight of its own, which must have given his shaky self-confidence quite a boost.

Soon, though, Hendrix picked up one of his most substantial and long-running pre-stardom sideman stints, as a member of the band backing **The Isley Brothers**, the great gospel-fired soul group best known at that point for their classic 1962 hit "Twist and Shout". Hits were actually thin on the ground for the Isleys when Hendrix was with them, but they were getting plenty of live and studio work, and he seems to have played with them for much of 1964. In addition, he was able to do at least a little recording with the group, one such track being the Isleys' mid-1964 single **"Testify"**. Here, for the very first time, you can hear a strong hint of the Hendrix the world would come to know and love. It's undeniably Jimi in both his speedy, nearly unhinged riffs and – particularly when he takes a brief solo just past the one-minute mark – a hint of burning distortion in his tone.

Apparently, however, that brief solo was about as much space as Hendrix was given to shine behind the stars of the show. Restless by nature anyway, he soon tired of the set performances, uniforms and limited opportunities for soaring guitar leads. Before long he was picking up work on various R&B tours again. Even during his short stint with the Isleys, though, his sheer dedication to his instrument obviously made an impression. "He played all the time", Ernie Isley told *Guitar Player*. "He would practice phrases over and over again, turn them inside out, break them in half, break them in quarters, play them slow, play them fast … So when it came time to play, it was virtually automatic. He didn't talk too much – the instrument was the talker." Later Ernie himself would become one of the more notable Hendrix-influenced guitarists on powerhouse 1970s Isley Brothers funk-rock hits like "That Lady".

Given Hendrix's impressively fluid playing on "Testify" and another soul session he managed to get onto in 1964, **Don Covay's "Mercy, Mercy"** (soon covered by The Rolling Stones, and later featured in Jimi's own early live sets), it may seem a little surprising that he didn't find more studio sideman gigs. But organization was never Hendrix's forte – even less so before he began his solo career – and he probably wasn't cut out for the fairly regular hours and discipline required to make a living as a session musician. In something of a vicious circle, the itinerant lifestyle he favoured made him harder to track down if and when someone wanted to give him a break. Guitar (and studio multi-tracking) innovator **Les Paul** supposedly wanted to do so after seeing him at a club around this time, but couldn't find Jimi again.

Sometime around late 1964, Hendrix signed up for another fairly extended – by his standards, at least – sideman job with **Little Richard,** one of the greatest of all 1950s rock'n'rollers. One of the highlights of Hendrix's musical youth, in fact, had been managing to get front-row tickets to a Little Richard concert in Seattle. It was now the mid-1960s, however, and with Richard's big hits in the past, he was reduced to taking what work he could get, largely on the black-oriented chitlin' circuit. Even though he no longer enjoyed the same chart success, however, Little Richard – who had only returned to rock'n'roll a couple or so years before, after renouncing the devil's music for the church – had an ego just as big as when he had been one of the hottest stars in the business. Clashes between Richard and Jimi were inevitable, not just because Hendrix played his guitar more assertively than the singer might have liked, but also because of Jimi's increasingly flamboyant dress and hairstyle, which was already pushing the mid-1960s boundaries of acceptable length. "He said *he* was the only one allowed to be pretty", Hendrix explained to *Melody Maker* a few years later. Still, Hendrix managed to hang on in Richard's group until around mid-1965, apparently playing in a few shows with **Ike and Tina Turner** during this period as well. (The earliest surviving piece of footage to capture Jimi performing – in the backup band for the obscure Buddy and Stacy duo on the *Night Train* TV show – also dates from around this time.) Although he did a bit of recording with Little Richard too, it's difficult to determine which tracks he appears on, and at least as difficult to hear much indication of Jimi's personality in the guitar work on the cuts on which he's often reported to have played, such as the deep soul opus "I Don't Know What You've Got (But It's Got Me)". During a stopover in Los Angeles, he did manage to play on an obscure soul single by his temporary girlfriend **Rosa Lee Brooks, "My Diary",** though his playing (as on Don Covay's "Mercy, Mercy") is relatively restrained, in the style of **Curtis Mayfield** – a substantial and often overlooked influence on Hendrix's approach.

Also taking part in the session (and writing the song) was a young **Arthur Lee,** soon to form and lead the great L.A. psychedelic-folk-rock band **Love,** and – shortly before Jimi's death – do some more recording with Hendrix. Characteristically, both Lee and Little Richard would later make much of what Hendrix had learned or even taken from them during their relatively brief collaborations. Whether by chance or design, however, there are some interesting similarities between Lee and Hendrix in that both men, despite being black, would lead great integrated rock bands that were willing to draw from outside R&B and found a much bigger audience among whites than African-Americans, though Lee and Love would never quite rise above cult status to the stardom that Hendrix and his bands enjoyed.

New York Session Man

By around mid-1965, Hendrix had apparently decided both to make New York a more solid base of operations, and direct his energies more towards breaking into the world of recording, adopting the pseudonym of Maurice James for a time. "There's a few record companies I visited that I can probably record for", he wrote on 8 August in a letter home (as quoted in Tony Brown's *Jimi Hendrix Concert Files*). "I think I'll start working toward that line."

Though accounts differ as to precisely when it occurred, the first figure in the New York business to offer him a contract was **Juggy Murray** of **Sue Records,** a fairly well-respected New York soul-oriented label with some national success. Murray was unsure of how to work with a brilliant but raw guitarist who was yet to sing or write his own songs, however. Nothing came of the recordings they attempted, although Jimi was lucky that the artist and management contract he signed with Murray wouldn't prevent him from taking up a far more attractive offer in late 1966.

He wouldn't be so lucky with the next record man he signed with, producer **Ed Chalpin,** to whom he was introduced by the leader of a local soul journeymen outfit he was playing with live, **Curtis Knight and the Squires.** Not only did this association produce no music of consequence, but Hendrix was paid a mere dollar to affix his name to a three-year contract. Far worse, the deal would cause unforeseen and massive legal headaches for Jimi after he became a star, running up to and even beyond his death. He was so desperate to gain studio experience of any kind, however, that appar-

Jimi Hendrix with Curtis Knight and the Squires

ently he was rather oblivious to the unfair financial conditions and legal ramifications of the papers he was signing.

Hendrix did play on a number of sessions for Knight (including a rewrite of "Like a Rolling Stone" retitled "How Do You Feel"), but few of the tracks appeared on disc at the time. That would change, much to Jimi's displeasure, in a year or two, when many of them were unearthed and deceptively marketed under his name after he had become a star leading a band of his own. Also while recording for Chalpin, he somehow got roped into playing backup on a session by the Marilyn Monroe of B-movies,

Jayne Mansfield, which could hardly have been chalked up as even useful experience.

As much as he wanted to do his own thing, until about mid-1966, Hendrix still had to resort to finding live work backing up Knight, The Isley Brothers (whose band he briefly rejoined in mid-1965), twist kings **Joey Dee and the Starliters**, and top session saxophonist **King Curtis** (who also had a fairly successful recording career under his own name). He was also finding occasional studio work on tracks by Curtis, his old employers The Isley Brothers and others. But even with some continued support from Fayne Pridgeon, he had problems providing himself

The Story

with the basic necessities. By the beginning of 1966, however, Pridgeon had married someone else. Above all, there was the frustration of not being able to play what he wanted. On his session work of the time, there's almost always the feeling that either somebody is keeping a lid on Jimi, or that Jimi is simply keeping a lid on himself, so little does his rather functional and perfunctory playing resemble what he would become revered for in the years ahead.

At this point, most guys in Hendrix's position would simply have given up, either going back home or taking a menial job while gig-ging for spare change with cover bands at night and weekends. Had that happened, he would be totally unknown today, save for soul collectors who might wonder who was responsible for that quick burst of a weird solo on The Isley Brothers' "Testify".

But Hendrix wasn't like most guys – even those not enamoured of his playing at this point would confirm that – and if the past three or four years hadn't seen him gain much head-way in the industry, at least it taught him to persevere in the face of odds that most sensible youngsters would have stopped defying.

Move to Greenwich Village

The first step in reinventing himself from Jimmy Hendrix, fairly anonymous sideman, to Jimi Hendrix, star, was taken when he moved from Harlem to **Greenwich Village** around spring 1966. **Richie Havens** – perhaps unco-incidentally, one of the few black musicians of the era, along with Hendrix and Arthur Lee, who would find a greater audience among white rock fans than black listeners – takes credit for instigating the move after seeing Jimi play with a little-known club band at the Cheetah in midtown Manhattan.

"I told him ... he didn't need to be playing for Little Richard or anyone else", Havens remem-bers in his autobiography, *They Can't Hide Us Anymore* (written with Steve Davidowitz). Havens thought Hendrix was the best guitar-ist he'd ever seen, and he advised Hendrix to check out the Village, where he could find a lot of young cats eager to play music.

This was not a hip thing to do for a young black musician in the mid-1960s. Harlem was the epicentre of New York's African-American musical and cultural community. Greenwich Village, on the other hand, though welcoming and tolerant of outsiders, was not where soul and R&B reigned supreme.

Yet Hendrix was becoming increasingly inter-ested in rock and folk, and most particularly in the revolutionary sounds of a newly electrified **Bob Dylan**. He went as far as to have Dylan's recording of "Blowin' in the Wind" played at a black club in Harlem, to instant negative feed-back from the other patrons.

Jimi gravitated toward such music nonethe-less – and it wasn't just because Dylan, and other mid-1960s white rockers, were coming out with youthful, personal and poetic lyrics which expressed things that had previously been unheard of in popular music, and weren't far

Jimi Hendrix, Session Man

Although Jimi Hendrix's discography is as chaotic as any back catalogue in the history of rock, no portion is as painfully scrambled as the numerous recordings he made as a sideman to other artists prior to his departure for London in September 1966. In part this is because many of them have been misleadingly packaged under the Hendrix billing, when in fact quite a few of them feature him in such a secondary, almost anonymous role that you'd never guess he was actually present. As a related caution, even the most dedicated Hendrix fanatic would have a hard time claiming greatness for most of them, especially as he rarely sings or even spins off guitar solos. As a general rule, it's wise to avoid the numerous tracks he cut with Curtis Knight, but even some of his better recordings with other artists are really of interest only to obsessive historians.

Nevertheless, a few glimmers of greatness are to be heard here and there, and a few of the tracks are fine soul records. The best of them is easily The Isley Brothers' **Testify**, and not only because it has Hendrix's only truly ripping solo in his pre-UK catalogue. This six-minute, two-part 1964 single – issued on the Isleys' own T-Neck label and now, thankfully, available on Isley Brothers CD compilations – is one of those rare raveups that's both propulsively infectious and downright hilarious, devoted as it is to the brothers affectionately mimicking James Brown, Ray Charles, Jackie Wilson, Stevie Wonder and even The Beatles. Not hit material by any means, but a lost classic for sure.

Another, less celebrated Isleys gem on which Hendrix plays, albeit with much less flash, is their more straightforwardly raunchy 1965 single **Move Over and Let Me Dance**. Here Jimi unleashes the twangy, almost mellifluous, and almost definitely Curtis Mayfield-influenced blues-soul runs that he would, with some refinements, use as counterpoints to his more roaring excursions, notably his figures in the intro to "Hey Joe". Although the young Hendrix's playing verges on the over-busy on "Move Over and Let Me Dance", it still gives a kick to hear him squeezing in his licks beneath the blaring horns and the Isleys' impassioned wailing.

More disciplined guitar lines in the same vein can be heard on Don Covay's 1964 soul classic **Mercy, Mercy**, especially at the very beginning of the track. Again there are echoes foreshadowing not only the kind of R&B-based riffing heard in the intro to "Hey Joe", but also throughout Hendrix's less heralded but similarly brilliant early UK hit "The Wind Cries Mary". It's been reported that a bold unknown Hendrix impressed Steve Cropper on an impromptu mid-1960s visit to Stax Records by telling the Booker T. and the MGs' guitarist that he had played on the single, though if so, it's strange that Jimi didn't manage to pick up some session work at the Memphis label.

A concise compilation of the best dozen or so pre-fame tracks on which Hendrix plays would do a great service to fans, eliminating the need to sift through so much rubbish for representative examples of his nascent talents. Owing to the usual licensing hurdles involved in assembling anthologies from the vaults of several different labels – some of whom have a vested interest in deceptively exploiting the Hendrix catalogue – it seems unlikely that a legitimate collection along these lines will appear in the near future.

off the lyrics that Hendrix would soon start to write. It was also because Dylan's voice, like Hendrix's, was hardly conventional or pretty. If Dylan could succeed sounding the way he did, without smoothing out his vocal kinks and idiosyncratic mode of expression, so could Jimi.

The Story

Jimi Hendrix and Bob Dylan

For all **Bob Dylan**'s huge influence in the pop world in the mid-1960s, relatively few young American blacks were big fans of the folk-turned-folk-rock singer-songwriter. Hendrix was a notable exception, and his passion wasn't a bandwagon he jumped onto when he moved to Greenwich Village in his last months in the US. He had already been besotted by Dylan's first out-and-out rock LP, *Highway 61 Revisited*, in 1965 while still living in Harlem. Dylan's contribution to giving Hendrix the courage to write and sing his own off-the-wall tunes has already been noted. It could also be that Jimi felt an especially strong bond with Dylan in general, and Bob's huge 1965 hit "Like a Rolling Stone" in particular, by sensing that Dylan was as much of an artistic outsider as himself. And like Dylan, Hendrix would change,

musically and personally, in ways not always approved of by the audience which had first acclaimed him. The stress of dealing with the subsequent attention might have come close to killing Dylan in 1966; it almost certainly played a part in leading to Hendrix's own death by misadventure four years later.

Hendrix, of course, would make **Like a Rolling Stone** his own onstage, most famously at the Monterey Pop Festival. Any doubt that he was a serious Dylan fan is dispelled by a far more obscure song Jimi covered on the BBC, **Can You Please Crawl Out Your Window?** The original version – never included on an album in Jimi's lifetime – was issued as a non-LP single in late 1965, only reaching number 58 in the US charts, so Hendrix must have been a

It might well have been Dylan's hit "Like a Rolling Stone" he had in mind when he wrote the following in that letter back home in August 1965: "Every day people are singing worse and worse on purpose and the public buys more and more records." He told his folks not to feel ashamed of him if they heard him sounding terrible on a record, because the money would be rolling in.

With that in mind, along with his ever-blossoming skills as a guitarist beginning to push electrical amplification to its limits, Hendrix at long last set about forming bands to play the Village which featured himself as front man. Another crucial and generally under-credited catalyst for these decisions was **Linda Keith**, girlfriend of Rolling Stones guitarist **Keith Richards**. Although Linda and Hendrix were

not romantically involved, she encouraged him to step out on his own after catching him playing guitar behind Curtis Knight. Knowing that Village clubs might be more amenable to the kind of music he wanted to play, Jimi began appearing at venues like the **Cafe Wha?** as leader of **Jimmy James and the Blue Flames** (an engagement which Havens also takes some credit for facilitating). Even with little original material, and a scraggly band including a fifteen-year-old guitarist named Randy Wolfe (and, occasionally, bassist Jeff Baxter, later of Steely Dan and The Doobie Brothers), Hendrix's makeovers of blues, soul and Dylan tunes were radical (and loud) enough to start attracting attention.

The most frustrating missing chapter in the history of Hendrix's development has to be dedicated fan to even be aware of it in the first place. Jimi certainly continued listening to Dylan attentively after he'd made it big, as evidenced by another rather obscure cover, **The Drifter's Escape**, which appeared on Bob's *John Wesley Harding* album at the tail end of 1967 (though Hendrix's outtake version would only be issued after his death).

But the most celebrated of Hendrix's batch of Dylan covers, of course, is **All Along the Watchtower**, originally on *John Wesley Harding*. A highlight of *Electric Ladyland*, it was Jimi's only US top-twenty single, reaching number five in the UK. Beyond its commercial success, however, it stands as one of the greatest illustrations of Hendrix's ability to rearrange a song from top to bottom and make it seem like

his own handiwork, without violating the original integrity of the composition. So highly regarded is his interpretation, in fact, that it's now considered the definitive version – so much so that Dylan himself eventually adopted its arrangement for his own live performances of the song.

"It overwhelmed me, really", said Dylan – never one to shower praise on cover versions lightly – of Hendrix's treatment in a 1995 interview. "He had such talent, he could find things inside a song and vigorously develop them. He found things that other people wouldn't think of finding in there. He probably improved upon it by the spaces he was using. I took licence with the song from his version, actually, and continue to do it to this day."

these crucial few months around mid-1966, from which no live or studio recordings have emerged to document what must have been a remarkably accelerated artistic growth. It was almost certainly at this point that Jimi began truly pushing available technology to the limit, experimenting with and refining **fuzz** distortion and the more far-out **feedback**, then just starting to get harnessed to devastating effect by **Jeff Beck** of **The Yardbirds** and – in a noisier, more abstract fashion – **Pete Townshend** of **The Who**. Although his set still included covers like "Mercy, Mercy", "Land of a Thousand Dances", Dylan's "Like a Rolling Stone" and The Troggs' new smash "Wild Thing", Hendrix was twisting them into something different with note-bending improvisations that were both elegant and aggressive.

Perhaps the best testament to Hendrix's sound and impact at the time was supplied by **Mike Bloomfield**, then himself a newly anointed guitar hero through his work for The Paul Butterfield Blues Band and his keening blues-rock licks as a sideman on Dylan's early electric recordings (including, as it happens, "Like a Rolling Stone"). "H-bombs were going off, guided missiles were flying – I can't tell you the sounds he was getting out of his instrument", Bloomfield told *Guitar Player* in September 1975. "He was getting every sound I was ever to hear him get right there in that room with a Stratocaster, a Twin [amp], a Maestro fuzz tone, and that was all – he was doing it mainly through extreme volume. How he did this, I wish I understood ... I didn't even want to pick up a guitar for the next year."

For all the lack of original material in Hendrix's set, it was one of his imaginative covers, **Hey Joe**, that would be primarily responsible for bringing him to the attention of the man who did more than anyone else to launch Jimi to stardom. Linda Keith had already tried to hustle some of her high-level connections in the rock scene into taking notice of the new kid on the block. But Rolling Stones manager-producer **Andrew Loog Oldham** was uninterested, possibly mindful of fostering jealousy between Hendrix and Linda's boyfriend, Keith Richards. Seymour Stein, soon to form Sire Records, declined as well. Probably in early August (though some biographers have dated the meeting as taking place about a month earlier), she persuaded **Chas Chandler**, then bassist with the great R&B-soaked British Invasion band **The Animals**, to see Jimi at the Cafe Wha?

By a remarkable coincidence, Chandler – then looking to retire as a musician and enter production/management – was looking for someone to cover "Hey Joe" with in the studio. "Hey Joe" was played by Hendrix that very show, based not on the classic garage-rock version which had been a fairly big US hit for Los Angeles band The Leaves, but a slower, more folk-rock-ish version by Tim Rose. But even if Jimi hadn't played or known about "Hey Joe", it's likely that Chandler would have seized on Hendrix as an ideal artist with whom to start his new career, so impressed was he with the singer-guitarist. Chandler couldn't believe that nobody had yet discovered Jimi, and if Hendrix was anywhere near as good as

he was by the time he recorded "Hey Joe" with Chandler in the producer's chair a few months later, it is indeed mystifying that he hadn't yet been snapped up. Not to sell Chandler short, however, it's a tribute to his good taste and shrewd judgement that he was immediately able to recognize Hendrix's potential – something no other industry figure had yet managed to suss.

Although some accounts might leave the impression that Chandler whisked Hendrix off to London almost overnight, a good deal of groundwork had to be laid before the two men took what would amount to a radically risky venture for both of them. First, Chandler had to finish his American tour with The Animals, who would break up when it ended (though lead singer Eric Burdon soon formed a new version of the group). Displaying a considerable amount of foresight for 1966 – a time when musicians were even more routinely exploited than they are now – Chandler also asked Jimi if he was signed to any contracts. Hendrix told him about his deal with Juggy Murray of Sue Records, which Chandler and his future management partner, **Mike Jeffery** (then managing The Animals), were able to buy out. Jimi, however, either forgot or neglected to tell Chas about his deal with Ed Chalpin, a mistake that would cost both parties dearly in the years to come.

While Chandler was wrapping up his commitments with The Animals, Hendrix, perhaps not wholly certain that his new benefactor would deliver the goods, continued to play the Village. For a brief time he played in the band

The Story

Chas Chandler

Born in Newcastle-upon-Tyne on 18 December 1938, **Bryan "Chas" Chandler** had himself been an international star for a couple of years immediately before becoming Hendrix's manager. True, relatively few rock fans could have told you Chandler's name in 1966, as the only personality in **The Animals** to impress the media as a star in his own right was their lead singer, Eric Burdon. Some biographers have downplayed Chandler's musical skills, seeing him as a merely adequate bassist who was glad enough to lay down his instrument to enter the business side of his profession when the opportunity presented itself. The last part might have been true, but in reality the hulking (six-foot-four) Chas was quite a good bassist. He held the fort admirably on a series of great mid-1960s Animals hits, their arrangement of the biggest of them (the folk standard **The House of the Rising Sun**) being covered by Hendrix himself in his Greenwich Village days. Indeed, if Chandler had wanted to play bass alongside Jimi in the new group Hendrix would form in

London, he wouldn't have been the ideal choice, but he wouldn't have been a bad one.

As the man who "discovered" Hendrix, Chandler's contribution to Jimi's achievement was absolutely crucial, but it went far beyond that. Along with Experience drummer Mitch Mitchell, Chas was arguably the greatest force in helping to make Hendrix's music as brilliant and lasting as it was. Not only did he produce Jimi's finest recordings, but he also made his home Jimi's own during Hendrix's uncertain early months in London; took almost reckless financial risks to make sure his protégé had a fighting chance to become a star in late 1966; and was the person, more than any other, who spurred Jimi to take songwriting seriously. Above all, despite some decisions that may seem a bit questionable in retrospect, Chandler truly seemed to have Hendrix's best musical and personal interests at heart. If he had been Jimi's sole manager, or been able to take on a partner who was more artistically inclined (like The Who's Kit Lambert) or more ethical (like Brian Epstein) than Mike Jeffery, the Hendrix story would doubtless have turned out very differently. Even with a less hard-hearted, more efficient mogul like Led Zeppelin's manager Peter Grant, or impresario Robert Stigwood (who looked after Cream) as Chandler's partner, Hendrix would probably have been better off.

Unlike many of the central figures of that story, Chas Chandler escaped from the turmoil of Jimi Hendrix's final years relatively unscathed. Bailing out of his production/management role in 1968, he went on to great financial (if hardly the same level of artistic) success as the manager of **Slade** in the 1970s, also becoming involved in other media and property ventures. He participated too in a couple of reunions of the original Animals, dying in his Newcastle home town in 1996.

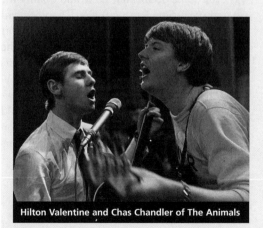

Hilton Valentine and Chas Chandler of The Animals

of young white bluesman **John Hammond** at the **Cafe Au Go Go**, and although it might seem a bit odd that Jimi would retreat to the role of sideman, Hammond was obviously prepared to give him more space for soloing than he had ever been able to get on similar gigs. Following an inclination to sit in with other musicians that would continue to the end of his days, Hendrix also played with the band of opening act **Ellen McIlwaine** (who would start her own solo recording career as a bluesy singer-songwriter in the early 1970s), taking the opportunity to showboat and win some more fans even in a backup role.

Then Chandler, true to his word, came back to New York after The Animals' tour had finished to find Jimi and bring him back to London. Though not unheard of, it was (and to a degree remains) rare to break an unknown American with no records under his own name on the British music scene. Even with so many of his hopes having been dashed over the previous five years and no definite prospects at home, it must still have been an enormous leap of faith for Hendrix to leave New York behind and take his chances abroad. And he would be going alone, not with any of the Blue Flames or any of the other musicians with whom he had worked, though Jimi wanted Randy Wolfe to come along. Wisely, Wolfe didn't, and not only because it would have been foolhardy to try and

take a fifteen-year-old overseas. Frankly, the sound Hendrix was generating was so immense and expansive by this point that it would have been superfluous to have any other guitarist, no matter how good, playing in the band as well. It didn't work out badly for Wolfe, in any case: as **Randy California**, he would become guitarist in one of the more successful West Coast psychedelic bands of the late 1960s, **Spirit**. Hendrix also invited his old pal Billy Cox to come to London, but Cox declined, though their paths would meet again a few years later under drastically different circumstances.

With no record deal – or at least one that looked as though it would never amount to anything – at home, and with little money despite his growing notoriety in Greenwich Village, it was time for Hendrix to take his chances across the Atlantic. Such little standing did he have on his native ground that there was even some doubt that he would qualify for a passport in time for his flight. Chandler had to get an American songwriter friend, Scott English (co-writer of Eric Burdon and The Animals' hit "Help Me Girl" and later co-writer of Barry Manilow's first smash, "Mandy"), to claim that he had known Hendrix for several years before the precious document could be secured. Jimi left for London with Chas on 23 September 1966, with little more than his guitar for luggage.

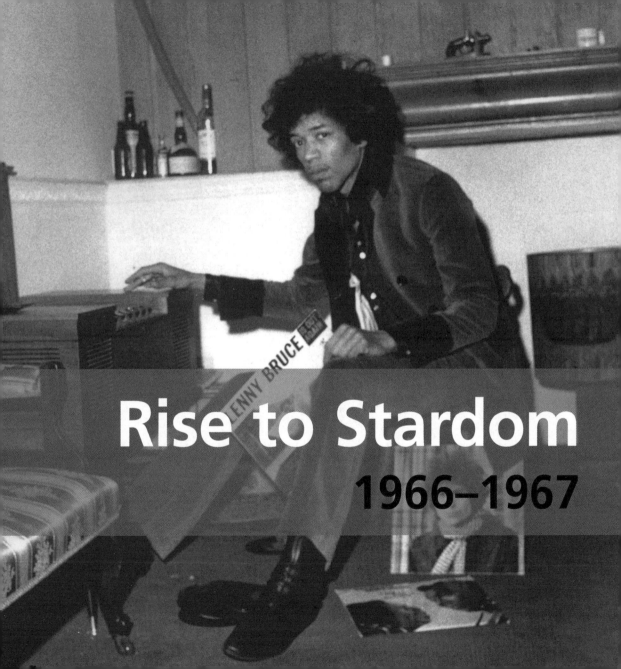

Rise to Stardom
1966–1967

"What this man does to a guitar could get him arrested for assault."

Keith Altham, *New Musical Express*, January 1967

Rise to Stardom
1966–1967

When Jimi Hendrix landed in London in late September 1966, nobody knew who he was, apart from his managers, Chas Chandler and Mike Jeffery. Yet when he flew back to the US nine months later, he was one of the hottest recording stars in the UK and Europe, and on the verge of conquering his home country as well. It was a remarkable metamorphosis, sparked mostly by the explosively heightened creativity of Hendrix's music, but also aided and abetted by canny management and a series of fortuitous breaks – which, finally, were mostly going Jimi's way.

Arrival in London and Formation of the Experience

When Hendrix first cleared customs, he must have been wondering whether he would be in London long enough to take out his guitar, as he was only given a visa to stay for one week. Indeed, Jimi nearly didn't make it into the United Kingdom at all. Animals roadie Terry McVay carried Hendrix's guitar through customs so that Jimi wouldn't be suspected of entering England in search of work, and even so, Chandler had to do some quick talking to convince the authorities that Hendrix should be allowed into the country. According to the story he came up with, Jimi was an American songwriter coming to the UK to collect his royalties – which, even in the unlikely event that some of his Curtis Knight sides had sneaked into Great

Britain, probably wouldn't have amounted to enough to pay his bus fare back to the airport.

Here again, Chandler deserves credit for taking pains to try to make Hendrix feel comfortable in highly uncertain circumstances the best way imaginable: by getting him to play music as soon as possible. Even on the way back from the airport, they stopped at the home of jazzy R&B musician **Zoot Money** to allow Hendrix to play some riffs for those who happened to be around, including a young member of Money's band, future Police guitarist Andy Summers. Also living in the Money household was **Kathy Etchingham**, who almost immediately became Hendrix's new girlfriend after catching him jamming at the elite Scotch of St

James club that same night, with **Eric Burdon** of The Animals in the audience.

While word of the new American phenomenon began to spread right away, Hendrix and his managers knew they had to get a band together and a recording contract as soon as possible to make their gamble pay off. Somehow, a work permit was wangled, and a bass player soon obtained through unlikely means when **Noel Redding** showed up to audition for the position of guitarist in the new version of The Animals being formed around Eric Burdon. Although the slot had already been filled, Chandler asked Redding if he could play bass. Noel, a multi-instrumentalist who had even been considering selling his guitar and amps to focus on drums in the hope of getting more work, jammed along with Hendrix and a couple of other musicians for a bit. Jimi liked what he heard well enough to offer Redding the bass gig after talking with him afterwards in a nearby pub. He also wanted Redding in his band because, of all things, he liked Noel's haircut, a curly mop somewhat similar to the one being sported by Jimi's hero Bob Dylan around the time of *Blonde on Blonde*.

The auditions to find a drummer were somewhat more considered, the candidates narrowing down to **Mitch Mitchell**, who had recently been playing as part of jazz-R&B-pop star **Georgie Fame**'s band, and **Aynsley Dunbar**, who had just joined John Mayall's Bluesbreakers. With Hendrix unable to decide, a coin was flipped, Mitchell emerging the winner. One thing had been decided even before the auditions, however – Jimi would be the clear leader of this new group, which was christened **The Jimi Hendrix Experience**, the spelling of his first name now permanently changed from Jimmy to Jimi.

If Hendrix's choices of bandmates seemed impulsive almost to the point of arbitrariness, it's difficult to imagine how they could have worked out better. Although Redding was an unknown who had barely recorded (on non-hit singles as guitarist of the Loving Kind) or even played bass, in a way his lack of experience on the instrument worked out to his advantage. Jimi wasn't looking for a conventional bassist, of whom there were plenty on the London scene: he wanted someone who would push and challenge him, and in turn be receptive to Hendrix's own unorthodox ideas. On all these counts, Redding fitted the bill well, playing with an edgy and unpredictable verve (perhaps heard best on the classic "Fire"), almost as if he was getting his bass to function as an additional guitar. In time, Noel's frustrated ambitions to be a guitarist and songwriter in his own right would cause tension within the Experience, but for the time being, these were channelled to the group's advantage.

While Mitchell was somewhat better known, his prior experience with Georgie Fame and on a few singles by obscure group The Riot Squad gave little indication of his true abilities. Not only was Mitch the fastest drummer this side of Keith Moon, but he also brought a jazzy, unpredictably irregular creativity to his rhythms virtually unknown to that point in rock music. In this sense, Mitchell's role was more like that of Elvin Jones – a drummer to whom he was often compared – in John Coltrane's cutting-edge 1960s modern jazz group than that of an orthodox R&B or rock'n'roll sticksman.

Because Redding and Mitchell followed Hendrix's lead in playing their respective instruments far louder than in most rock bands of the time, it also meant that there was no need – or, to be blunt, room – for additional members. At first, Hendrix had wanted a larger group, and guitar-bass-drums **power trios**, as they would soon come to be called, were still rare in rock (the newly formed **Cream** being the most notable exception). The three-man format of the Experience, however, balanced the players' muscular volume with a leanness that forced each musician to play as hard as they could while preventing the overall sound from getting too busy and cluttered. To cap it all, the integrated black-and-white line-up – and, at least at first, the Afro hairstyles that both Redding and, for a while, Mitchell adopted – made the Experience look as different from other bands as they sounded.

So shy was Hendrix about singing that – hard as it might be to believe now – Redding and Mitchell were actively considered as vocalists for the group. It was quickly realized, however, that Jimi would have to be the lead singer, though even after he had become a star, he would insist on doing his studio vocals behind screens, with the lights turned low so that nobody could see him and make him feel even more embarrassed about his vocal abilities. "After taping a lead vocal, Hendrix would poke his head around the screen with this bemused look on his face, asking, 'How was that? Was that okay? Was it all right?'" revealed Eddie Kramer, who worked on many of Jimi's sessions as an engineer, in *Hendrix: Setting the Record Straight*. "Jimi needed every bit of encouragement because he lacked confidence in his voice. I would say, 'Yes Jimi, it was great, but if you want to do another one, go ahead.'" But even after half a year of fronting a band, Hendrix remained unconvinced, telling Chris Welch of *Melody Maker* in April 1967, "I just wish I could sing really nice, but I know I can't sing. I just feel the words out. I just try all night to hit a pretty note, but it's hard. I'm more of an entertainer and performer than a singer."

Even as the Experience were forming, word of Hendrix continued to spread among insiders in the rock community and music press. In late September, when he jammed with respected jazzy R&B outfit the **Brian Auger Trinity**, onlookers' jaws dropped in amazement. As Auger later recalled in Charles R. Cross's *Room Full of Mirrors*: "The difference between him and a lot of the English guitar players like Clapton, Jeff Beck and Alvin Lee, was that you could still tell what the influences were in Clapton's and Beck's playing. ... But Jimi wasn't following anyone – he was playing something new."

The momentum snowballed after Hendrix jammed with **Eric Clapton** and the aforementioned Cream at Regent Street Polytechnic on 1 October, with Beck in the audience as well. As Chas Chandler told John McDermott in McDermott and Eddie Kramer's *Hendrix: Setting the Record Straight*, Clapton suddenly stopped playing and stumbled offstage. When Chas asked him if he was all right, Clapton replied: "'Is he that fucking good?' He had heard ten bars at the most. Within a week, he had his hair frizzed and would come by our

Almost Experienced

Although the choice of Mitch Mitchell and Noel Redding to complete the Experience trio seemed almost arbitrary in its haste and reliance upon chance and intuition, there were a few other musicians who were at least briefly in the running. If Hendrix had had his own way, of course, both bassist **Billy Cox** and guitarist **Randy California** (then known as Randy Wolfe) would have come with him to London. Jimi's desire to bring along a second guitarist shows that he wasn't thinking of constructing the group as a guitar-bass-drums power trio – still a novel concept in rock music in 1966.

When Redding did his brief and successful audition for the bass position, he was accompanied by Hendrix, keyboardist **Mike O'Neill**, and drummer **Aynsley Dunbar**. O'Neill is the real mystery man of the embryonic Experience, having first played (and sung) in **Nero and the Gladiators**, who had a couple of minor instrumental hits in the pre-Beatles early 1960s and performed in Roman costumes. In the late 1960s and early 1970s, O'Neill would play piano in a couple of bands including that of another, albeit lesser-known British guitar hero, **Albert Lee**.

There is no evidence to suggest that O'Neill was seriously considered for membership in the Experience, but his very presence does suggest that Hendrix might have been thinking of including other instruments besides guitar, bass and drums. According to Charles R. Cross's *Room Full of Mirrors*, Jimi even initially wanted a nine-piece band with horns, in line with many of the soul bands with whom he had worked in the US. Chas Chandler even called keyboardist **Brian Auger** to ask about the possibility of Hendrix fronting the band Auger was currently leading, The Brian Auger Trinity. The jazz-R&B organist might actually have made a fine occasional contributor to Hendrix's recordings, but as a front man himself, he would have found it hard to play second fiddle (so to speak) to a guitarist, and was soon scoring hits of his own with featured vocalist **Julie Driscoll** in Julie Driscoll, Brian Auger and the Trinity. In addition, Chandler wanted to ensure that Hendrix would stand out as the star of whatever group formed around him, and having just two other band members certainly helped in this respect.

In another move indicating the initial uncertainty about making the Experience a threesome, David

flat anytime that he had a spare moment, to be with Hendrix."

For all the impact Jimi was having at such unannounced jams, however, it was crucial that the Experience should get off the ground as a band. Dates were fixed up in Paris as an opening act for, rather weirdly, **Johnny Hallyday**, a sort of French equivalent to Elvis Presley, after Hallyday had seen Hendrix in London. In what might be the first Hendrix review ever, a writer for the French regional newspaper *L'Eure*

Éclair described him as "a singer and guitar player with bushy hair, a bad mixture of James Brown and Chuck Berry, who pulled a wry face on stage for a quarter of an hour, and also played the guitar with his teeth sometimes".

Contracts were also signed binding the Experience to **Chas Chandler** and **Mike Jeffery.** For anybody looking for a villain in the Jimi Hendrix story, Jeffery – whose surname, confusingly, has also been spelled in biographies and elsewhere as Jeffrey, Jeffries, or Jeffreys – is

Knights was briefly auditioned on bass, the idea being to allow Redding to remain on guitar in a two-guitar/bass/drums line-up. By this point, however, there really wasn't any room for another guitarist in a group that Jimi would lead. Things worked out okay for Knights, however, as he would soon join **Procol Harum**, who had a lot of success on both sides of the Atlantic with their blend of psychedelia and early progressive rock.

Although the competition for the drum seat eventually narrowed down to Aynsley Dunbar and Mitch Mitchell, it's sometimes been reported that John Banks – then part of the short-lived duo **John and Johnny** with fellow ex-Merseybeater Johnny Gustafson (who would later play bass on several Roxy Music albums) – was also in the running. Another variation of the story has it that Banks was considered as a replacement for Mitchell very early on; Redding even claimed in Sean Egan's *Jimi Hendrix and the Making of 'Are You Experienced?'* that "Hendrix loved him. He fitted in well because he was a powerful type drummer. He wasn't as flamboyant as Mitchell, but he fitted in well with what we were doing." Banks's recordings as part of the relatively tame Liverpool pop-rock group **The Merseybeats**, however, give little indication that he was capable of coming up with anything to match Mitchell's kinetic energy. Again according to Redding, Banks wasn't hired because he hated flying, which would have been unworkable in a band that toured as heavily as the Experience did.

Dunbar lost out to Mitchell purely on the toss of a coin, although it's also been reported that he got turned down for asking for £10 more a week than the position would pay. However, his drum work on records by Liverpool band The Mojos and more esteemed blues-rockers **John Mayall's Bluesbreakers** (alongside future original Fleetwood Mac guitarist **Peter Green**), while solid enough, similarly lacks any of Mitchell's flash. Dunbar didn't do too badly for himself, though, leading his own reasonably popular late-1960s blues-rock band, The Aynsley Dunbar Retaliation, before playing with **Frank Zappa and the Mothers of Invention** and American AOR stars **Journey** and **Jefferson Starship**. Ultimately, although Hendrix's habit of making rushed business decisions has sometimes been criticized, in the case of the Experience, the gods must have been smiling.

the leading candidate for the role. The morality of his business decisions, and the pressures he exerted upon Jimi, have been questioned so often in subsequent accounts that it's tempting to wonder why Chandler hooked up with him in the first place, especially as Jeffery has been reported to have exploited The Animals as badly as he did Hendrix.

Chandler, however, wasn't in much of a position to be choosy about his sources of funding. Despite The Animals' success, he had been left with little money after the original line-up folded, and needed quite a bit of financial backing if he was to get anywhere with the unknown quantity he had imported from the States. Chas also later claimed that, as he himself was still signed to Jeffery, The Animals' manager was entitled to a cut of whatever he did anyway. Whatever the case, Jeffery was probably the only person with both the money and the high-level music biz connections willing to fund Chandler's enterprise.

The Story

Mike Jeffery

It's a measure of the mystery of the origins of the shadiest figure in the Jimi Hendrix story, **Mike Jeffery**, that decades of diligent research into Jimi's life have still failed to firmly establish where Jeffery came from and how exactly he managed to rise to such a prominent position in the music business. He had supposedly worked for British intelligence, earning considerable sums on the side in the 1956 Suez crisis by selling imported newspapers to soldiers stationed in Egypt. He found his way into the music industry through owning clubs in the Newcastle area, including the famous Club A Go Go, where his clients **The Animals** built their following. Some observers and biographers feel that he would use many of the same tactics he employed to exploit The Animals – pitting members against each other, working them to the point of exhaustion and funnelling money into offshore accounts – with Hendrix and the Experience, where the money and stakes were considerably higher.

Defending Jeffery is an unenviable task, as there's been a near-unanimous avalanche of criticism and accusations against the man by those who worked with him and/or Hendrix. Without in any way justifying the morality of his behaviour, however, it can be noted that some of his methods weren't uncommon in the jungle of the 1960s music business. He may have set up offshore tax shelters for The Animals and Hendrix in the Bahamas, but so had The Beatles (which explains why they filmed part of *Help!* there). He might have set up an unreasonable touring schedule for Hendrix, but squeezing as many shows as possible into criss-crossing continental journeys was par for the course for many big rock acts. His hard-headedness and negotiating skills were also undeniably crucial to getting Hendrix huge opportu-

nities in the record and concert world that he might not have otherwise had, although characteristically Jeffery sometimes twisted these to his own advantage rather than his client's. Some who worked with him, especially Noel Redding, never gave up questioning where much of the money Hendrix earned had gone, believing the funds to have vanished into the black hole of Jeffery's offshore setup, never to be distributed properly among those who had earned them.

The most objectionable difference between Jeffery and some other prominent British rock managers who made their share of questionable business decisions – such as The Beatles' Brian Epstein, The Rolling Stones' Andrew Loog Oldham, The Who's Kit Lambert and Chris Stamp, and, closer to home, Jeffery's partner Chas Chandler – is that he had little apparent empathy for Hendrix's aesthetic vision and personal well-being. For all their flaws, all of the other managers mentioned were usually devoted to their star clients as friends, and willing to bend and take risks to ensure that the musicians could advance themselves artistically. Although Jeffery paid some lip service to the hippie/alternative/drug-oriented lifestyle that came to dominate the counterculture by the end of the 1960s, most of those around him at the time found his apparent embrace of those values creepily hypocritical. Jeffery must also take part of the blame for kick-starting the posthumous exploitation of the Jimi Hendrix brand virtually before the superstar was buried. He wouldn't profit from this after his death in a 1973 plane crash, but such was his octopus-like grip on Hendrix's affairs that the deals he made continue to affect Jimi's musical and monetary legacy to this day.

And to be fair, each went to some lengths to pay for the Experience's expenses in the group's early days. Chas sold some of his bass guitars and it's been claimed that Jeffery undertook some behind-the-scenes machinations to ensure that Hendrix could stay and work in the UK. Jeffery may have had some prior experience in this regard with Goldie and the Gingerbreads, an all-girl American rock group he had managed in the mid-1960s, who had been able to base themselves in the UK for quite some time.

"Hey Joe" and Other Hits

The Experience still didn't have any original material by the time they came to give their first live performances. In fact, their repertoire was limited to a handful of R&B covers, all hangovers from Hendrix's days fronting the Blue Flames back in Greenwich Village. Fortunately, one of these was the song Chandler was sure would be a hit, **Hey Joe**, which they recorded in October at Jimi's first proper studio date as an independent musician. Even at this stage, the whole plan to get Hendrix a foothold on the UK music scene was very much a hand-to-mouth operation: there was no record deal in place, and although Chandler hoped to interest a label in releasing it as a single, he wasn't even sure that his cash would last long enough to cut a B-side.

Fortunately, the session was highly successful, even if "Hey Joe" might seem relatively restrained in comparison to the torrential noise that Hendrix would soon be routinely creating. His mastery of fluid blues-rock licks was established right from the intro, but it was in the instrumental solo break where he really took off, showcasing the shrieking sustain that would become one of his trademarks. And for someone so shy about taking on lead vocals, his singing sounds remarkably assured on this maiden effort, projecting a cocky, knowing sensuality that oozed hipness.

In retrospect, the B-side – so often an afterthought in the 1960s – was just as important. Hendrix wanted to do one of the cover versions that he was still including in his stage act, such as "Mercy, Mercy" (having played on Don Covay's original back in 1964), "Land of a Thousand Dances" or Howlin' Wolf's "Killing Floor". Chandler, however, forcefully told Hendrix that he would have to write a song of his own, and not only because he was intent on prodding Jimi into more original territory. Quite simply, the whole operation sorely needed to make money, and if the single was a hit, a self-penned B-side stood to generate valuable publishing royalties (in which, it has to be said, Chas had a stake).

Almost backed into a corner – he certainly couldn't escape Chandler's watchful eye, as he and Kathy Etchingham were now sharing a flat with Chas and his girlfriend – Jimi quickly came up with **Stone Free**. If this really was his first complete songwriting effort, it made for a remarkably fine initial outing, demonstrating his capacity for combining bluesy rock and pop hooks, as well as unveiling the breezy, devil-may-care individualism that would colour many of his subsequent lyrics. If his guitar sorcery was still somewhat subdued at this point, the distorted waves of notes on the instrumental fade-out – which probably paid homage to similar experiments by both The Who and The Yardbirds – gave fair warning that he had plenty more tricks up his sleeve.

More important in the long term was the fact that Hendrix – under much pressure from Chandler – finally seemed to have tapped into his ability as a songwriter, a role which, like that of lead singer, he seemed to lack the confidence to take on until forced. Many other songs would follow over the next few months, almost all of them good at the least and quite a few of them classics. But of all the manifestations of Hendrix's incredible potential in the mid-1960s, this particular one is the most amazing and mysterious, even more so than the quantum leap his instrumental skills were taking at the same time. Some who knew Hendrix in his New York days maintain that Jimi was working on writing songs, or at least outlines of songs, which were prototypes for ones he would eventually record (including "Red House", soon to be cut for his first LP). If that were truly the case, though, you would think that he would certainly have had a song like "Foxy Lady" at the ready when challenged by Chandler for a B-side. The balance of evidence suggests, however, that Hendrix didn't start writing seriously until the sessions for this debut single. The apparently instant blossoming of his facility in this respect – not arrived at gradually, but virtually fully formed on his first attempts – is, more than any other aspect of his art, a burst of

magic that seems to defy rational explanation.

"Hey Joe" itself was actually rejected by a few labels before Chandler placed it with **Track Records**, a new imprint formed by Who managers **Kit Lambert** and **Chris Stamp**. Lambert and Stamp actually had hopes of getting involved in Jimi's management, but seeing as though the job was already taken, settled for what seemed the next best thing. So eager were they to get Hendrix's first disc out, in fact, that the single would actually appear on Polydor, the label of Track's distributor, the Track label itself not being quite ready for launch at that point.

In the meantime, the Experience managed to play a few shows in Munich and some more club dates in London, the buzz about Hendrix spreading through more of the capital's top rock musicians, and Jimi starting to pick up some of his first mentions in the British music press. The first of these actually appeared a good six weeks before the release of "Hey Joe", when *Record Mirror* reported that Hendrix was already "being hailed in some quarters as a main contender for the title of 'the next big thing'". To the same magazine, Jimi pointedly observed: "We don't want to be classed in any category. If it must have a tag, I'd like it to be called 'Free Feeling'. It's a mixture of rock, freak-out, blues and rave music."

It was a gig in Munich in early November that led Hendrix, through a combination of chance and Chandler's egging-on, to add another attention-catching gimmick to his live act. Accidentally breaking his guitar neck when he threw it onstage, an angry Jimi reacted by grabbing hold of it and deliberately swinging

Hendrix at the Speakeasy
Club, 19 January 1967

the body of the guitar down on the ground like an axe. Noting the audience's enthusiastic response, Chandler decided that Hendrix should make smashing guitars part of his performances. Pete Townshend of The Who had already been doing this for a good couple of years or so, but even if it wasn't exactly an original gimmick to incorporate into the Experience's act, it was undeniably an effective one.

Perhaps hardened by years of failure and disappointment, even at this point Hendrix wasn't taking success for granted and still felt the need to justify himself to his oft-disapproving father. "I have my own group and will have a record out [in] about two months named 'Hey Joe' by The Jimi Hendrix Experience", he wrote to his father from Munich; "I think things are getting a little better." It might have also been around this time (though some have dated the incident to just after his arrival in the UK) that Jimi called Al Hendrix from England, only to get scolded by his unimpressed dad for having the nerve to reverse the charges. There would be a more satisfying reunion with a ghost from the past when Hendrix tracked down Little Richard to a London hotel, letting him know that his ex-sideman now had a band of his own.

Released in mid-December, "Hey Joe" was promoted by an appearance – which Kit Lambert and Chris Stamp were instrumental in securing – on the TV pop programme *Ready Steady Go!* Although a surviving photo from the occasion shows the band dressed relatively soberly in comparison with the outlandish outfits they would soon be wearing, Hendrix's appearance and music were so alien that many viewers must have felt as though they were watching a broadcast from another galaxy. "Hey Joe" itself rose to number six in the British charts, although insiders have since admitted that this impressive performance was aided – as was often the case in those days – by arranging for numerous copies to be bought at shops which provided the returns on which the UK charts were based.

Such media exposure and promotional shenanigans were considered crucial, however, to giving Hendrix wider exposure than the in-crowd London circuit. As much as those gigs and jams at elite clubs frequented by rock stars had helped Jimi to make a name for himself, they weren't going to enable him to support himself financially. And the Experience needed money, especially as CBS Studios refused to allow them to continue recording there until Chandler had paid the bill. Chas did settle up, but never recorded at CBS with Hendrix again, cutting the Experience's follow-up single elsewhere.

Nonetheless, there were still a few more in-crowd appearances in London clubs before the Experience took off on the road to pop stardom, such as one at Blaises in late December with various Beatles and Rolling Stones in the crowd. No shows were more legendary than a couple of subsequent gigs at the **Bag O'Nails** in Soho on 11 January, attended by many top British rock musicians (and particularly guitarists). Although the list may have been embellished with time, it probably included John Lennon, Paul McCartney, Pete Townshend, Mick Jagger, Brian Jones, Donovan, Georgie Fame, Jeff Beck, Jimmy Page and members of The Hollies, Small Faces and Animals.

Several of the above returned during Hendrix's shows at the 7½ Club over the following week. These were followed by a performance at the hippest London club of all, the **Speakeasy**, where Hendrix tried to pull **Marianne Faithfull** right under the nose of her very famous then-boyfriend, Mick Jagger. Faithfull would later lament her gallant rebuff of Jimi's pass as one of the biggest regrets in her very colourful life.

Other key London dates in this eventful January included one at the legendary **Marquee** club, where the queue to get in ran for several hundred yards, and the **Saville Theatre**, owned by Beatles manager Brian Epstein. It was the latter gig, Eric Clapton told *Rolling Stone*, which inspired the genesis of Cream's early hard-rock classic "Sunshine of Your Love", as Jimi "played this gig that was blinding. I don't think [Cream bassist Jack Bruce] had really taken him in before. I knew what the guy was capable of from the minute I met him. It was the complete embodiment of all aspects of rock guitar rolled into one. I could sense it coming off the guy. And when [Jack] did see it that night, after the gig he went home and came up with the riff. It was strictly a dedication to Jimi. And then we wrote a song on top of it." Jimi would return the favour with a surprise performance of this very song on BBC television two years later, specifically dedicated to the just-disbanded Cream.

Curtain call at the Saville Theatre, 29 January 1967

The Jimi Hendrix British Boys' Club

Judging from retrospective accounts, it seems difficult to exaggerate the impact of Jimi Hendrix on leading British rockers in the heady days of late 1966 and early 1967. **Eric Clapton**, **Pete Townshend** and **Jeff Beck** – probably the top three UK rock guitarists at the time – have all enthused over Hendrix's revolutionary style. ("It was like a bomb blowing up in the right place", said Beck in the mid-1990s rock history documentary series *Rock & Roll*, of seeing Hendrix for the first time.) Jimi also deeply impressed some heavy hitters not known as lead guitarists, including **Paul McCartney**, **Eric Burdon** and Rolling Stones guitarist/multi-instrumentalist **Brian Jones**. Such was the hyperbole of their praise that you might think that they were cowed into a submission that made them want to give up competing in the guitar wars, much as Mike Bloomfield had felt it hopeless to match such an obviously superior guitarist when he had seen Hendrix in Greenwich Village.

Nonetheless, the impact does seem to have been exaggerated a bit. For one thing, Clapton, Townshend and Beck hardly hung up their axes or stopped trying to pull out all their own stops after the arrival of Hendrix. Clapton (with Cream) and Townshend (with The Who) did some of their greatest work in the late 1960s *after* Hendrix's emergence, and if Beck's wasn't as great, it certainly wasn't anything to be ashamed of. Moreover, none of them tried to beat Hendrix at his own game, or even overtly reflected his influence in their own wild effects-riddled solos. As highly talented players themselves, they probably realized that it was pointless to try and out-Hendrix Hendrix, and were secure enough in their own abilities to follow their own muses.

Rather less attention has been given to the influence that British guitarists like Clapton, Beck and Townshend might have had on Hendrix himself. Chas Chandler would later claim that the very first time he met Hendrix in New York, the guitarist asked him whether he knew

Recording *Are You Experienced?*

The success of "Hey Joe" was vital not just for increasing the number and quality of the Experience's bookings, but also for giving them the impetus they needed to complete an entire album. Even before its release, they had started work on more tracks, with Chandler producing (as he would for another year and a half). It was soon clear that there would be more than enough new Hendrix originals to make an exciting album, fired not just by Chandler's encouragement, but also by his collection of **science-fiction** books. Although songs like

"Purple Haze" and "Third Stone from the Sun" are often believed to have been generated by the psychedelic drugs that Jimi – like many top London rock stars – was taking, it's equally if not more likely that they were inspired by the books lying around the flat he shared with Chandler, as Chas often claimed. Chandler also made an underappreciated contribution by acting as an editor of Hendrix's lyrics. Jimi himself later admitted (to the London underground paper *International Times*) that even his early songs could often be "about ten pages long",

Clapton and that Chas's promise to introduce Jimi to Eric clinched his decision to move to London. There may be a bit of poetic licence in this oft-repeated story, given that Clapton – then just starting to perform with Cream – was almost as unknown in the States as Jimi was. Clapton had yet to visit the US, and the first studio album on which he was prominently featured, John Mayall's *Blues Breakers with Eric Clapton*, didn't even come out until mid-1966 in the UK, not getting issued in the States until the following year. (Although Clapton did play on about an LP's worth of Yardbirds tracks issued in the States in the mid-1960s, he was uncredited on these, his place having been taken by Jeff Beck by the time they were issued.) There again, Hendrix might have been sufficiently clued-up to find out about *Blues Breakers* via an import LP in the Village – for all his poverty, he was obviously somehow finding a way to hear out-of-the-way records at the time, as evidenced by his later cover of the non-LP Dylan single

"Can You Please Crawl Out Your Window?".

It seems inconceivable, on the other hand, that Jimi could have been unaware of Jeff Beck, who was the guitarist most responsible for developing the use of feedback and distorted sustain in rock music prior to Hendrix's emergence. In the *Rock & Roll* documentary, Beck confirmed that Jimi had specifically confessed to swiping a lick from the fabulous but relatively modest-charting late-1966 Yardbirds single "Happenings Ten Years Time Ago", which highlighted one of Jeff's most searingly psychedelic solos. The possible influence of Pete Townshend on Hendrix is less clear, especially as The Who had yet to score any US hits by the time Jimi moved to London. Again, however, it seems likely that Hendrix would have picked up on the ferocious feedback that Pete introduced into early Who records such as "My Generation", since there were very few other rock discs of the mid-1960s featuring such effects.

and such epics simply wouldn't fit onto commercially releasable recordings in late 1966 and early 1967.

From the early sessions for the album, it was clear that Hendrix was developing a remarkable knack for coming up with riffs that both rocked harder than granite and were immediately memorable. It was also clear that he was becoming a formidable lyricist, able to tap into almost absurd psychedelic imagery ("Purple Haze") with a likeably goofy, slightly spacey charm, as well as exude red-hot sexuality ("Foxy Lady", "Fire"). Yet other songs displayed a surprisingly sensitive, poetic side,

one capable of both tender romanticism ("The Wind Cries Mary") and vulnerable self-doubt ("Can You See Me", "Manic Depression", "Love or Confusion", "I Don't Live Today"). His grounding in the blues was nonetheless evident in **Red House** and, more subtly, **Highway Chile,** while the mostly instrumental **Third Stone from the Sun** acted as a vehicle for the mind-blowing howls, shudders and squeals he was learning to coax from his guitar.

Very much in parallel with his expanding abilities as an instrumentalist and singer-songwriter, Hendrix was also developing a ravenous appetite for experimenting with new kinds of gui-

The Story

tars, **amplifiers**, **effects** and **studio techniques**. By now it was apparent that the kinds of sounds he wanted to translate into reality, or at least onto vinyl, were not just testing the limits of the era's available technology, but in some cases totally beyond its capability. It was a challenge to capture a band on tape which almost certainly played louder than any previous group, especially when Hendrix brought stacks of **Marshall amps** into the studio. Such was the Experience's sheer volume that one of the early studios in which they worked, De Lane Lea, was reluctant to book them after the noise screwed up the computers in a bank on the next floor.

Hendrix also enlisted the help of **Roger Mayer** for then-futuristic gadgets like the **Octavia** and the **Fuzzface** fuzz box in what was already a never-ending quest for the most far-out effects that could be conjured from his guitar. Although he would take these to considerably further extremes on his later recordings, even on this first batch of tracks, there were sounds – the bee-buzz that starts "Foxy Lady", the almost pre-rap scratches of "Are You Experienced?", the fuzz-fests of "Purple Haze" and the whole catalogue of roars, scrapes and squiggles throughout "Third Stone from the

Sun" – that had never been heard before on a record of any sort. Hendrix was also starting to experiment with **overdubbing** and **multitracking** to create soundscapes that would have been utterly impossible to produce in live performance, although actually Jimi could come pretty close to recreating even some of the more elaborate of these onstage.

For the time being, however, it was important for any band, no matter how far-out, to try for hit singles as well as create album-length statements. This was even true of the most creative psychedelic bands emerging from London's underground scene in late 1966 and early 1967, like **Pink Floyd** and **Soft Machine**, the latter of whom were also signed by Chandler and Jeffery. Actually a good half-dozen of the fifteen or so songs the Experience would work on over the next few months would have made fine, commercial hit singles, and it still surprises some people that "Foxy Lady" and "Fire" weren't released as such at the time. But few could argue with the choice of "Purple Haze" as the follow-up single, and it solidified The Jimi Hendrix Experience's position as a major act on the UK music scene when it reached number three in the spring of 1967.

Today London, Tomorrow the World

By this time, the Experience were touring around the country, and occasionally on the Continent, with a regularity that was punishing even by the standards of the day. From the New Year through to the end of May, in fact, they played a show on nearly every single date, and

often more than one set. The notoriety they were accumulating wasn't solely due to their innovative music, either. Even in a nation that had revolutionized fashion and hair length through "beat groups" (as they were called in Britain) or British Invasion acts (as they were known

The Story

in North America) like The Beatles, Kinks and Rolling Stones, Hendrix stood out as something quite different. Outrageous fashion statements were *de rigueur* in Carnaby Street's heyday, but Jimi took things to a higher level with increasingly florid scarves, shirts, headbands, floppy hats and jewellery. For quite a long spell, he also donned military jackets, something not every conservative Englishman took a liking to, although any anger usually dissipated when it was learned that Hendrix himself had served in the US Army. Topped by his puffed-up flowing hairdo, it was almost as if he was living out the vivid imagery of his songs in real life.

There was also Hendrix's onstage **showmanship**, which saw his moves becoming progressively bolder and wilder. Playing behind his back, with his teeth and while somersaulting wowed the crowds, as did humping the amplifier with his guitar and, on less regular occasions, even smashing or burning it. Even when Jimi wasn't humping the amp, his sexual postures were often so explicit that few members of the audience could have missed them, even the young teenage girls attending the Experience's first nationwide package tour that spring with a young **Cat Stevens,** fellow American expatriates **The Walker Brothers** and (believe it or not) **Engelbert Humperdinck,** the unctuously smooth middle-of-the-road balladeer whose recent cover of the country ballad "Release Me" had managed to keep The Beatles' classic "Penny Lane"/"Strawberry Fields Forever" off the top of the UK singles charts.

As for not only singing about "Fire" but literally setting fire to his guitar, that particular

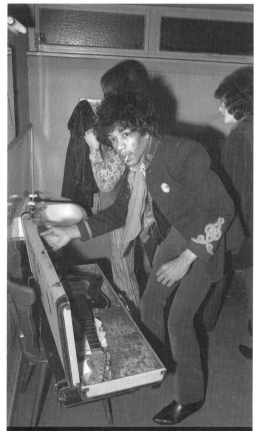

Hamburg, March 1967 – backstage with guitar case.
Photo: Friedhelm von Estorff

stage move was cooked up on the very first date of the tour, at the suggestion of rock journalist Keith Altham. Altham was joking – Jimi would have needed a blowtorch to get his instrument to burn properly. Chas Chandler, however, came up with the idea of using lighter fuel to create the illusion of setting fire to the guitar without actually burning it, and after a few successful try-outs in the dressing room, Jimi had another eye-catching gimmick for his act.

It wasn't an easy thing to pull off onstage – on this occasion and at least one other (at the Monterey Pop festival), it took a few attempts for the match to catch after Jimi poured lighter fluid on his instrument. That Hendrix was willing to risk injury to produce such flash testifies not only to his genuine onstage wildness, but also the need that was still felt by musicians and their handlers in early 1967 to get press attention with stunts that had little to do with the music – even if, in this first instance, Jimi *did* set his axe on fire at the end of an actual *song* called "Fire".

Some critics have felt that such showmanship was more or less what both Hendrix and numerous other soul/R&B entertainers had been doing on the chitlin' circuit for years, putting down the crowd reaction to the inexperience of callow white Europeans who had rarely seen African-American performers of any sort, let alone such uninhibited ones. There's some truth to this, but realistically, Hendrix's show wasn't a mere mimic or even extension of the extravagant spectacles mounted by such legends as Bo Diddley or his old boss Little Richard. It was truly wilder than just about any rock show previously done anywhere, on any continent. It was also rather at odds with an offstage demeanour almost unfailingly remembered by those who knew and encountered him as soft-spoken, polite, humble and even a bit shy. The dichotomy would soon cause its own problems

as Jimi felt pressured to live up to the image he had created, both in concert and offstage.

Whether or not Chandler might have had this in mind when he asked Jimi to come to London, it's fortunate that Hendrix was able to develop this persona in the UK rather than his native US. Dressing like he did and having white girlfriends might have been okay for a young African-American in Greenwich Village, but it would have been tolerated in few other neighbourhoods in the United States, and might well have risked not only insult but personal injury in the Southern towns Hendrix played on the chitlin' circuit. In a British society where prejudice was less ingrained, Jimi was freer to do as he pleased, though even there he was sometimes viewed as a specimen or novelty act of sorts; the "wild man of Borneo" tag applied to him on some occasions in his early UK days would certainly be judged as politically incorrect today.

In the early spring of 1967, with two hit singles behind them and a third ("The Wind Cries Mary"/"Highway Chile") in the wings, the Experience assembled their debut album from various sessions stretching over a period of several months. For all its magnificence and long-ranging influence, the sessions for *Are You Experienced?* were pretty piecemeal and, if not exactly rushed, certainly not allowed to run nearly as long as subsequent recording dates, where Hendrix was given a long leash to fiddle around with and perfect his tracks. When "The Wind Cries Mary" was cut, in fact, Mitchell and Redding were recording without even having had a chance to hear the song in advance. Sessions had to be fitted in here and there in the few times Hendrix's hectic touring schedule would allow, at various studios around London. At one of these, Olympic Studios, Jimi would meet and work for the first time with staff engineer **Eddie Kramer**, who would play a significant role in many of Hendrix's recordings throughout the rest of the guitarist's career.

Considering the relative haste and stop-start manner in which it was recorded, *Are You Experienced?* was a remarkably cohesive-sounding, mature work. Even with three of the best of Hendrix's late-1966/early-1967 recordings having been skimmed off for singles, it contained several tracks ("Foxy Lady", "Fire", "Manic Depression") that even back then immediately became nearly as well known as his chart hits. There might have been the odd relatively unmemorable song like "Remember" and "May This Be Love", but that was only in comparison to the shinier jewels that surrounded them.

So different was it to anything that had preceded it that Chas Chandler was still nervous when the time finally came to present the fruit of the group's labours to Horst Schmaltze, head of A&R at Polydor, the company that would distribute the LP in Europe and the UK. As Chas recalled in *Jimi Hendrix: Sessions* (written by John McDermott with Billy Cox and Eddie Kramer), Schmaltze played the whole album through without uttering a single word, then told the terrified Chandler: "'This is brilliant. This is the greatest thing I've ever heard.' I let out a loud, 'Aaah!' Horst became a great supporter of the band from that point forward."

Neither Schmaltze nor Chandler would have to worry about whether the public would feel the same way. With *Are You Experienced?* reaching number two in the British album charts, where it stayed for more than half a year, and "The Wind Cries Mary" becoming their third straight top-ten single, The Jimi Hendrix Experience were now upper-echelon superstars in the UK. Their influence now extended not just to the leading rock musicians who witnessed the group's early shows, but to scores of bands and recordings which reflected the innovations and reckless volume of Jimi's guitar work in particular.

With the near-simultaneous release of *Are You Experienced?* and "The Wind Cries Mary" in May 1967, the Experience's increased status saw them spending much of the month touring the European continent. One particularly odd gig found them sharing a bill at the Star Palast in Kiel, Germany with **The Monks**, American ex-soldiers who had shaved their heads and donned monk costumes to perform furiously minimalist rock, their sole album belatedly finding a fervent cult following decades later. Typically, an open-minded Hendrix took it as an opportunity to learn something from a support band many would have dismissed as a novelty act.

"We'd always buy the newest electronic stuff, because one of our premises to make the music was to experiment", Monks bassist Eddie Shaw told the author in an interview about thirty years later. "We had the wah-wah pedals, and the only way to do them, is you had to move 'em from left to right. They didn't go up and down, they went left to right, and [Monks

The Jimi Hendrix Experience play *Top of the Pops*, March 1967

guitarist Gary Burger] had to give his knee an awkward movement to do that. I used to stand down at the edge of the stage and make fun of him when he did it, and he used to hate it. But Hendrix was genuinely interested in it. And he didn't see anything humorous about it at all. I remember on break he was asking Gary, 'Where'd you get that?' And Gary told him it was shipped from the States." Within a couple of months, Jimi was using **wah-wah pedals** as yet more tools in his attempts to stretch electric guitar textures to their upper boundaries.

There were also more prestigious TV bookings to fulfil that spring, including slots on the BBC's *Top of the Pops*. Such was the Experience's prestige that they headlined over Cream, Pink Floyd and The Move on 29 May at a festival

of sorts billed as "Barbecue 67", in the unlikely location of Spalding, Lincolnshire. In an antici-pation of things to come, Hendrix showed his frustration, both with the imperfections of his equipment and the expectations of the crowd. As a young Germaine Greer reported in the British underground paper *Oz*, the audience "didn't even care whether 'Hey Joe' was in tune or not. They just wanted to hear something and adulate. They wanted him to give head to his guitar and rub his cock over it. They didn't want to hear him play. But Jimi wanted, like he always wanted, to play it sweet and high. So he did it, and he fucked with his guitar and they moaned and swayed about, and he looked at them heavily and knew that they couldn't hear what he was trying to do and never would."

Jimi Hendrix's Lonely Hearts Club Band

Although The Beatles probably didn't have as much influence on Hendrix as more guitar-oriented British acts, there's little doubt that he, like most premier 1960s rock musicians, paid close attention to each new Beatles release. He certainly did so when *Sgt. Pepper's Lonely Hearts Club Band* came out in the UK on 1 June 1967.

When Hendrix played London's Saville Theatre on 4 June, he opened – to the surprise of the audience, not least of an actual Beatle in the seats, Paul McCartney – with the title track of *Sgt. Pepper*. As McCartney later marvelled to Barry Miles in *Paul McCartney: Many Years from Now*: "To think that that album had meant so much to him as to actually do it ... three days after the release." Describing it as "a pretty major compliment in anyone's book", McCartney put it down as one of the great honours of his career.

Perhaps Hendrix decided to give a nod to The Beatles not just because McCartney was in the audi-

ence, but also because the Saville was owned by the group's manager, Brian Epstein. There can be no doubt that Jimi liked the song, however, as he would continue to give it his rough'n'funky spin in concert for years. Even shortly before his death, he was still playing it onstage, as shown by its inclusion in his set at the 1970 Isle of Wight festival. And it was obviously not the only Beatles record that had caught his ear, as his radio performance of "Day Tripper" in December 1967 (available on the *BBC Sessions* CD) confirms.

Incidentally, it's widely known that McCartney helped Hendrix get on the bill for the Monterey Pop festival, but not nearly as well known that Paul also wanted the Experience to play in The Beatles' late-1967 TV special, *Magical Mystery Tour*. Although he was grateful for the offer, by that time Jimi didn't need the exposure, and the only other group to appear in the movie would be Britain's top comedy-rock act, The Bonzo Dog Band.

The big prize, however – and where the biggest money lay – was the US market, home of the largest and most affluent record-buying population in the world. In a day when international communications were far slower than they are in the twenty-first century, and UK vinyl imports far less available than they would be in just a few years' time, Hendrix remained almost as unknown in his homeland as he had been on his departure. One commendably far-sighted action Mike Jeffery was apparently instrumental in taking on Hendrix's behalf was securing a deal for US distribution of his recordings with **Reprise Records**, a subsidiary of Warner Bros.,

in early 1967. Although Jimi had yet to become a superstar abroad and was an unproven quantity in the US, his management also obtained an advance (reported to be as high as $120,000) and promotional commitment that was impressive by the standards of the day. Although Reprise did issue The Kinks' records in the US, the label was better known for middle-of-the-road pop by its founder Frank Sinatra and his buddy Dean Martin. Shrewdly, however, they saw Hendrix as a chance to establish themselves in the rock market.

In breaking Hendrix in the US, Chas Chandler and Mike Jeffery were – like Jimi with his own music – moving into unknown territory. They had already pulled off a difficult enough feat in helping to make Jimi into a star in the UK; The Walker Brothers and P.J. Proby were the only other American artists of the mid-1960s who had managed to become big in Britain before having hits at home. Making the trip in reverse had proved difficult, however, for both The Walker Brothers (who had just a couple of medium-sized hits in the US) and Proby (who had just one). But Hendrix was clearly a bigger phenomenon, and was probably hungrier than most such artists would have been in his position to return home as a conquering hero, given the many indignities he had suffered there as a struggling sideman in the early-to-mid-1960s. Even though "Hey Joe" failed to chart following its belated US release on 1 May, plans were already afoot to have Jimi create just as big a sensation there as he had in the UK and Europe.

The astonishing impact Hendrix had made on London's rock aristocracy paid off when, partly thanks to the lobbying of The Beatles' **Paul McCartney**, the Experience gained a slot at the **Monterey Pop festival** in mid-June. Taking place in northern California, this was the first true big modern rock festival, and although The Beatles themselves weren't appearing, McCartney wielded some influence as a member of the board for the event. It would also serve as a good launch pad for the Experience's first US tour, as it was thought – correctly – that Jimi's dynamic concert act would be immensely valuable in making his name known, especially in the absence of hit records. While not planned as a thank-you gesture, in a way Hendrix paid back McCartney in kind by making the title track of the just-released *Sgt. Pepper's Lonely Hearts Club Band* the opening number of his final British concert before taking off for the States, with Paul himself in the audience.

Ten days later, on 13 June, the Experience flew to the US. It had only been nine months since Hendrix had left, but musically and even visually, he was unrecognizable from the struggling guitarist who had been spotted in New York the previous year. Although in one sense he was starting again from scratch, this time he was doing it from a position of strength.

International Stardom

1967–1968

"I enjoyed his soundcheck more than anything else. He walked on, plugged into one of his pedals, turned the whole volume up as loud as possible, smashed the guitar once, and that was it."

Bert Jansch recalls Hendrix's preparing for the "Guitar-In" at the Festival Hall, London, 25 September 1967

International Stardom 1967–1968

In spite of his mammoth success in the UK over the previous six months or so, Hendrix must have been more than a little nervous when the Experience flew to California to make their US debut at the Monterey Pop festival.

The Monterey Pop Festival and the First American Tour

Although he had a deal in place for major-label distribution of his recordings, Jimi was still virtually unknown Stateside, except by a few music-industry insiders. And yet his unveiling would take place, not in the sort of relatively small clubs that had hosted his first British performances, but in front of the biggest crowd ever to attend a rock concert up to that point. Yet at the same time, Hendrix's self-confidence as a musician and performer must have grown enormously since he had last set foot on American soil. With such a prestigious initial gig, he would have been justified in feeling like a conquering hero returning home, even if few if any members of the audience would have known him when he was still called Jimmy Hendrix. As in London, his very anonymity remained an asset of sorts – there was no previ-ous track record to judge him against, making his allure all the more alien and exotic, as if he had shot onto the scene from nowhere. And for all his shyness, Hendrix also had a burning, competitive ambition. He wasn't going to let anything or anyone stop him from making the maximum impact he could muster, using the theatrics he had developed to such a fine art in his time away to make a permanent imprint on his first big US audience.

The Monterey Pop festival certainly boasted an impressive line-up, both in terms of estab-lished stars and hot newcomers. Organized by John Phillips of **The Mamas and the Papas** and the group's producer, **Lou Adler**, it was conceived as a charitable event, with the per-formers (apart from Ravi Shankar) being paid expenses only. Although there were a

The Story

few big pop-rock acts such as The Mamas and the Papas and Simon and Garfunkel, the accent was more on new Californian folk-rock and psychedelic groups like The Byrds, Buffalo Springfield, Country Joe and the Fish, and Jefferson Airplane. A number of San Francisco-area groups who had yet to break nationally would be there (The Grateful Dead, Big Brother and the Holding Company, and Quicksilver Messenger Service), and while Otis Redding was already a soul star, this would be his biggest exposure yet to a white audience. Probably the only other acts on the bill that Hendrix was relatively familiar with were **Eric Burdon and the Animals** and **The Who**. Even though The Who had already played some American shows, they were just as eager to play Monterey as Jimi was, having yet to make a big US breakthrough. A film crew headed by documentary maker D.A. Pennebaker (previously responsible for the Bob Dylan documentary *Don't Look Back*) would also be on hand to capture the event for posterity.

As it happened, the Experience were scheduled to play on the final day of the festival, 18 June, around the same time as The Who. Although – as is the case with many crucial events in Hendrix's career – there are different versions of what happened backstage, neither group was keen to follow the other, especially since both of them relied upon some of the same sensationalistic onstage routines. The most commonly accepted account has the toss of a coin deciding the issue (as with the selection of Mitch Mitchell as the Experience's drummer), with The Who taking the stage

Jimi mentally prepares backstage at Monterey with John Entwistle of The Who looking on

first, to be followed by Hendrix. The Who's performance, as illustrated when much of the set was finally issued on an expanded DVD edition of the *Monterey Pop* film, actually wasn't one of their best. However, their final number, "My Generation", ended with explosive scenes of guitar-and-equipment smashing which understandably wowed an audience still largely unfamiliar with the band.

The Experience vs. The Who

Over the decades there have been varying accounts of the argument about which act should go on first at Monterey, the Experience or The Who. What seems clear is that neither was eager to follow the other, and that the argument was primarily between Hendrix and The Who's lead guitarist and chief songwriter, Pete Townshend. Given the similarly aggressive exhibitionism of their acts – climaxing in the destruction of their guitars – it might have made more sense to schedule them on different days of the festival, or at least not right after each other. Lumped together they were, however, and backstage there was some heated discussion as to who should go first.

"Before the show at Monterey, we were starting to talk about the running order", Townshend recalled about five years later in the *Jimi Hendrix* documentary. "He said, 'I'm not gonna follow you on.' So I said, 'Listen. *We* are not gonna follow *you* on, and that is *it*.'" Whereupon, according to Townshend, Jimi stood on a chair and played some astonishing guitar to onlookers like Janis Joplin, Brian Jones and Eric Burdon before getting off and warning Pete: "If I'm gonna follow you, I'm gonna pull all the stops."

In a 1987 interview for VH1, however, Townshend told a rather different story. Jimi was sky-high on acid,

claimed Pete, and wouldn't even discuss the matter. Townshend, however, was hoping that, as friends, the pair would talk it over, especially as it would probably be the first time most people in the crowd had seen how they ended their acts. When Townshend finally confronted Hendrix, however, Jimi said that he would go on first, whereupon Pete told him: "I think you are a great artist, and I think I'm not. I think I'm gonna have trouble with that. Would you go on after us?"

The dispute was finally resolved when, according to Townshend, either Brian Jones or John Phillips suggested tossing a coin: "And then everything was okay. But I saw him at the airport on the way home the next day and tried to talk to him about it, and he was still pretty pissed." When Townshend met Hendrix later in Los Angeles, however, Jimi had forgotten all about it.

In the end, the running order didn't matter either way, since Monterey turned out to be a key stepping stone to great US success for both Hendrix and The Who, with neither triumphing at the expense of the other. "I remember I sat down with Mama Cass [of The Mamas and the Papas] to watch Jimi, and Jimi started to pour lighter fluid over his guitar", Townshend added. "She turned to me and said, 'Isn't that your act?' And I said, 'It's our act.'"

Now Hendrix somehow had to top them, a feat that, to his enormous credit, he managed to pull off. Introduced by his friend **Brian Jones** of The Rolling Stones (who weren't actually on the bill, though Jones came to watch, as did Paul McCartney), Jimi delivered a tight and electrifying set. Alongside all three of his British hit singles, Hendrix performed "Foxy Lady" and radical reinterpretations of Dylan's "Like a

Rolling Stone" (to which he admitted forgetting the words at one point), B.B. King's "Rock Me Baby" and Howlin' Wolf's "Killing Floor".

Hendrix brought the set to a climactic close with another cover: a mauling of The Troggs' 1966 chart-topper "Wild Thing" which ended with Jimi setting fire to his guitar – probably the only way to upstage The Who's autodestruct act. He had talked about sacrificing something

Jimi onstage at Monterey

he loved in his spoken introduction to the number, but only the very few who had seen or heard about him doing it before could possibly have anticipated that he would actually set his instrument alight. For good measure, he also smashed the guitar to smithereens on the stage before tossing its remnants into the audience. With little or no advance warning about what they were about to see, the Monterey audience was astounded, and Hendrix almost immediately started blazing a path to US stardom that would be nearly as rapid as the one he had just completed in the UK. Only The Who, Janis Joplin (as lead singer of Big Brother and the Holding Company) and Otis Redding – all also highlighted in the *Monterey Pop* film – rivalled him in the breakthrough performance department at the three-day festival.

For all its subsequent notoriety, however, Monterey wasn't an instant passport to American success. The performance wasn't televised, the film wouldn't come out until the following year and – hard as it might be to believe today – Hendrix's set wasn't universally praised. *Billboard* magazine, the leading US music trade publication, gave it a negative review. More surprisingly, Robert Christgau, the doyen of American rock critics, found Hendrix "terrible", describing him as "a psychedelic Uncle Tom" who couldn't sing. Christgau would radically revise his opinion of Hendrix soon enough, but his piece – written for *Esquire* – demonstrated that Jimi's showmanship wasn't to everybody's taste. "I suppose Hendrix's act can be understood as a consistently vulgar parody of rock theatrics", the critic sniffed, "but I don't feel I have to like it."

But the vibes from the audience at Monterey – and, perhaps even more importantly to Hendrix, from fellow musicians – were almost wholly positive, sometimes ecstatically so. The Experience's elation continued when they immediately followed the festival with a week of well-received, two-sets-a-night concerts at **San Francisco's Fillmore West**, then not only the top psychedelic venue in the US, but an epicentre of international youth counterculture in general. As if that weren't enough, there was also a free concert at Golden Gate Park; more shows in southern California, including the famed Whisky A Go Go; and then a triumphant return to New York, with a couple of shows at the Scene Club in early July, followed by a concert in Central Park with top hit-makers The Rascals. Around this time Hendrix also made his first US recordings with the Experience (in both L.A. and New York), now as a hot property, rather than as a mere sideman.

In retrospect, perhaps Hendrix should have followed the same path for the rest of this initial US tour, playing in the underground-oriented venues and liberal cities in which he was most likely to be appreciated. Or, if not many such gigs were available – and the psychedelic "ballroom" circuit of clubs and auditoriums such as the Fillmore was only just starting to get off the ground – maybe the Experience should have gone back to touring the UK and Europe until such time as their records penetrated the American market. Instead, Mike Jeffery opted for a strategy that has come to seem even more senseless with the passage of time. He arranged for the Experience to work

The Experience vs. The Monkees

The aborted July 1967 tour which saw The Jimi Hendrix Experience playing as one of the opening acts for The Monkees was memorably described by John Morthland in *The Rolling Stone Illustrated History of Rock & Roll* as a combination "that must have been conceived in a lunatic asylum". In fact, it was largely the brainchild of the lunatic running the asylum, Hendrix's co-manager, Mike Jeffery. Jeffery had arranged the slot through **Dick Clark**, then the most powerful personality in the US rock media through his television programme and other business ventures, including concert promotion. Chas Chandler thought the idea was crazy and was very upset about it, and one imagines that Hendrix, Noel Redding, and Mitch Mitchell were hardly any happier, especially after they had won over the audience at both Monterey and the Fillmore West.

It was Chandler who came to the rescue when it became increasingly evident that the combination wasn't working. Jeffery was afraid that Clark would sue if the Experience pulled out of the tour, but fortunately Chas already knew Dick from his Animals days and was able to work something out, especially as Clark agreed how poorly the two acts meshed. To provide a convenient excuse, and no doubt to boost the Experience's notoriety, a story was invented that the conservative women's group **The Daughters of the American Revolution** had objected to young Monkees fans being exposed to Hendrix's overtly sexual onstage antics. Rather surprisingly, nobody from the Daughters of the American Revolution ever seems to have challenged this fabrication, which ultimately seems to have done both them and the Experience little harm.

Some accounts claim that Hendrix got on better with The Monkees than has usually been reported. "We loved it, we had a great time", Monkees drummer/singer Micky Dolenz recalled in Andrew Sandoval's *The Monkees*. "He was a fan of ours, that's why he went on the tour. He liked what we were doing. I think he recognized the kind of show business carnival atmosphere. The kids I think quite liked it. It's probably the mothers that objected the most when he started pissing [*sic*] on his guitar and stuff like that." Dolenz, who – along with fellow Monkee Peter Tork – had seen Hendrix at Monterey, has also said that he helped get Jimi on the tour, feeling that the different forms of theatricality of the two acts would complement each other well.

In an interview given to the *New Musical Express* shortly after the Experience pulled out of the tour, however, Hendrix himself painted a rather different picture. In his phrase, the Experience were initially given the "death" spot in the programme, having to play right before The Monkees were scheduled to appear, forcing Jimi to perform over impatient screams for the headliners. Finally, however, the Experience were allowed to go on first, which made for a big improvement. "We got screams and good reaction, and some kids even rushed the stage", he claimed. But then "some parents who brought their young kids complained that our act was vulgar. We decided it was just not the right audience."

Hendrix added that he had got on well with Dolenz and Tork. Obviously, his outlook had softened since he had given his opinion of The Monkees to *Melody Maker* before the US tour: "God, I hate them!" he exclaimed. "Dishwater. I really hate somebody like that to make it so big."

The Story

Herman's Hermits, whose audience was scarcely more mature and sophisticated than the Monkees'. Jeffery might well have also reasoned that The Monkees were so huge at the time that the Experience stood to benefit substantially from *any* exposure on what was guaranteed to be a hugely successful, massively attended tour. Hendrix and The Monkees were just too different, however, for such a combination to do Jimi much good; the audiences were too young, and in any case, only there to see their TV heart-throbs.

Equally importantly, the Experience and Chas Chandler were disgusted by the charade as well. Playing in front of such inappropriate and uninterested audiences was little short of humiliating for musicians who had just wowed the *crème de la crème* of the rock cognoscenti. Yet judging by Lillian Roxon's description of one of their final shows with The Monkees in mid-July at Forest Hills Stadium in New York, Jimi wasn't exactly toning down his act for the teenyboppers. As she later recounted in her *Rock Encyclopedia*, he was still turning up the amplifiers as loud as they could go, and performing in a manner many upstanding citizens would find downright indecent in its sexual suggestiveness. Comparing Hendrix to Christ, Roxon described how the star did things to his guitar "so passionate, so concentrated and so intense that anyone with halfway decent manners had to look away. And that was the way the act began, not ended. By the time it was over he had lapped and nuzzled his guitar with his lips and tongue, caressed it with his inner thighs, jabbed at it with a series of powerful

as the supporting act on a nationwide tour by **The Monkees**, then the biggest-selling group in the US, albeit a manufactured one which appealed primarily to the teenyboppers who watched their TV sitcom show.

Although Jeffery's decision may seem indefensible, it should be noted that such chalk-and-cheese combinations were then far from unknown. At the very same time, The Who undertook a two-month tour as one of the opening acts for chirpy British pop-rockers pelvic thrusts." As Roxon observed, even the little girls who had come to see their TV idols could hardly fail to understand what this was all about. "What Mick Jagger and the early rockers had so saucily promised and hinted at", she concluded, "Jimi Hendrix delivered."

After only about ten days, Hendrix was taken off the Monkees tour, his management inventing a story which claimed that he had been forced off by the conservative women's movement **The Daughters of the American Revolution**. The next month, the Experience played more suitable venues, principally hip clubs in New York, although there were also shows in Washington, DC, and the prestigious **Hollywood Bowl** in Los Angeles on 18 August (albeit as support act for The Mamas and the Papas). Once again, however, someone had screwed up and *Are You Experienced?* wasn't released in the US until 23 August, a few days after the group had flown back to London. Reprise Records lost out by not having the record available at a time when hip rock fans were getting blown away by Hendrix in concert, and one imagines that the UK edition of the LP must have done incredibly brisk business in the few American shops selling import albums at the time.

At least Jimi and his bandmates were able to do some more recording in New York with Chandler and engineer Gary Kellgren, including their next single, **The Burning of the Midnight Lamp/The Stars That Play with Laughing Sam's Dice.** Kellgren would work on other Hendrix sessions in the US, and Jimi welcomed the chance to catch up with old New York friends,

now as an amazing success story. One was Charles Otis, a drummer for John Hammond from whom Jimi had borrowed $40 before leaving New York. Now Hendrix was able, as Hammond later told it, to pull out a roll of hundred and thousand dollar bills and ask Otis to take what he needed, although the drummer simply took the $40 that he was owed.

Another of those old friends was Curtis Knight, with whom Hendrix unfortunately and inexplicably made some more recordings for Ed Chalpin, who was already trying to stop Jimi from releasing more discs with the Experience until the dispute over his old contract with Chalpin was settled. The incident also illustrated some character traits that would cause Hendrix even more problems as his success grew: a willingness to entrust some of his career to unsavoury figures, a disregard for the niceties of business matters in general, and a reluctance to stand up to those who were using him for their own personal gain – which seems surprising in view of his supreme confidence in his own musical and performing abilities.

When the Reprise Records version of *Are You Experienced?* did come out in the US, it was somewhat altered – as was customary for the time – from the original UK release. Three of the songs ("Can You See Me", "Red House" and "Remember") were removed and replaced by the A-sides of Hendrix's first three British singles, "Hey Joe", "Purple Haze" and "The Wind Cries Mary". Including tracks on LPs that had previously been released on 45s was something that was usually avoided by major acts in the UK, and their inclusion on the US

Jimi Hendrix, Michelle Phillips and Cass Elliot sit together backstage at the Hollywood Bowl in 1967

version of Hendrix's debut album could be seen as tampering with what the artist had originally intended. In addition, a question mark was added to both the title of the LP and its title track, and, less explicably, the spelling of "Foxy Lady" was changed to "Foxey Lady".

Nitpicking apart, the substitutions actually made the LP even stronger, and as the three tracks from British singles weren't American hits anyway – though "Purple Haze" struggled to number 65 – very few US fans would have already owned the material in a different format. A new sleeve design was used as well, and again, while this was a departure from the original, the distorted fish-eye lens photo of the Experience was superior to the rather flat UK version, as well as being far more in tune with the psychedelic image of Hendrix that was helping to attract many American fans.

Ultimately, Reprise's delay in issuing *Are You Experienced?* didn't seem to matter. Even with the Experience out of the country for the rest of 1967, and even without the boost from a hit single, the LP began to sell well straight away, reaching number five and staying in the top forty for a remarkable 77 weeks. Hendrix thus became the very first major rock artist to sell enormous numbers of albums in the US without the benefit of big chart 45s. Partly, this was down to fortuitous timing: album-oriented, youth counterculture-targeted FM radio was just taking off in the country, as was the underground rock press, and rock-loving youth itself was growing up and shifting their purchasing power from singles to LPs. Much of Hendrix's success, however, was due to the sheer strength of his debut and the albums that followed it.

In this, as in so many other respects, Hendrix was a trailblazer whose influence is still felt throughout the rock world. Yet despite his deep roots in blues and R&B, he was selling much more heavily to a white audience than a black one, and getting far more airplay on radio stations targeted toward white psy-chedelic rock listeners than outlets aimed at the African-American community. Jimi would have much rather been equally popular with both constituencies, but this imbalance would remain for the rest of his life, and has since been only partially redressed.

Yet for all its glitches, the Experience's first US tour must be considered a highly successful one, both in helping them to break into the all-important American market and in providing Hendrix with a great sense of personal triumph. Soon, indeed, the States would be his primary market, but for now the Experience needed to return to the UK, which was still their commercial stronghold as *Are You Experienced?* hit American record shops.

Back to London

No sooner had the Experience got back from the US than they resumed a heavy touring schedule. The first concert, headlining at Brian Epstein's Saville Theatre on 27 August, was no doubt intended to be one of the most triumphant. It turned tragic, however, when the second show was cancelled after news had spread of Epstein's unexpected death earlier that day. (Incidentally, while he's sometimes caricatured as a stuffy sort more interested in Sibelius than rock, Epstein was undoubtedly a Hendrix admirer, calling him "an ace guitarist" in a February 1967 interview with famed New York radio DJ **Murray the K** – possibly the first major piece of publicity Jimi ever got in the United States.)

One high point was the Experience's participation in what was billed as a "Guitar-In"

at the **Royal Festival Hall** on 25 September. Hendrix and his group were the only rockers on the bill, which also included classical duo Tim Walker and Seb Jorgensen, flamenco player Paco Peña and the great British folk guitarist, Bert Jansch. "I enjoyed his soundcheck more than anything else", Jansch told biographer Colin Harper in *Dazzling Stranger: Bert Jansch and the British Folk and Blues Revival*. "He walked on, plugged into one of his pedals, turned the whole volume up as loud as possible, smashed [a chord on] the guitar once, and that was it." In what might have been their most unusual photo opportunity, the Experience were also snapped fooling around with then British Liberal Party leader Jeremy Thorpe, the politician even holding Hendrix's psychedelic

Jeremy Thorpe meets the Experience at the RFH

Hallyday. They were filmed on- and offstage for a TV documentary, *Experience*, narrated by British blues godfather Alexis Korner. There was also an end-of-year package tour – an institution that was beginning to decline with the rise of the university/alternative circuit – with **Amen Corner, The Move, The Nice** (with Keith Emerson) and new psychedelic stars **Pink Floyd**, then struggling to cope with the breakdown of their initial leader, **Syd Barrett**.

Today it sounds like a bill 1960s music fans would die to see, but it still wasn't the ideal showcase for the Experience (or for any of the bands except perhaps Amen Corner): the audiences were too young and – at just twenty minutes per act – the sets too short. Hendrix's massive popularity and the mushrooming of more suitable venues, however, meant that the Experience would never have to play a package tour again. Numerous multi-artist **festivals** were also starting to sprout up in the US and Europe, one precursor being a "Christmas on Earth" show the Experience played at London's Olympia exhibition arena on 22 December, with The Animals, The Move, Pink Floyd, Soft Machine, The Who and others.

guitar as he shared a laugh with the boys.

In addition to British gigs and TV/radio shows (at one of which the Experience jammed off-mike with Stevie Wonder), there was also quite a bit of work in Sweden and Holland, and a TV programme in Paris, where they played L'Olympia again – this time as headliners, rather than as a support act to Johnny

Recording *Axis: Bold as Love*

Even before *Are You Experienced?* reached the peak of its sales, Hendrix was clearly already itching to scale new sonic heights. "We have other sounds to make, other singles and LPs to cut", he emphasized to the Los Angeles underground paper *Open City* just before the end of the American tour, a few days prior to the belat-

ed US release of *Are You Experienced?* "Critics are already classifying us on the basis of ten months ... one album and perhaps one or two concerts they've heard. I think it's time for these people to understand that we are not always in the same bag with each performance. How can you be – when you are constantly reaching,

The Story

Jimi Hendrix, Science-Fiction Fan

Much of the imagery in Hendrix's lyrics is so other-worldly that many fans assume that it must have been the product of regular acid trips. No doubt Hendrix took his share of LSD, as he made all too obvious on the title of one of his B-sides, "The Stars That Play with Laughing Sam's Dice". No doubt, too, his imagination was already vivid enough that it didn't need to be jump-started by acid or any other drug. Some of his most colourful and fantasy-strewn lyrics, however, turn out to have fairly specific sources in the world of **science fiction**, Chas Chandler's collection of literature in that genre probably doing as much to fire Jimi's muse as any exotic substances did.

Such was the case with one of Hendrix's first and most psychedelic songs, **Purple Haze** – not the slang term for a particularly potent pill or a description of hallucinogenic effects, but said by Jimi himself to derive from a science-fiction tale he had read in which "purple death rays" played a part. The source in question was probably Philip Jose Farmer's 1957 story "Night of Light", which refers to a "purplish haze" in the nocturnal sky. The story was expanded into a novel of the same name, which was first published in June 1966 – just in time, perhaps, for Jimi to come across it in Chas's collection.

Chandler himself made it clear that he thought both **Third Stone from the Sun** and *Axis: Bold as Love*'s **Up from the Skies** were inspired by the books Hendrix

improvising, experimenting? It's impossible. It is just going to take time to reach these labellers with our sounds." Throughout the rest of his career, Hendrix always seemed to be planning to move in new directions and explore new concepts way beyond what he had managed to record and release, even if he sometimes had a hard time translating these ambitions into reality, or even clearly explaining what he had in mind.

As busy as the Experience were, there was a bit more time to fit in recording sessions, by now the work that mattered the most to Hendrix. The sessions for *Axis: Bold as Love* themselves, too, were allowed to go on for longer, and Jimi was given more freedom to fuss over every stage of the recording process. Though impressive, his **perfectionism** could be frustrating for his fellow musicians and studio staff, whose patience was

increasingly tried as Jimi insisted on redoing parts that most people would have been satisfied with on the first or second take.

In contrast to the ad hoc nature of the sessions for his first album and singles, more stability was ensured by the use of just one studio, London's **Olympic Studios**, and one engineer, the reliable **Eddie Kramer**, who shared Jimi's appetite for sonic experimentation and refinement. **Phasing, reverse guitar** and the **wah-wah pedal** – first used by Jimi in the studio on "The Stars That Play with Laughing Sam's Dice" – were all added to Hendrix's already large palette of effects. For all his attention to detail, however, Jimi somehow managed to leave the masters for the mixes of the songs on side one in a taxi, necessitating a rushed last-minute remix of the tracks.

The dozen Hendrix originals that made the cut for *Axis: Bold as Love*, indicated that like borrowed from his library. Both might have been at least partially prompted by the first book Jimi read in Chas's collection, George R. Stewart's 1949 sci-fi novel *Earth Abides*, in which a disease decimates the Earth's population, leaving the survivors to build an entirely new civilization. Apart from a few enigmatic spoken utterances, Hendrix didn't need any lyrics at all to make the instrumental "Third Stone from the Sun" seem like something utterly extraterrestrial. Crucially, however, the song's narration doesn't replicate the book's scenario, Jimi instead taking the role of an amused alien who decides to destroy the people on Earth, who will famously "never hear surf music again". On "Up from the Skies", meanwhile, Hendrix takes the point of view of a pre-historic man returning to find an Earth he finds weirdly changed, and not wholly for the better.

Hendrix would go on to write other songs with images of futuristic environments which, if not traceable to specific sources, certainly seemed to draw from science-fiction-like tableaux. This is most notable on *Electric Ladyland*'s **1983... (A Merman I Should Turn to Be)**, which refers directly to Atlantis. Also worth an honourable mention of sorts is **Astro Man** (first heard on Jimi's first posthumous release, *The Cry of Love*), which seems not so much a homage to science fiction as a satire of the genre's comic-book superheroes – although its reference to Superman as a "faggot" would nowadays be considered a politically incorrect faux pas.

all great artists, Jimi was growing in unexpected directions. Even the "Burning of the Midnight Lamp" single that had preceded the album had indicated that he wasn't quite as concerned with grinding out the elemental, super-catchy riffs that had so dominated his early singles and much of *Are You Experienced?* The single's relative commercial failure – reaching just number eighteen in the UK – likewise seemed to signal a shift in his priorities from 45s to albums, and although he would continue to have the odd hit single, from now on LPs would be his primary focus.

Yet for all their less obviously commercial appeal, the songs on *Axis: Bold as Love* were still relatively concise, just a couple of them exceeding the four-minute barrier (and even then, not by much). In part this is a tribute to the discipline producer Chas Chandler still imposed on the sessions, though to a far lesser extent than he had when the Experience began their recording career. But it also reflects the very song-oriented format in which Hendrix was still working, despite the increasingly multi-faceted sophistication of his compositions, equipment and overall ideas. Within that format, however, he was beginning to shade his basic riff-centred, piercing-guitar-dominated approach with more funk, returns to his soul/R&B roots and even hints of jazz here and there.

He had already established his mastery of the delicate romantic ballad with "The Wind Cries Mary", but continued to explore a surprisingly tender and mystical side with **Little Wing**, destined to become the album's best-loved song. There was still some cosmic rock that both roared and purred with **If Six Was Nine**, probably the runner-up to "Little Wing" as the record's most popular cut, due in part

Eddie Kramer

Born in South Africa, **Eddie Kramer** moved to England when he was nineteen and rose through the music-engineering ranks at various studios, first meeting Hendrix when the Experience worked at Olympic Studios in London in early 1967. Kramer would go on to engineer more Hendrix sessions than anyone else, in both London and New York.

Kramer was not quite a producer or co-producer when working with Hendrix, and his considerable involvement with posthumous album releases, books and video projects may have led some to feel that his role has been exaggerated. It's undeniable, however, that he was the non-musician with whom Jimi felt the most artistic sympathy in the studio. As George Chkiantz (who worked on some Hendrix sessions with Kramer as a second engineer) told Sean Egan in *Jimi Hendrix and the Making of "Are You Experienced"*:

"A lot of the engineers at the time would have – and to my pretty certain knowledge did – absolutely hate the racket that Hendrix was making." In contrast, Kramer – who had a taste for avant-garde jazz – didn't merely tolerate the noise Jimi was cranking out, but positively relished it, both for its quality and the interesting challenges it presented in getting the music recorded in the best sound possible.

In addition to working with other major British-based musicians of the late 1960s such as Traffic, John Mayall, Led Zeppelin, and The Nice, it was Kramer who recorded the Woodstock festival for the album and movie it spawned. Like many top engineers, he also went on to work as a producer, with credits ranging from Carly Simon and Kiss to jazz-fusion guitarist John McLaughlin and bluesman Buddy Guy.

---

to its prominent use on the soundtrack of the 1969 counterculture movie classic *Easy Rider*. Whatever musical idiom he was working in, the tone of Hendrix's lyrics – referencing science fiction, utilizing dream-like imagery, affecting carefree and slightly spacey stances with tinges of melancholy underneath – was fairly constant, further cementing his image as the ultimate space-age hippie.

Song for song, *Axis: Bold as Love* simply isn't as strong as *Are You Experienced?* and Hendrix's initial trio of singles, and its innovations not as breathtaking. It's also diluted a bit by the inclusion of a bit of indulgent electronic cosmic whimsy, "EXP", as the first track, and a relatively pedestrian, sub-par Noel Redding-sung composition, "She's So Fine" – probably a sop to the bassist to appease his increasingly restless ambition to be recognized as a songwriter and performer in his own right. As impressive an album as *Axis* is on its own terms, it's not as impressive as either its predecessor or its more sprawling but more striking successor, *Electric Ladyland*.

But by the time *Axis* was issued at the beginning of December, the Hendrix phenomenon had gathered so much steam that any solid follow-up was guaranteed to be a huge success. Accordingly, the record went to number five in the UK and, after getting issued Stateside the following month, number three in the US. Its prospects were also bolstered by another eye-catching psychedelic cover (this time used in both the US and UK), this one showing Hendrix as the central figure of a three-headed, multi-arm-sprouting Experience, crowned by cobras and against the background of exotic Indian faces. So in line was it with Hendrix's public image that many must have assumed it to be Jimi's idea, but actually it was done without the band's input, and apparently not wholly to their leader's liking. He was more approving of the inner gatefold – still in itself a rarity for single-disc releases in 1968 – which had a large black-and-white photo of the Experience, as well as an orange insert that put the lyrics in red type.

More Touring, More Hassles

As the Experience prepared for an all-out assault on the States in early 1968, a serious problem was brewing with Hendrix's old producer Ed Chalpin, whose legal proceedings against Jimi were becoming more than a mere nuisance. Far from appeasing Chalpin, the recordings Hendrix had made with Curtis Knight over the summer seemed to fire his ex-producer's hunger to make some money out of their association, as some of the tapes (along with some recorded before Jimi's success) were used on a late-1967 Capitol release titled **Get That Feeling**. As much as Hendrix loathed confrontation, his dissatis-faction with its appearance was made clear in a deposition in January 1968, which stated: "The label creates the impression that Knight and I recorded as at least equal performers, which is untrue. My involvement was completely subor-dinated and accommodated to Knight's musical personality and ability, which are the obliga-tions of a 'session man.' The record therefore conveys a completely erroneous, unflattering and unfavourable impression of my talents and abilities."

While it was obvious from a casual lis-ten that the album wasn't representative of Hendrix's abilities, it was nonetheless marketed as a genuine Jimi Hendrix LP, and didn't sell all that badly, making the *Billboard* top hundred. Being released just before *Axis: Bold as Love* in the States, there was understandable concern that the appearance of such old, substandard product could not only hurt Hendrix's cur-rent sales, but also tarnish what would today be considered his "brand". Despite efforts to settle the whole business, Chalpin wouldn't go away, and *Get That Feeling* would be just the first of many deceptive Hendrix packages that proliferate to this day.

In part as a reaction to the stress this caused, Jimi's indulgence in both drugs and – espe-cially on the road – sex with groupies began to increase. Without minimizing his indulgence in such pastimes, it's fair to observe that Hendrix was hardly exceptional in this regard among his peers in the top strata of rock, or even among his own band (as Noel Redding sub-sequently confessed). He did maintain a fairly steady if somewhat tempestuous relationship with the London girlfriend he had met right after his arrival in 1966, Kathy Etchingham, but was never the type to be tied down, as

The Wind Cries Kathy

Hendrix was not a one-woman man; even excluding the groupies with whom he had casual one- or two-night stands, he had several more girlfriends over the last five years or so of his life, sometimes simultaneously. Nor was he one to settle down into a steady domestic or long-term arrangement in general. If he was too shy to say so in person, he certainly said it loud and clear on his first two B-sides. **Stone Free** is a forthright protest against being tied down in any way, with one line referring to women who try to keep him in a "plastic cage". The far less celebrated **51st Anniversary** – used as the UK B-side of "Purple Haze" and for many years difficult to acquire in the US – is even more explicit: Jimi states that he's going to change his woman's mind about getting wed, offering not one but two verses detailing bad marriages and ending with a plea to let him live a little longer, as he's definitely not ready for any such commitment. Perhaps he had his own parents' rocky marriage in mind when he wrote the song.

If there was any one woman to whom Hendrix can be said to have been attached, it was probably **Kathy Etchingham**. Jimi hooked up with her within days of arriving in London, and would stay in a relationship with her, albeit a fairly off-on one, until early 1969. A twenty-year-old who had already had flings with celebrated rock musicians by the time she met Hendrix, she is best known for inspiring "The Wind Cries Mary" – actually written, she told Hendrix biographer Charles R. Cross in *Room Full of Mirrors*, after a vicious quarrel sparked off by, of all things, the quality of her cooking. No doubt she was a subtle influence on several of his other more romantic early songs, and the relationship must have helped Hendrix to make the difficult transition to living in the UK. However, Etchingham also had a fiery, independent streak, which, while a good match for Jimi's own moods, meant that she didn't put up with Hendrix's unpredictable behaviour lightly. Although the relationship

songs like "Stone Free" suggested. And like many artists of humble origin who rocketed to fame after years of struggle, Hendrix was not immune to foolish spending sprees – some, to Redding's and Mitchell's annoyance, charged to the band's account – such as buying expensive cars even though he didn't have a driver's licence. (Jimi would almost kill himself behind the wheel in one 1968 accident in Los Angeles, writing off the car but luckily escaping without serious injury.)

At the beginning of a Scandinavian tour in January 1968, Hendrix committed the first act that got him into any serious sort of trouble with the law since he had become a celebrity, smashing up his hotel room in Gothenburg. The damage to his career was minimal: staying in Sweden for an extra week to appear in court, he got off with a fine, and if anything, the incident probably helped to reinforce his image as something of an outlaw. But it was symptomatic of the toll the hectic last year and a half had taken, especially as the outburst seemed so out of character for a man remembered by most as an exceptionally gentle, even reticent personality offstage. Sadly, such violence was

Hendrix and Etchingham at home in Mayfair, 1969

was made public in January 1969 and there were plans for her to accompany him on his US tour a few months later, ultimately his increasingly serious dalliances with Devon Wilson, drugs and shady hangers-on sparked a permanent split that spring. They kept in touch, however, even after she married later in 1969.

Etchingham has kept the flame burning for Hendrix since his death, most notably by organizing a sale of his memorabilia for charity and by mounting a successful campaign to get a building at 23 Brook Street, Mayfair where the couple lived honoured with a **blue plaque** recording the fact. More messily, she also brought libel proceedings against the woman Jimi was with when he died, **Monika Dannemann**, over material in the latter's book *The Inner Life of Jimi Hendrix*. Dannemann died shortly after the case (see box on page 123); Etchingham's account of the times she and Hendrix shared can be found in her memoir, *Through Gypsy Eyes*.

not limited to inanimate objects, and there are reports of Jimi occasionally hitting women in the final years of his life; while such incidents were infrequent and might have been a symptom of the stress he was under, it doesn't make them excusable.

It had only been a year since Hendrix had become famous, yet such was the pace of his life in the fifteen months since he had been whisked to London in September 1966 that he was already showing signs of exhaustion. At the same time, he was becoming increasingly frustrated by his inability to realize some of his

more ambitious, but – given his heavy commitments – largely unworkable ideas. "I'd like to take a six-month break and go to a school of music", he told *Melody Maker*. "I'm tired of trying to write stuff and finding I can't. I want to write mythology stories set to music based on a planetary thing and my imagination in general. It wouldn't be similar to classical music, but I'd use strings and harps with extreme and opposite musical textures ... I'd play with Mitch and Noel and hire other cats to supplement us."

Perhaps Jimi could have alleviated some of the pressure of feeling as though he was repeat-

The Fillmore West, San Francisco, 1 February 1968

ing himself onstage by introducing some of these new compositions and ideas in a live setting. In a 6 January interview in Copenhagen, he told Carsten Grolin of *Ekstra Bladet* that he had thought about completely changing the Experience's stage act: "In the future, I will present a stage play with colours, which is going to play one part, dancers and other groups, who are going to play different parts.

And we will play different parts, either with or without instruments. I'd like to have Procol Harum with me. They appear like a troupe of Shakespearean actors when they get on stage."

Perhaps Hendrix, who had pulled himself out of poverty just a year and a half before, lacked the confidence to tinker with what was obviously a successful formula, and to risk the ire of managers who had struck it very rich with their gamble on this unknown American. Whatever the case, he would in some respects be surprisingly unadventurous not only as regards altering his presentation (which would never incorporate the ideas he had floated in Copenhagen), but also in the material selected for his live sets. Curiously, only a few songs from *Axis: Bold as Love* appear to have been played onstage, and even some of those played quite rarely, although it seems that his audience would have been eager to hear some of the LP's other highlights, such as "If Six Was Nine". According to Noel Redding's autobiography *Are You Experienced: The Inside Story of the Jimi Hendrix Experience* (co-written with Carol Appleby), Jimi wasn't as eager to fix the problem as he was to complain about it: "he kept saying: 'We never do anything new', but refused to rehearse".

But if Hendrix was showing signs of fatigue, there would be no break to recharge his batteries in the months ahead. He had yet to tour the States as a bestselling recording star, and in the wake of the chart success of *Are You Experienced?*, a second American tour was planned which was gruelling even by 1960s standards. The Experience played 60 cities in 66 days, starting on 1 February at the scene of the first non-Monterey triumph, San Francisco's Fillmore West. Supporting them on many dates were fellow Jeffery-Chandler clients **Soft Machine**, then yet to release their first album, although various other acts were featured on the bill, depending on the city.

Although the tour crammed too much into too little time, it also showed some concerted plan-

ning, taking in major venues on the now-thriving psychedelic circuit such as Philadelphia's Electric Factory and Los Angeles's Shrine Auditorium as well as universities and more conventional auditoriums, stadiums and civic centres. Hendrix's commercial stature was such that he could now fill much bigger venues than most headliners, and his equipment so cutting-edge that it could produce the volume needed to be heard by large crowds.

While "arena rock" and "stadium rock" would come to be somewhat odious terms associated with impersonal, mass-manufactured entertainment, here again Jimi was a pioneer, mapping out and defining territory that had yet to be explored until he and fellow major touring attractions such as Cream came along. By promoting concerts themselves, Hendrix's management was also able to get a considerably greater cut of the proceeds than many other big touring acts, although the distribution and investment of those proceeds would subsequently give cause for much complaint.

Of special significance to Hendrix was the tour's stop in **Seattle** on 12 and 13 February, giving Jimi a chance to see his family for the first time since he had joined the army nearly seven long years before. Jimi had kept up a written correspondence with his father Al all the while, but the relationship still seemed strained at best, Al offering little if any appreciation of his son's accomplishments, perhaps not quite believing what he was reading. By now, however, Jimi's superstardom was undeniable and the Experience sold out the Seattle Center Arena. Hendrix was properly feted by

The Story

The Story

family and friends, Al included, before putting in a rather chaotic appearance at the high school from which he had never graduated. By this time Al had remarried, eventually adopting his new wife's daughter, **Janie**, who would eventually play a huge role in administering Jimi's estate.

As a testament to Hendrix's unpredictably eclectic taste, the following month he gave his approval to a then little-known singer-songwriter he met on tour in Ottawa, Canada. "Talked with **Joni Mitchell** on the phone", he wrote in his diary on 19 March. "I think I'll record her tonight with my excellent tape recorder ... Went down to the little club to see Joni. Fantastic girl with heaven words." So it was that the loudest musical legend of the 1960s enthusiastically crossed paths with one of the quietest, then just on the verge of releasing her first album.

A far tenser segment of the tour took place a couple of weeks later in the aftermath of **Martin Luther King**'s assassination. Rioting in Newark, New Jersey (near New York City), meant that the first of the two shows the Experience were supposed to perform there on 5 April were barely attended. The second show was cancelled, even though both performances had been sold out in advance. Although Hendrix had managed for the most part to make his music separate from the ugliest political clashes of the time, it was a sign that he couldn't remain untouched by such racial tensions for much longer.

After the tour ended in early April, the Experience stayed on in New York to undertake concentrated work on their next album. (A few scattered dates followed in April and May, including a headlining spot at the Miami Pop festival, an event overseen by future Woodstock co-promoter Michael Lang.) Yielding some of the crowning accomplishments of Hendrix's career, the sessions would also help sow the seeds for the dissolution of the musical and management relationships that had brought him to such prominence in the first place.

The End of the
Experience
1968–1969

"Things had to be done Jimi's way or no way, and Jimi's way was getting more and more unproductive."

Noel Redding, in *Are You Experienced: The Inside Story of the Jimi Hendrix Experience*

The End of the Experience
1968–1969

There were several enticements for Jimi Hendrix to stay on in New York in the spring of 1968 to work on the Experience's third album. The most important was the availability of a new studio, the Record Plant, with what was then state-of-the-art twelve-track equipment. The Experience would be the first big-name act to use the facility, where Jimi would continue to work on numerous occasions over the next couple of years.

Just as strong a factor might have been the presence of **Eddie Kramer,** now working as an engineer at the Record Plant after having been an important contributor to Hendrix's London recordings. It's also likely that Jimi appreciated the chance to spend some extended time in his native US, in the city that, considering his wandering ways, was as much a home to him as any could be, with many old and new friends around with whom to both jam and socialize. The list of luminaries with whom he informally jammed included Larry Coryell, Stephen Stills, Johnny Winter, the McCoys, and future bandmate Buddy Miles. Unfortunately, the jam with which listeners are most likely to be familiar is one in which a drunken Jim Morrison was inspired to slur along with Jimi, as the results found their way onto releases of dubious legality, the most notorious of which was titled *Woke Up This Morning and Found Myself Dead.*

Buddy Miles

The Story

Electric Ladyland Begins; Chas Chandler Leaves

Actually the sessions for the album that would eventually take shape as *Electric Ladyland* had started back in late 1967 in London, with a bit of work done at the just-opened Record Plant on a tour rest-day in March 1968. Just as *Axis: Bold as Love* had marked a different way of recording from *Are You Experienced?*, so the *Electric Ladyland* sessions would mark a continuing evolution in Hendrix's music, songwriting and methods of track construction. Not all of these were to his producer's and bandmates' liking, and this heightened tensions which had already begun to surface at some of his more painstaking 1967 recording dates.

First and foremost, there was the increased presence of many **hangers-on and groupies** that Chandler, and to a lesser extent Redding and Mitchell, felt were unnecessary distractions. Hendrix always had a hard time saying no to or getting rid of people who wanted to get to know him better, get high with him or generally feed off his aura, whether due to his innate shyness or an inability to assert himself. He even invited a cab driver to jam with him in the studio, probably not anticipating that the guy would actually show up and get in the way of that day's work.

Now that he was one of the most famous and charismatic young celebrities in the world, the flocks of hangers-on grew into unmanageable crowds, especially when Jimi let them trail along with him into the studio. Letting friends into the studio was hardly unknown in the rock world, of course, and was becoming much more frequent in the late 1960s, when studio practices had loosened up quite a bit as young hipsters gained commercial ascendance. The problem was, apparently, that many of Jimi's buddies weren't there to listen to or contribute to the music so much as to party with him as if they were in his hotel room. Chandler and the Experience were primarily there to work, and resented so much of Hendrix's energy being siphoned off by non-musical matters, as well as the attendant delay in the star of the show's comings and goings.

Also, Hendrix was using more and more **guest musicians** from outside the Experience to increase the colours available to his progressively more complex sound paintings. In and of itself, this wasn't a bad thing. Most major rock bands of the time, from The Beatles and The Rolling Stones to Jimi's friends in Cream, made occasional-to-frequent use of outside players. In the case of the Experience, whose primary instruments were limited to one guitar, one bass, and drums, it was especially necessary and desirable to add keyboards and other textures not available in the power-trio format. Members of fellow top British bands Traffic and The Move had already been called in to sing backing vocals on some 1967 sessions. With someone as eager to jam as Jimi was, it wasn't difficult to attract high-calibre musicians, both famous and not-so-famous, eager to pitch in on his US studio recordings.

Yet at times the Experience felt cluttered and hemmed in when too many of these musicians showed up, or their additions were superfluous or led to unproductive jams which were a distraction from the songs they were working on. Noel Redding in particular got annoyed when other bass players were used, or, worse, when Jimi himself recorded bass parts, or re-recorded ones that Redding had already cut. In part this was a by-product of Hendrix's perfectionism. He was stopping at nothing to get the sound he wanted, and nobody could do it quicker than Jimi himself, especially when Redding, as was increasingly the case, wasn't around, worn out by the long studio hours and the uncomfortable vibe in general. Perhaps Hendrix could have handled the situation more sensitively, but when he was determined to get his material out of his head and onto tape, such niceties weren't always observed. In a band that was still touring intensively as a three-man unit, this couldn't help but fray some nerves and open the door to serious long-term problems. And Redding still wanted to write and sing more of the Experience's material – which, given Jimi's obviously superior abilities, just wasn't going to happen.

Noel much preferred their working methods in their earlier days, when they would work out the basics of their material before going into the studio. "Now Jimi got into the habit of hanging out in the studio, taping everything, and hoping for inspiration", observed Redding regarding the shift in the group's approach to recording in *Are You Experienced: The Inside Story of the Jimi Hendrix Experience*. He noted feeling particularly concerned that

Jimi was letting the standard of his lyrics slip: Hendrix would make noises to accompany his guitar playing and eventually replace them with proper lyrics, but Redding felt they didn't really fit.

At the Record Plant in particular, Redding felt that Jimi's fascination with the new frontiers opening up in overdubbing and electronic effects was leading to a loss of the simplicity of the earlier Experience recordings, which Noel much preferred. In Redding's view, it would have been better to just run through the songs a couple of times before trying to get a take.

Now, however, Jimi was doing dozens of guitar overdubs and, according to the bassist, failing to clearly articulate what he wanted from his rhythm section, often moving on to something else before he had finished what he had started doing. "I could nip out to a club and pull a chick and return only to find Jimi still hadn't finished tuning his guitar", he wrote. "I told him he was being silly to try to do so much at once – writer, producer, singer, guitarist, arranger – but he took no notice. Things had to be done Jimi's way or no way, and Jimi's way was getting more and more unproductive."

Jimi's perfectionism, while an asset in helping him navigate previously uncharted waters in the art of recording, was finally reaching what Chandler in particular felt to be unreasonable extremes. A session at which 41 takes of "Gypsy Eyes" were attempted seems to have been one of the last straws. A few days later, around early May, Chandler stepped down as Hendrix's producer. Shortly afterward, he opted out of his management role as well, get-

The Story

ting bought out by Mike Jeffery for $300,000. To his displeasure, he didn't even get a production credit for *Electric Ladyland*, although he had produced some of the LP's earlier tracks, including its two most popular ones, "All Along the Watchtower" and "Crosstown Traffic".

Although Chandler's departure ultimately had little effect on the overall quality of the *Electric Ladyland* album, long-term it might have been the single biggest contributing factor to the business and musical hassles Hendrix would suffer in the final two years of his life. Chas's role as a producer, manager, and friend had not just been crucial to establishing Jimi as a star. Chandler had also been the person most able to channel Hendrix's prodigious but mercurial, oft-unfocused talents into songs, recordings and performances that were concise and accessible without compromising Jimi's originality.

Left more to his own devices, Hendrix would often have trouble distilling his ideas and piles of tapes into a clearly expressed and finished product, in part because few if any people in the studio were as willing to check Jimi's excessive impulses as Chas was. Perhaps Chandler could have been more flexible in growing along with Hendrix in the studio and indulging some of his more ambitious whims.

As excessive as forty-one takes might have been in 1968, it means nothing forty years later, when major artists sometimes slave over albums for years. But apart from The Beatles' recent efforts, however, there was little precedent for such extended studio experimentation back then, and Chandler may well have felt that the whole enterprise was in danger of stalling or going off the rails. The truth is, however, that at this point Hendrix was becoming so obsessed with getting his way in the studio that it's doubtful whether anyone could have stopped him. In effect, Jimi was bound to become his own producer, at least until such time as it might be decided that another approach was more suitable.

Electric Ladyland Continued ...

Now Jimi's career was left in the hands of Mike Jeffery, who cared relatively little for his music, but a lot for the money Hendrix was generating. Much of that money, however, was being eaten up by the massive costs of the sessions at the **Record Plant**, especially as they were not being underwritten by a record company. Hendrix's earnings took another hit when, as part of a settlement with his pre-fame producer, Ed Chalpin's **PPX** company was given royalties on Jimi's Warner Bros. recordings over the next

few years, as well as large cash payments.

Jimi would have almost certainly liked to have finished his third album before going out on the road. But in what was developing into a vicious circle, there seemed no alternative but to undertake more concerts to raise the money to keep the elaborate Hendrix operation afloat. The latter Record Plant sessions for *Electric Ladyland* were thus intermingled with shows at the Miami Pop festival, at the Fillmore East and in Italy and Switzerland, as well as a brief return visit to the UK. With Jeffery moving his office to New York, however, and the most lucrative concert opportunities remaining Stateside, Hendrix was again becoming more of a US-based artist than a British one. (Some of his studio and live work that May, incidentally, was filmed by ABC television in the US for a planned documentary, the footage of which unfortunately has been stolen or lost.)

Partly as a consequence of spending so much time in the Record Plant – but also, to give him his due, as a product of Hendrix's prodigious songwriting output – *Electric Ladyland* ended up being a two-LP set, which was still a fairly rare format for rock releases in 1968. And, partly as a consequence of his less disciplined approach but also owing to the musical directions in which he was naturally evolving anyway, it was simply a heavier record than its predecessors, and not only in the sheer weight of the package. There was a funkier gait to many of the rhythms; a more diffuse sprawl in the songwriting; a denser multitrack depth to the sonic texture; a jazzier feel to some of the arrangements; and a fuller, harder growl and squeal in Hendrix's guitar work.

Although the album's been noted for its length and somewhat more scattered approach, however, only three of the tracks exceed five minutes in length (and one of those only just). What's more, Hendrix hadn't entirely lost his knack for tight numbers that could make great commercial singles. One of the songs, **Burning of the Midnight Lamp**, had already been issued on 45 in the UK a good year or so previously. Another – a masterful rocked-up interpretation of Bob Dylan's **All Along the Watchtower**, from Dylan's then most recent LP, the folk/country-based *John Wesley Harding* – would restore Jimi to the top five of the British singles charts, and become his only top twenty Stateside hit. Despite disappointing sales, on the other hand, **Crosstown Traffic** was a driving soul-rock number that would be picked up years later for use in a TV advert. There was an unexpected tribute to Jimi's formative years with a cover of New Orleans R&B guitarist Earl King's "Come On (Let the Good Times Roll)", and Noel Redding, perhaps to appease his dissatisfaction with the way things were going, was allowed to contribute the token and pedestrian "Little Miss Strange".

For all the non-Experience musicians who drifted through the studio during the recording of the album, the guest spots – at least those credited on the LP – were both relatively infrequent and purposeful. Traffic's **Stevie Winwood** (on organ) and Jefferson Airplane's Jack Casady (on bass) played on "Voodoo Chile", with fellow Traffic men Dave Mason (singing backing vocals on "Crosstown Traffic") and Chris Wood (playing flute on "1983... (A Merman I Should Turn to Be)" also lending a hand. **Al Kooper**, late of The Blues Project and founder of Blood, Sweat and Tears, added piano to "Long Hot Summer Night", and the relatively unknown **Mike Finnigan** played some super-cool organ on "Rainy Day, Dream Away" and "Still Raining, Still Dreaming". Of most long-term significance was the presence of drummer **Buddy Miles** on these two latter tracks, as Miles would often play with Hendrix over the next two years.

The relative economy of most of the songs, and the judicious manner in which outside musi-

Noel Redding

Though rarely seen as one of the bad guys in the Jimi Hendrix story, assessment of **Noel Redding**'s role in the tale is mixed, if seldom negative as regards his musical ability. Redding's personal relationship with Hendrix is sometimes characterized as rather remote and cool, or – only slightly more charitably – as more of a business collaboration than a genuine friendship. Some accounts tend to emphasize his complaints about Jimi's leadership and the Experience's management, as well as unjustified attempts to get more of his songs and lead vocals recorded than the mere two such outings – "She's So Fine" and "Little Miss Strange" – he was allowed on the group's LPs (*Axis: Bold as Love* and *Electric Ladyland* respectively).

Ultimately, however, the proof of Noel's value to Jimi is in the grooves, not in whether Redding might have been as much a buddy to Hendrix as Billy Cox or the many musicians with whom Jimi jammed live and in the studio. And on that basis, it must be said that Redding, like Mitch Mitchell, was an excellent foil for Jimi in that he was not content to merely follow his leader. Like Mitchell, he challenged and pushed Hendrix to new heights, his restless, pulsating, melodic bass proving a suitable match for the guitarist's own ceaselessly probing sonic flights.

Admittedly, judgement on Redding's contributions to Jimi's recordings might be clouded a bit by Hendrix's reported playing of some of the bass parts on record, particularly on the later Experience sessions. It's reasonably certain, however, that the bass on most if not all of their pre-1968 recordings is Redding's handiwork, and many tracks feature strikingly powerful bass lines worthy of praise in their own right. Some of his best playing can be heard on "Fire", where he propels the infectious chorus with runs that seem to bubble out of the earth with a geyser-like force; "If Six Was Nine", where he does much to both anchor and swing a song otherwise in danger of vanishing in self-absorption; and "Third Stone from the Sun", where he both complements Jimi's anthemic leads and swoops like a roving spaceship as appropriate. As with John Entwistle in The Who, such was the presence of Redding's bass that at times it almost functioned as a second guitar – a necessary device in the stripped-down power trio format, perhaps, but none the less effective for that.

Less flatteringly, as much as Redding might have wished otherwise and like many sidemen with frustrated ambitions to do their own thing, he proved rather undistinguished when he was finally free to pursue those ambitions. To the surprise of Hendrix fans, Fat Mattress's eponymous 1969 debut didn't sound at all like the Experience, but rather like a competent but run-of-the-mill psychedelic folk-rock/vocal

cians were employed, suggests that Hendrix, at least at this point, did know how to curb his overindulgences after all, even without Chandler around for the latter part of the sessions. There were, however, a couple of lengthy selections that both allowed Jimi to stretch out much more than he ever had before on record, anticipating the direction that much of his onstage and studio music would take over the next couple of years. The first was the sixteen-minute **Voodoo Chile,** to which the closing five-minute "Voodoo Child (Slight Return)" was a sequel of sorts. Here Hendrix was going back to his deepest blues roots, but wedding them to an almost avant-garde elasticity which left plenty of room for extended soloing and improvisation. The

Fat Mattress, 1969

– the album only managed to reach number 134 in the US, where a headlining tour by the group was cut short after just a few dates. The LP's poor performance must have come as a jolt to their record company, Polydor, which had unwisely paid a $150,000 advance to the band in the vain hope that its sales might be comparable to an Experience release.

Redding left Fat Mattress midway through the recording of their second and final album, later working with a heavy-metal group, Road, and – after moving to the small town of Clonakilty in West County Cork, Ireland – The Noel Redding Band, a.k.a. The Clonakilty Cowboys. In 1973, a hard-up Redding was persuaded to give up his entitlement to ongoing royalties from the Experience recordings on which he had played for just $100,000. Exceptionally bitter over what proved to be a costly mistake, he spent much of his energy in his final years trying to retrieve some of the rights he had signed away, even announcing plans to sue Experience Hendrix for up to $5 million in lost earnings. A few months later, on 11 May 2003, Noel Redding died at his home in Ireland, from complications arising from cirrhosis of the liver; he was 57. His account of his ups and downs in the rock business can be found in his autobiography *Are You Experienced? The Inside Story of the Jimi Hendrix Experience*, co-written with Carol Appleby.

harmony band. To be fair, Redding deserves credit for doing something different, and – considering his complaints about his contributions to the Experience not being valued – not seeking a dominant role in what seemed to be a pretty democratic outfit (he was neither the lead singer nor the only songwriter for the group). The public wasn't all that impressed, however

second was the nearly fourteen-minute **1983... (A Merman I Should Turn to Be)**, which had an epic grandeur that Jimi never matched in any of his similarly long outings, and a soaring, almost horn-like tone to the guitar lines, nearly akin to the flights taken by avant-garde jazz players. Also close to free jazz were some of the instrumental sections, which left behind most sem-

blance of melody and structure for a splashing interplay between guitar, bass, drums, flute and miscellaneous sounds. Less radical but funkier was the much shorter song that preceded and segued into it, **Rainy Day, Dream Away**, which set up a psychedelic soul-jazz groove.

Naturally, Hendrix's flighty romanticism remained a strong feature of many of the lyr-

Hendrix's Session Musicians

Although Jimi seemed to enjoy playing with other musicians outside his official bands, surprisingly few truly noteworthy contributions from outsiders found their way onto his records. If his jam sessions – which were, frankly, more often than not unremarkable – had their uses, they might have principally been as a way for Jimi to socialize and let off steam away from the hothouse pressure of his main projects. The great bulk of his significant recordings were made with the Experience and (to a markedly lesser degree) the Band of Gypsys, and despite all the friends who dropped in at some point (especially after 1967), not many of their contributions actually made the cut for official release.

It's perhaps unsurprising that some of the most valuable outside help came in the guise of session singers, background vocals being perhaps the weakest link in Hendrix's sound. His very first true solo recording, "Hey Joe", featured ethereal harmonies by the all-woman British group The Breakaways, who had releases of their own but were mainly known as some of the most frequently employed session vocalists in the UK. Hendrix probably wouldn't have chosen The Breakaways on his own, but almost certainly approved of the use of **Trevor Burton and Roy Wood** of The Move and

The Move, 1969 – Roy Wood (l) and Trevor Burton (r)

ics, especially **Gypsy Eyes** and the soul-soaked, relatively overlooked **Have You Ever Been (To Electric Ladyland)**. At times, though, it seemed as though his world-view was on the verge of tearing loose from all its earthbound ties and alternately plumbing the depths of the ocean and flying off into the heavens like a stray balloon, particularly on the three cuts that made up a side-long suite of sorts ("Rainy Day, Dream Away", "1983... (A Merman I Should Turn to Be", "Moon, Turn the Tides... Gently Gently Away") and the one that immediately followed it (the wah-wah-drenched "Still Raining, Still Dreaming"). All of which, of course, helped to reinforce Hendrix's image as the ultimate space cowboy.

Graham Nash (then of **The Hollies**) for "You Got Me Floatin'" on *Axis: Bold as Love*. Nash, of course, went on to even greater stardom as part of Crosby, Stills and Nash; although they were barely known in the US, The Move were regular British hit-makers and would be one of the acts on Hendrix's package tour at the end of 1967. But the best backup singing on a Hendrix recording was probably heard on the boisterous background vocals on *Electric Ladyland*'s "Crosstown Traffic", to which (appropriately enough, given the title) Traffic's Dave Mason contributed – though even here, as on "You Got Me Floatin'", Noel Redding and Mitch Mitchell also pitched in.

Instrumentally speaking, Hendrix's most famous studio guests were Stevie Winwood of **Traffic** and Jack Casady of **Jefferson Airplane**, who acquitted themselves ably on organ and bass respectively on the same album's "Voodoo Chile". Perhaps the most memorable session appearance, however, was the relatively obscure organist Mike Finnigan's buoyant playing on "Still Raining, Still Dreaming". Hendrix met Finnigan when the latter's band, The Serfs, were recording at the Record Plant at the same time as the Experience were working on *Electric Ladyland*. (Uncoincidentally, The Serfs' sole, little-

known Capitol LP was produced by Record Plant co-founder/owner Tom Wilson.) Two other members of the band, Freddie Smith (on saxophone) and Larry Faucette (on congas), were brought in to play alongside Hendrix, Finnigan and drummer Buddy Miles on both "Still Raining, Still Dreaming" and "Rainy Day, Dream Away". Oddly enough, Finnigan would spend much of his subsequent career in the bands of two other Hendrix session men, Dave Mason and (with Crosby, Stills and Nash) Graham Nash.

The most famous Hendrix session appearance that's never been released has to be The Rolling Stones' **Brian Jones**' unused piano part on "All Along the Watchtower". Jones, a good friend of Jimi's then in the midst of a downward personal spiral that saw him cast out of the Rolling Stones shortly before his death in July 1969, apparently showed up at the session in such a state that it impaired his considerable musical abilities. "He was completely out of his brain. ... He got on the piano, it was take 21, and we could just hear 'clang, clang, clang, clang, clang'", revealed engineer Eddie Kramer in the recording magazine *Sound on Sound*. "It was all bloody horrible and out of time, and Jimi said, 'Uh, I don't think so.' Brian was gone after two takes. He practically fell on the floor in the control room."

It was a risky move to put out a double album in late 1968. Only a few major artists had previously done so, most notably Bob Dylan with *Blonde on Blonde*, The Mothers of Invention with *Freak Out!*, and Cream with *Wheels on Fire*. Even The Beatles' entry in the field, *The White Album*, was still a month away from release when *Electric Ladyland* came out in October 1968. The decision was vindicated, however, when the record went to number one within weeks of its release in the US, and if it didn't do quite as well in the UK, its number six peak was still a more than solid achievement. In a way, the timing was good: with the growth of FM radio and the live concert circuit, the US market was embracing heavy psychedelic rock

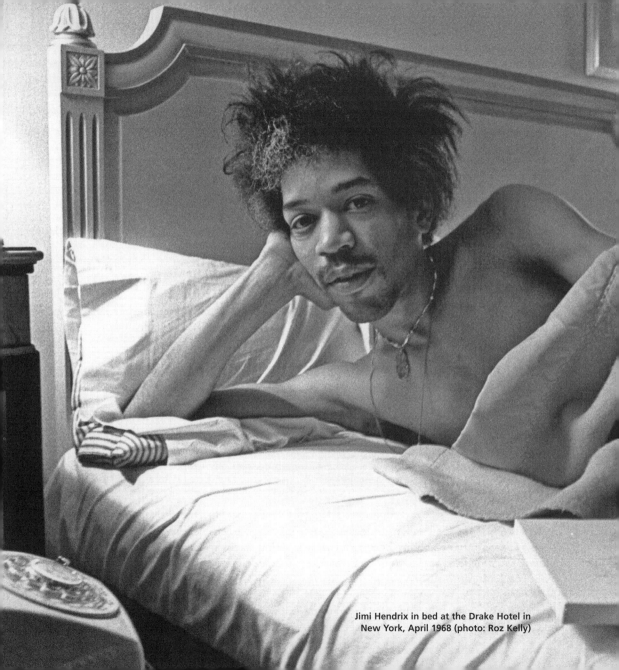

Jimi Hendrix in bed at the Drake Hotel in
New York, April 1968 (photo: Roz Kelly)

records with extended tracks that didn't rely on big hit singles. Indeed, two such albums, *Wheels on Fire* and Big Brother and the Holding Company's *Cheap Thrills*, had topped the charts in the US not long before *Electric Ladyland*.

Such was the perception of Hendrix as a wild'n'crazy stud at this point that it was probably assumed that the UK cover of a bevy of naked ladies – an extremely controversial, indeed unprecedented, choice of sleeve art – must have been his idea. In fact, as with *Axis: Bold as Love*, it was commissioned without Hendrix's knowledge, the women getting paid £5 each to go topless, and an extra £3 to take off their underwear. The sleeve prompted some bitterly derisive comments by Jimi in the press, an indication that there were still some basic career decisions that were somehow escaping his control. It also affected the LP's British sales at least slightly, with some shops refusing to stock it, or wrapping it in a paper bag. Although there were no such problems with the US cover – which used a fuzzy photo bathing Jimi's face in psychedelic lighting – Hendrix's instructions for the design were ignored, and the photo of the Experience with some children in Central Park that he had chosen was used on the inside sleeve instead.

Another US Tour, a New Recording Studio

Even before *Electric Ladyland* was in the shops, however, the Experience had had to mount another exhaustive US tour to keep up with both Hendrix and Mike Jeffery's prolific spending and expenses. From the end of July to mid-September, they played in about thirty cities, sometimes performing two shows a night. Again, Soft Machine frequently played in support, often joined by heavy New York rock band **Vanilla Fudge**. A handful of other US Experience concerts followed in October and November, and by the end of the year, it's hard to imagine the Experience's penetration of the American market could have been any more complete. Only about a year earlier, they had had a lukewarm response as the opening act at the 18,000-seat Hollywood Bowl for The Mamas and the Papas. In September 1968, however, they were the headliners at the same venue, many in the crowd risking electrocution to jump into an artificial moat separating the audience from the stage.

Also noteworthy were several concerts the following month at **Winterland** in San Francisco, as the shows were professionally recorded, much of the material finding release on the *Jimi Hendrix Concerts* and *Live at Winterland* albums, albeit not until the 1980s. Less noteworthy, and not very typical, was a 30 November concert in Detroit which Jimi initially refused to travel to in a fit of pique before he was persuaded to fly there. And most unusual of all was a 28 November concert at Philharmonic Hall in New York City on a bill which also included harpsichordist Fernando Valenti and the New York Brass Quintet. There had been hopes to fit in an appearance on the *Ed Sullivan* TV show that month too, but this

The Story

fell through, and it's a tribute to the enormous push given Hendrix by FM radio airplay and sheer word of mouth that he got as big as he did without playing on any major US television programmes prior to 1969.

Sometimes another Jeffery act, the Irish group **Eire Apparent,** were also on the bill, and Jimi would produce the band's only, and rather obscure and unimpressive, album. (Around this time he also produced the somewhat more successful, but likewise musically undistinguished debut album by **Cat Mother and the All Night News Boys,** although producing didn't develop into a substantial sideline of his.) Much of the Eire Apparent recording took place at **T.T.G. Studios** in Los Angeles, giving Hendrix a chance to do a lot of work on tracks of his own, both with the Experience and other musicians. While Jimi was obviously continuing to generate new songs, the sessions were more and more prone to jams with outside musicians which produced little in the way of useable recordings.

Unbelievably, although Hendrix recorded more tracks on tape in the last two years of his life than in any other, there would not be another studio album of new material issued under his name before his death. While this was in part due to legal hassles and complications from the break-up of the original Experience in 1969, it also reflected his increased difficulty in driving his songs through to completion and deciding what form he wanted them to take. Certainly his fans and record companies were chomping at the bit for new Hendrix albums, as was his management, Jimi by this time ranking among the world's top rock stars. Yet the greater their impatience, the more he seemed incapable of delivering finished product. It certainly wasn't for lack of opportunity: by this time, it seemed as though he was spending as much time in the studio as out of it, getting through tape almost as voraciously as he dallied with numerous women in various hotel rooms.

One way of both keeping a cap on the enormous recording costs Hendrix was incurring and allowing him complete creative freedom was to construct his own recording facility, **Electric Lady Studios.** Toward that end, he and Mike Jeffery went to look at a defunct club at 52 West 8th Street in New York City. The original idea, apparently, was to continue to operate the space as a club, with a small studio attached to record live performances. When common sense prevailed, however, it was decided to rebuild the premises to function exclusively as a recording studio.

In theory, the idea of Hendrix having his own studio was brilliant and far-sighted, and eventually proved workable when many other musicians followed his example. But in practice, building Electric Lady proved something of a headache, with massive delays and cost overruns. Long-term, Hendrix's thinking was on the mark: the studio would not only give him the time and space he craved, but also, hopefully, do the same for other musicians, generating some revenue while Jimi was away on tour or otherwise engaged. In the short term, however, it meant continued touring to keep out of debt, and tied him even more closely to Jeffery, now his partner in the studio as well as in other vital aspects of his career.

Mitch Mitchell

Some of the same criticisms levied against Noel Redding have also sometimes been applied in retrospective assessments of **Mitch Mitchell**'s role in Jimi Hendrix's career. It's been claimed that the Experience was essentially a manufactured group, the three men being hastily thrown together by a management eager to get Jimi on the commercial map, rather than spontaneously forging the personal and musical bonds which gave birth to definitive 1960s bands such as The Beatles, the Stones, and The Who. In the eyes of a few, it's also a drawback that the rhythm section happened to be young white Englishmen, rather than the seasoned African-American R&B players that some feel would have provided the best backing for Jimi – despite the fact that he had played with many such musicians over the previous five years, without his talents achieving proper recognition by either the public or, apparently, most of those same musicians.

Actually, in many respects Hendrix, Redding, and Mitchell seemed to get along okay as friends for much of the time, especially considering that they didn't know each other when they first began to play together, and were soon thrust into a media maelstrom for which none of them could have been prepared. In Mitchell's case in particular, what's more important is that he was, when all is said and done, the single musician with whom Hendrix played the most, live and in the studio. As annoyingly reluctant as he could be to stand up for himself, Jimi would not have suffered a musical or personal fool gladly. Quite the opposite – Mitchell was the musician he retained after the original Experience broke up, and when the Band of Gypsys didn't work out after that, Mitch was back behind Jimi until Hendrix's death.

Crucially, Mitchell was a great drummer who brought out the best in Hendrix, certainly more so than the Band of Gypsys' considerably less versatile or light-footed Buddy Miles. If there was a definite jazz bent to some of Jimi's work, some of it must be credited to Mitchell, who played in unpredictably imaginative and irregular, occasionally circular patterns rarely found in rock music. Rightly, it's often been noted that Elvin Jones (who played on many of John Coltrane's greatest recordings) was a big influence on Mitch, but so were fellow jazz drummers Max Roach, Philly Joe Jones and Tony Williams. Although he was adept at adding the more straightforward thrust necessary to put Hendrix's music over to the rock audience, Mitchell was also marvellous at devising multi-dimensional, all-enveloping rhythms which punctuated Jimi's vision perfectly, whether the stop-starts of "Fire", the alternations between swing and swirl in "Third Stone from the Sun" or the pure poetic thunder of "If Six Was Nine".

Mitchell seemed a little lost as to how best to employ his formidable musical talents after Hendrix's death, though fortunately he was able to contribute overdubs to some of the unfinished tracks that were released posthumously. Like Noel Redding, he sold his rights to the royalties from the Experience's recordings for a sum that turned out to be much less than they were worth, though publicly at least, he was not nearly as bitter as the bassist over the loss. Some of the musicians he played alongside in middle age included his other Hendrix bassist-bandmate, Billy Cox, and more strangely, the best-known and most faithful Hendrix tribute act, Randy Hansen. Mitchell's anecdote-slanted recollections of his days with the Experience can be read in his book *Jimi Hendrix: Inside the Experience*, co-authored with John Platt. Mitchell sadly died 12 October 2008, at the age of 61, in his hotel room in Portland Oregon, while touring with the Experience Hendrix Tour.

The Story

The Experience Falls Apart

Electric Ladyland turned out to be the final Jimi Hendrix Experience album, and Jimi fuelled rumours of a split when he told *Melody Maker* in November 1968 that "very soon, probably in the New Year, we'll be breaking the group, apart from selected dates ... there are other scenes we want to get into". But to all intents and purposes, the Experience remained very much a functioning entity as the New Year came around. They had played only one UK concert in the whole of 1968, but the group returned to London for a while as the year began. Noel Redding and Mitch Mitchell might have been getting a little homesick; Hendrix wanted to see Kathy Etchingham again; and all three were mindful of re-establishing their presence in the country that had seen the birth of their success.

A two-week European tour (mostly in Germany) was undertaken in January, and in Düsseldorf, Hendrix met **Monika Dannemann**, the woman who was with him when he died the following year. But the only chance British audiences had to see the Experience that month was on Lulu's BBC TV variety show, where the band famously launched into an impromptu cover of Cream's "Sunshine of Your Love", delighting fans but causing consternation among the programme's time-conscious, schedule-driven producers. Abruptly cutting short a performance of "Hey Joe", Jimi expressed both his admiration for Cream – who had just split up – and his impatience with retreading his first hit: "We'd like to stop playing this rubbish and dedicate a song to the Cream, regardless of what kind of group they may be in." It may seem odd today that the Experience was playing these sort of variety shows in the first place, but in the late 1960s it was still considered standard promotion for all popular rock acts: during a brief British stopover in June 1968, Hendrix had even appeared on Dusty Springfield's show to duet with the hostess on the early-1960s soul hit "Mockingbird".

Jimi Hendrix and Noel Redding performing on the *Happening For Lulu* **TV show**

Electric Lady Studios

Although in some ways it was an indulgent and fiscally foolish enterprise, **Electric Lady Studios** ultimately proved to be one of the soundest of Jimi Hendrix's many pie-in-the-sky ideas. True, some of its specific accoutrements seem a little like a confluence of hippie culture and *Star Trek* when viewed with forty years distance, like white walls that changed colour via a remote-control theatrical lighting setup, as well as abundant mirrors and large cushions. The psychedelic mural, oddly enough, was disliked by Hendrix, perhaps because it was Mike Jeffery's idea. Whatever his specific tastes, however, his goal was commendably practical: to make the studio a comfortable place in which to work, as opposed to the rather brusque and institutional atmosphere boasted by many major facilities of the era, all the way up to Abbey Road (whose sterility The Beatles would vocally complain about to staff towards the end of their career).

"He just loved being in the studio", stressed Eddie Kramer in *Hendrix: Setting the Record Straight*. "He would say, 'Give me red lights or yellow lights tonight', and wash the walls in a rainbow of different colours. It had always been his intent to have the studio loose and casual, yet at the same time we worked hard to maintain a high standard of professionalism." The equipment and acoustics were first-rate, including a

forty-mike input console and a large floating ceiling twenty feet above the floor, and in Kramer's view (as stated in *Jimi Hendrix: Sessions*), "Jimi could hear that *his* studio offered him a better bass sound, better drum sound, better everything. I think Jimi relished the challenge that the studio represented."

Hendrix was nonetheless frustrated that he couldn't use Electric Lady whenever he felt like it if the studio was booked by other artists, the initial rates being $155 an hour. He did get to do quite a bit of recording there in Studio A before Electric Lady was officially finished and opened to the public at a party he briefly attended on 26 August 1970, just before he left for a European tour. He would undoubtedly have done much more, of course, had he ever returned.

It was uncertain whether Electric Lady would survive after Jimi's death the following month. But its reputation really took off after Stevie Wonder, a studio perfectionist to rival Hendrix himself, used it in the early 1970s to cut the ground-breaking albums on which he first asserted total control over his recordings, *Music of My Mind* and *Talking Book*. David Bowie, The Clash, Led Zeppelin, Joni Mitchell, The Rolling Stones, Run-DMC and Patti Smith are just a few of the major rock stars since that time who have used the studio, which continues to thrive to this day.

There were also some proper concerts in February at the **Royal Albert Hall** in London, which marked the Experience's final UK shows (and for which Chas Chandler, as a favour, briefly returned to the fold to help out with the sound). These shows were also filmed by Jerry Goldstein and Steve Gold, as part of a planned documentary on the Experience. Unfortunately,

legal disputes between the filmmakers and the Hendrix estate have thus far prevented the appearance of any footage from the Albert Hall concerts, let alone a finished film.

In the case of the first show, this may have been for the best, as it's been roundly panned as one of the band's worst high-profile gigs, although the second went much better. Chandler for one

The End of the Experience

The Experience play the Royal Albert Hall

was wondering if the Experience were on their last legs, describing the first concert in *Hendrix: Setting the Record Straight* as one of the worst he'd ever seen Jimi give, though blaming Mitchell and Redding rather than Hendrix: "If I had still been in charge, Mitch and Noel would have been sacked the next day." There were also scattered attempts to record at Olympic Studios that month, and then at New York's Record Plant in April, but these were so fraught and unproductive that it began to seem a matter of time before the Experience imploded.

The Jimi Hendrix Experience's final US tour began in April, with a typically gig-crammed schedule that saw them play a couple of dozen venues in six weeks. It was a testament to Hendrix's popularity that he was now able to play large stadiums and arenas that had seen few rock shows prior to the late 1960s, such as the Spectrum in Philadelphia, the Forum in Los Angeles, Oakland Coliseum, Detroit's Cobo Hall, and New York's fabled Madison Square Garden. The band's radical reworking of "The Star Spangled Banner" was already attracting controversy, with police unsuccessfully demanding that the show be stopped when they played the song in Houston, and outraged Texans threatening (again unsuccessfully) that Jimi wouldn't make it out of the building alive if he played it in Dallas.

There was also a solitary show in Canada, at Toronto's Maple Leaf Gardens, which everyone involved soon wished had never been booked. For on 3 May, Hendrix was busted for heroin and hashish possession while going through customs on his arrival. He was freed in time for the concert that evening and allowed to return to the US to finish the tour, but a court appearance in mid-June, at which a trial was scheduled for early December, left a sword hanging over his head. Another troublesome legal situation, though not one that threatened to send Hendrix to prison, involved the ongoing disputes with Ed Chalpin, who was still chasing money from Jimi's overseas earnings after a settlement had been negotiated regarding his North American releases.

A further storm cloud hovering over the Experience was the imminent departure of Noel Redding to play with a band of his own, **Fat Mattress**. (The ungainly name, incidentally, might have had its roots in Hendrix's rambling rap before "Wild Thing" at Monterey, during which he observed that "America doesn't like us because, you know, our feet's too big, or we got fat mattresses, and we wear golden underwear.") Redding had already been using some Experience studio time to work on songs of his own that didn't make the trio's official albums, with Fat Mattress forming near the end of 1968, even as Noel kept up his position in the Experience. Perhaps as an olive branch

of sorts – though perhaps also in part because Jeffery wanted at least a cut of Fat Mattress's career – the group opened for the Experience at the Royal Albert Hall and at some dates on the spring 1969 US tour. Redding's status remained uncertain, however, when the tour ended in early June, although the Experience played a couple of festivals later that month.

Probably with an eye on needing a replacement – though just as probably in need of an old and trusted friend as his life threatened to spiral out of control – Hendrix met up with **Billy Cox** when the Experience played in Memphis on 18 April. By May, with the Hendrix-Redding-Mitchell line-up continuing to fulfil numerous tour obligations throughout the US, Cox was already working with and even doing some recording with Hendrix in New York, where Jimi admitted to Billy that he was running out of ideas. "He knew that I was familiar with his style, sound and creativity", Cox observed in *Jimi Hendrix: Sessions*. "I hadn't played with him in a long while, but when I first heard 'Foxy Lady', I knew that to be an old song of his we used to call 'Stomp Driver' in Nashville. Jimi's creativity had been stifled, and I guess he thought of me, because even in the early days we had always been able to make up stuff."

In interviews from around mid-1969, Hendrix talked about both wanting to take a breather and various projects that would never be completed, indicating both fanciful ambition and a seeming indecisiveness as to where to turn next. He told *NME* that he was thinking of taking a year off; in *Rolling Stone*, he mused about touring with musicians other than

Redding and Mitchell. He also told *Rolling Stone* that he was writing songs with twins Taharqa and Tunde-Ra Aleem, whom he had known since his pre-fame Harlem days (when they were known as Arthur and Albert Allen), with a mind toward producing an album for their group The Ghetto Fighters.

As Hendrix complained in *Beat Instrumental* in June, three years of nonstop work had taken its toll on the Experience both musically and emotionally, leaving him little time to pursue his creative ambitions. He also intimated that he might not want to be tied down to a group at all, praising the way in which jazz musicians were free to jam with each other or form temporary alliances without long-term obligations. "Maybe the group only exists for that one album, maybe they go on for a year or so together – but they don't stretch it out once it has started losing the sheer exuberance of jamming together", he noted. "Now it's happening on the pop side of things this can only be good."

Close to the end: portrait, October 1968, Bakersfield, California

Hendrix and the Black Power Movement

Seemingly against his will, Jimi Hendrix was co-opted by the burgeoning **Black Power** movement of the late 1960s, although his attitude towards them – like his attitude to many other things, musical and otherwise – is hard to determine with any certainty. It was obvious from the musicians he played with, the company he kept and the sounds he listened to, that Hendrix was about as colour-blind as a major cultural figure could be. He was also an African-American, however, and some black militants, perhaps suspicious of his enormous appeal to the white rock audience, felt that he should be demonstrating his solidarity with his own race and endorsing their political causes.

Hendrix, however, was rather apolitical by nature and – despite the occasional torching of his guitar – not someone inclined to think that violence offered a solution to social problems. "Quite naturally, I don't like to see houses being burnt", he told the Los Angeles underground paper *Open City* in August 1967. "But I don't have too much feeling for either side right now … Maybe I'll have more to say later when I get more political."

Jimi seemed to do just that when the assassination of Martin Luther King, Jr sparked rioting across the US (including in one city, Newark, which he played almost immediately after King's death). Shortly afterwards, he reportedly donated $5000 to an organization affiliated with King, also appearing at a Madison Square Garden concert with soul stars Aretha Franklin, Joe Tex, and Sam and Dave to raise money for the Martin Luther King Memorial Fund.

But although Black Panthers would sometimes corner Hendrix to try and coerce him into becoming more active – as they did at one of the original Experience's last concerts at the Newport Pop festival, in June 1969 – Jimi never endorsed them, still less advocated violence or any other radical measures to fight African-American oppression. While his Band of Gypsys project is seen by some as bowing to pressure to play with black rather than white musicians, its short life suggests that it wasn't a notion to which Hendrix was beholden, and he continued to play with – and make unrealized plans to play with – both black and white musicians until his death. Any changes Jimi wanted to make were expressed almost exclusively through his music, which he always seemed to view as a unifier of diverse ideas and peoples, not as a mouthpiece for any one cause or race.

Although nobody could know for certain that they would be the last shows by the trio, the two festivals the group played in late June weren't anybody's idea of a good way to wrap up what had truly been an incredible Experience. Jimi was in a foul mood at the **Newport Pop festival** in southern California, in part because he had just come back from his preliminary hearing for the Toronto case, and also because some Black Panthers had cornered Hendrix in his dressing room shortly before he was due to go on. As Redding recalled in his memoir *Are You Experienced?* (co-written with Carol Appleby): "He looked petrified and I was chilled to the bone by his appearance. I don't know what they were on about, but Jimi looked so relieved to see me that it was pathetic." Unfortunately, Hendrix took out his unhappiness on the audience, grumbling about their inattentiveness and playing much of the show with his back turned.

Shortly before the Experience's show at the **Denver Pop festival** at Mile High Stadium on 29 June, Redding heard a rumour from a reporter that he was out of the band. Confusingly, it's also been reported that although Hendrix wanted Billy Cox in the band on bass, it didn't necessarily mean there wasn't room for Redding to stay, indicating that Jimi might at least have been considering keeping him on as second guitarist. Be this as it may, the rumour couldn't have improved the vibe of this troubled final show of the tour, where fans rioted for free admission. There was more rioting inside the stadium, and when police used tear gas in an attempt to control the crowd, the band themselves were forced offstage; fans nearly crushed their truck as they fled the venue. Whether or not plans to disband or change the Experience line-up were underway – although Jimi's comment during the show itself that it would be their last gig seemed to confirm this – it was enough for Redding, who flew back to the UK the day after the concert. Despite a temporary effort to reunite the original Experience in early 1970, the show in Denver was the last time the threesome played together.

Now in musical and legal limbo, Jimi had to think about forming a new group or – more likely considering his recent penchant for jamming with numerous musicians – rotating ensembles with which to play. He would indeed perform and record with several different line-ups of musicians throughout the last year of his life, but without ever regaining the focus the Experience had brought to his increasingly erratic talents.

The Final Year
1969–1970

"He was very sophisticated; he knew what he wanted. But his main problem was that he wanted too many things at one time."

Alan Douglas

The Final Year
1969–1970

In mid-1969, despite the break-up of the Experience, Jimi Hendrix was in some ways in an enviable position. Unlike bandmates Noel Redding and Mitch Mitchell, he was a superstar in his own right. There was no shortage of world-class musicians dying to play with Hendrix, either in a proper band or on a more casual basis.

It all worked out differently, of course. Over the last fifteen or so months of his life, Hendrix could never quite decide what he wanted to do, and with whom he wanted to do it. Instead of vaulting into a clearer, more defined musical space, he fitfully roamed between different bands and studios, the personal and business turmoil that had surrounded his affairs for a couple of years threatening to engulf him. For all its instability, however, this period did see him both record and perform some highly worthwhile, adventurous music, highlighted by perhaps his most legendary live concert.

Woodstock

The dissolution of the Experience at the end of June 1969 left Hendrix without a band for the first time in almost three years. In a TV appearance on *The Dick Cavett Show* on 7 July, in fact, he was backed by members of the programme's orchestra when the host got him to play "Hear My Train A Comin'". When he appeared on *The Tonight Show* a few days later, Billy Cox was accompanying him on bass, but in the absence of Mitch Mitchell, the programme's house drummer, Ed Shaughnessy (sporting what *Rolling Stone* described as "pasted on sideburns"), had to make up the rhythm section. Clearly a more organized group was needed, and toward that end, Jimi asked another ghost from his immediate post-army days in Tennessee, **Larry Lee**, to join as rhythm guitarist.

Also for the first time since the formation of the Experience, Hendrix now had the clear break in his schedule that he had been pining for – sometimes vocally, in the press – ever since he had become a superstar. In the remaining six months of that year, he would play just three concerts and some scattered television dates. In keeping with the vogue among some top rock musicians at the end of the 1960s to "get it together in the country", he rented a large house near Woodstock in New York State, then famed as the home of Bob Dylan and The Band (as well as several other rock musicians seeking to escape from the rat race). He also asked two percussionists he had come across on the New York club scene, **Jerry Velez** and **Juma Sultan**, to join in rehearsals with him, Cox and Lee, the entire proto-band moving into the mansion.

In a way, this was a nod to both past and future ambitions. Hendrix's original idea when Chandler took him to London had been for a much bigger band than the power trio he had ended up leading. In addition, he had started talking about the notion of "Electric Church Music", a rather utopian concept in which people of all backgrounds could assemble and create almost as a religious exercise, not a commercial one. The large house at Shokan could have been an attempt at a church of sorts, the band not so much a set proposition as a loose collective, welcoming ideas not only from each member, but also from anybody else who might drop by with something to contribute.

Yet to an even greater degree than Electric Lady Studios (whose costly construction continued even as Jimi was chilling out in the country), there was a big gap between the scenario Hendrix envisioned and the cold reality of making it happen. Like some of his recent studio sessions, what the open-door ethos of Shokan led to was not inspired interplay between players at the top of their game, but seemingly endless and aimless jamming. The plain fact was that, as musicians, Lee, Velez and Sultan were no match for Redding, Mitchell or for that matter Cox. They were also fairly unnecessary for the

sort of sound Hendrix generated, cluttering up the arrangements rather than adding anything significant to them. As Velez and Sultan were conga players, not standard full-kit drummers, they were often in danger of being overwhelmed by Jimi's sheer volume anyway. It's quite possible that at this point, Hendrix was more concerned with surrounding himself with friends with whom he felt comfortable than the best musicians possible – an understandable decision given his recent stresses, perhaps, but not one conducive to the best artistic results.

Although his presence was desperately needed to give the project some cohesion, it was unclear whether Mitch Mitchell was still in the fold or not. When Mitchell finally checked things out, he was dubious, not only as to the need for a rhythm guitarist and conga players in the first place, but also as to whether the percussionists in particular could even keep time with the others. "The band was a shambles", he wrote candidly in *Jimi Hendrix: Inside the Experience* (co-written with John Platt). "Apparently, they'd been working for about ten days when I got there, but you'd never have known." Whether on impulse or in an attempt to temporarily remove himself from the mess he had created, Hendrix took an unscheduled trip to Morocco for a week or so at the end of July, leaving the others behind in Shokan to wonder whether the band – dubbed **Gypsy Sun and Rainbows** – had a future.

The group might never have performed had Jimi not committed to performing in mid-August at **Woodstock**, which was turning into the largest and most revered rock festival of all time. Hendrix would be closing the show – a in the half-million-strong crowd exhausted by a weekend that had seen heavy rain and other problems turn the site into something of a disaster area, he started his set shortly after dawn on a Monday morning (instead of Sunday night as planned), in front of a rapidly dwindling audience too exhausted to stick it out.

Having stayed up all night waiting to go on, Hendrix and his band may well have been exhausted too. Frankly, their set was fairly ragged, as confirmed when much of it finally became available on both disc and video. In part, this was because Lee, Sultan and Velez were surplus to requirements. But it was also due to the fact that, alongside familiar favourites such as "Foxy Lady", "Purple Haze" and "Fire", Jimi indulged in some disorganized, over-long jamming, indicating not only his confusion about where he wanted to take this band in particular, but also about his entire musical vision. Indeed, before his plans were vetoed by Woodstock's promoters and/or Mike Jeffery, Hendrix had originally intended to perform a couple of acoustic songs – which would certainly have been a radical and interesting change from his usual approach, but which would probably have made for an even more incoherent set.

"Quite frankly, I never thought his performance, save for 'Star Spangled Banner' and a few other highlights, was any good", divulged Eddie Kramer, who was responsible for recording the performance, in *Hendrix: Setting the Record Straight*. He recalls watching the rushes and listening back to the performance with disappointment, given Hendrix's considerable talents. "I distinctly remember worrying that

Woodstock – a physical and musical marathon

high honour, considering that the roster also included major icons like The Band, Creedence Clearwater Revival, Jefferson Airplane, Janis Joplin, Santana, Sly and the Family Stone, The Who and Crosby, Stills, Nash and Young. When Jimi and his band-in-progress (Mitchell fortunately aboard) finally took the stage, however, circumstances beyond their control meant that it came as something of an anti-climax. With the show running way over schedule, and many

Waving his Freak Flag High: Hendrix's "Star Spangled Banner"

Even before it was immortalized in the *Woodstock* movie and soundtrack, Jimi Hendrix's unique instrumental interpretation of **The Star Spangled Banner** at the festival had generated quite a bit of attention, not all of it positive. To put it in context, particularly for non-US residents, "The Star Spangled Banner" is not just a patriotic song honouring the country's flag, but the official national anthem, played with considerable solemnity at many political and military ceremonies (and before most professional sporting events). So often is it heard in fact, that it's become banal through repeated exposure.

Its multi-octave tune also renders it legendarily difficult to sing well, so Hendrix was wise to make his an instrumental treatment. Even without singing – let alone changing – any of the words, however, his stinging interpretation of the melody stood the familiar song on its head, and to some minds totally twisted the original intention of the anthem. Rather than playing it as a homage to his native land, it was sometimes argued, Hendrix was actually deliberately sabotaging it, much as those new-fangled hippies were bent on destroying the very fabric of American life. At the very least, some claimed, his aggressive assault on the tune was meant to mirror the violence of the war the US government was waging abroad (in Vietnam) and at home (against young protesters and, in the eyes of many, African-Americans such as Hendrix himself).

But though it's often assumed otherwise, Hendrix himself was not particularly anti-military or anti-US in his attitudes, at least until the very end of his life (and then, only subtly so). Part of this, no doubt, was attributable to his own background as a soldier in the early 1960s. Although it might not have seemed entirely reasonable to some passionate anti-war protesters, attacks against the US military as a whole could be seen by some vets as an unfair slur against soldiers, of which Jimi had been one (if only briefly, and never in combat). Perhaps Hendrix felt a kinship with forces serving in Vietnam, knowing that, then as now, those risking death in US uniform were disproportionately African-American in number, including some blacks Jimi had known before he became famous. This would seem to be the case from the onstage dedication he gave to soldiers fighting in Vietnam when introducing "Machine Gun", although he made it clear he was concerned with young people caught up in conflict everywhere by extending the dedication to "soldiers" fighting in various American cities.

Though it could been more out of naïveté than enthusiasm, in 1967 the Experience even took part in a **US Army** public service radio spot urging youngsters

Woodstock might be the beginning of the end for Jimi Hendrix."

The Woodstock performance is usually remembered as a great triumph, however, for the very good reason that it featured Hendrix's definitive deconstruction of "The Star Spangled Banner". As a film crew was also on hand to capture his set for what became the ultra-successful rockumentary **Woodstock**, his rendition also became a centrepiece of the ensuing movie, doing as much to propagate his legend as any other recording or film footage of the guitarist. It's not clear to what extent Hendrix intended his "cover" of the US national anthem to be a to enlist (as did, that same year, Hendrix's friend/rival/fellow Woodstock star Pete Townshend in an ad for the US Air Force). Following a short interview with the singer-guitarist, DJ Harry Harrison urged listeners: "It's your future, it's your decision, choose army!" In an interview with the Dutch magazine *Kink*, indeed, Jimi sounded not so much like a free-spirited hippie as a spokesman for the Pentagon: "The Americans are fighting in Vietnam for the complete free world. As soon as they move out, they'll be at the mercy of the communists. For that matter, the yellow danger [China] should not be underestimated. Of course, war is horrible, but at present, it's still the only guarantee to maintain peace."

By the beginning of 1969, on the other hand, he seemed to have become more sympathetic to the anti-war movement, dedicating a show in Stockholm on 9 January to "the American Deserters Society" – a possible reference to the growing number of young Americans moving to Sweden to avoid the draft.

It's also not universally known that Hendrix did not unfurl his particular brand of "The Star Spangled Banner" specifically for Woodstock, but had been playing it live for a while, also recording a studio version in March 1969 (posthumously released on the *Rainbow Bridge* LP). Most likely Jimi was

attracted to the song not for its (frankly unimpressive) aesthetic qualities or out of a specific intention to desecrate the flag or criticize the government, but for the opportunity it afforded to create some high-spirited musical mischief that was more artistically than politically subversive. After all, he did the same thing, albeit to less notorious and memorable effect, to the hallowed standards "Auld Lang Syne", "Little Drummer Boy" and "Silent Night", not to mention "God Save the Queen" at the Isle of Wight festival. When the controversy over his unorthodox Woodstock interpretation of "The Star Spangled Banner" was brought up by talk show host Dick Cavett on national television shortly after the festival, Hendrix's response – "I thought it was beautiful" – seemed sincere, not sarcastic.

And for all the criticism it provoked at the time, Hendrix's "arrangement" of "The Star Spangled Banner" has itself come to be seen as something of a national standard. When the fortieth anniversary of the Summer of Love was commemorated with a special day at a San Francisco Giants major league baseball game in the summer of 2007, the national anthem was performed prior to the first pitch by a Hendrix imitator, replicating Jimi's Woodstock version of the song note-for-note.

commentary on the stormy times in which he lived (see box). But with the imitations of falling bombs, explosions and sheer sonic mayhem that Jimi mixed in with the siren-sweet notes of the melody, it was hard for most people to take it as anything but a savage critique of the manner in which the US was failing to live up

to its idealistic principles, both in the Vietnam War and the violence erupting in protests and race riots at home.

It wouldn't be until well into 1970, however, that most of the world got to hear and see Hendrix's performance via the *Woodstock* soundtrack and film. In the immediate aftermath of the festival, Jimi still had to contend with a floundering band and impatient, unsympathetic management. Within a decade or two, a multi-year break between albums would be considered unexceptional for major recording artists, but back in the late 1960s, a minimum of an LP a year was expected. With almost a year since the release of *Electric Ladyland* and no follow-up in sight, a rather premature "greatest hits" collection, *Smash Hits*, was issued in the US in the summer of 1969 to fill the gap. (A live LP assembled by Eddie Kramer from various performances had actually been submitted to Reprise as a possible stop-gap in mid-June, but *Smash Hits* was given the go-ahead instead.) A similar collection with an identical title had been issued in the UK way back in April 1968, but the new version at least contained a few tracks previously unavailable in the US.

The line-up from Woodstock did cut some sessions in New York City over the next few weeks, but the results weren't entirely satisfactory. To be fair, it wasn't entirely the fault of Hendrix's accompanists. Although Hendrix, Mitchell and Cox (who had done session work in Nashville before teaming up with Jimi again) were studio veterans, it was a lot to be asking of the less experienced Lee, Sultan, and Velez to gel with one of the world's top musicians under this pressure.

More arrows came flying at Hendrix in the shape of increased pressure from **African-American militants** to become more political. As radical as he was in his music, dress and lifestyle, Jimi had shown little interest in politics and moved easily in integrated musical and social circles from the mid-1960s onward. At a time when race riots were erupting in the inner cities and groups such as the Black Panthers were asserting African-American power and identity, however, some fellow blacks felt that Hendrix, as one of the most visible and famous African-Americans, should be throwing in his lot with their cause. Black activists might have felt that Jimi was somehow kowtowing to the Establishment by virtue of being far more popular with white rock fans than African-Americans, although this gap has probably been overestimated, as some of his albums actually rose to fairly high positions on the *Billboard* R&B charts.

Perhaps to placate his political critics (though it's also been speculated that he did so to avoid conflicts with Harlem gangsters trying to force him into giving a concert), Hendrix and his new band played a closing set at a free festival in **Harlem** on 5 September, in front of just a few hundred people. Some eyewitnesses have depicted the concert as a musical success, and others as a failure – the crowd was apparently geared up for a soul-style revue (in line with the other acts on the bill) rather than a hard-rock outfit. But as it turned out, the tentative aggregation known as Gypsy Sun and Rainbows would play just one more show, at New York's Salvation Club a few days later, before it was dissolved by mutual agreement. Although Jimi had originally intended to play a series of concerts in the South at the end of September, these were cancelled. There was still time, however, for a jam with Sultan and keyboardist Mike Ephron

Jimi Hendrix performs at a street concert in Harlem

to be recorded that month – which, to Jimi's dismay, became the very first Hendrix bootleg the following year.

Meanwhile, Mike Jeffery was not only anxious to get another album out: according to some accounts, he was also aggrieved by the relatively uncommercial turn Hendrix appeared to have taken with his new personnel arrangements. Although, given the wildly varying accounts that have been published, there seems no way of getting to the bottom of the incident, it's been reported that Hendrix was **kidnapped** after the Salvation show by organized criminal elements that wanted to threaten him, shut him up or somehow get something out of the musician. It's also been speculated that Jeffery orchestrated the whole thing so that he could pretend to "rescue" Jimi from his abductors, thereby binding Hendrix closer to his own interests and/or letting his client know that Jimi had better stay in line to avoid very serious trouble.

Alan Douglas and the Band of Gypsys

Without a band again after just two months, Hendrix managed to coax Billy Cox into re-enlisting for whatever his next venture was going to be, although Mitch Mitchell returned to the UK. Slotting in as a replacement of sorts was **Buddy Miles**, who had already played with Hendrix on several occasions in the studio, most notably on *Electric Ladyland*'s "Rainy Day, Dream Away" and "Still Raining, Still Dreaming". As corpulent as Mitchell was pencil-thin, Miles had an impressive track record in both the R&B and rock worlds, having played in the great soul singer Wilson Pickett's band before joining The Electric Flag, who were spearheaded by blues-rock guitar hero Mike Bloomfield. Miles also had a substantially heavier, more funk-oriented approach than Mitchell, which, combined with Cox's soul background, began tilting Hendrix's entire sound in a more R&B-oriented direction.

The new group wasn't always intended to be a trio. Miles later recalled that both he and

The Electric Flag – Buddy Miles on drums, Mike Bloomfield on guitar

Hendrix wanted to get British rock star Stevie Winwood into the band, although it's unclear how such a major vocal and instrumental talent could have comfortably fitted into such a set-up. For that matter, Cox almost got ousted in favour of Billy Rich, who had played bass with Miles in The Buddy Miles Express, although Rich turned out to be unavailable.

For all Jimi's ambitions to form a larger ensemble, however, he always seemed to end up with a trio format, albeit sometimes embellished by other musicians in the studio. It was as a threesome that Hendrix, Miles and Cox made some generally halting and unsatisfactory progress on recording in New York in late 1969, often with producer **Alan Douglas** and engineer Stefan Bright. Although Douglas's main background was in jazz, he had broadened his range with his Douglas Records label, working on spoken-word recordings by Malcolm X and comedian Lenny Bruce, as well as albums by proto-rappers The Last Poets and emerging jazz-fusion guitarist John McLaughlin. None of the 1969 recordings he made with Hendrix were issued at the time, but his role in Jimi's career was far from over, Douglas later becoming a major (and extremely controversial) force in the completion and packaging of many of Hendrix's posthumously released recordings.

In Douglas's defence, it might not have been possible for anyone to get much out of Hendrix in the studio at this point. "I never saw such disorganization in all of my life", is how Douglas described his first visit to a Hendrix session in John McDermott and Eddie Kramer's *Hendrix: Setting the Record Straight*. While Hendrix,

Cox and Miles spent the entire night jamming, Douglas was aghast to see that nobody seemed to be giving Jimi useful feedback or direction. "The engineer just kept putting rolls of tape on the machine and pressing the record button. ... I wondered why he [Hendrix] had asked me to come because I didn't know what he was trying or even wanted to do."

In an interview with *Record Collector*, Douglas stated that he went on to spend four months in the studio with Hendrix, trying to help him to produce himself. According to Douglas, this was the best way to work with Jimi: "He was very sophisticated; he knew what he wanted. But his main problem was that he wanted too many things at one time."

It's around this time that **Miles Davis** apparently expressed some interest in recording with Hendrix, with another major jazzman, Tony Williams, on drums. Though Davis's and Hendrix's backgrounds were very different, there's some logic to the combination, as Miles had recently begun to make a controversial and highly influential move into jazz-rock fusion, which, if not exactly rock'n'roll, used powerful rock-influenced instrumentation. How exactly the two giants might have melded with each other remains unknown, since – according to Douglas – Davis and Williams wanted $50,000 each before coming into the studio. Davis is also said to have hoped to do a concert with Hendrix at Carnegie Hall, another intriguing project that never came to fruition.

This near-collaboration, along with jam sessions involving **John McLaughlin** and organist **Larry Young**, has given rise to speculation that

The Story

Jimi Does Jazz

Of all the uncertainties surrounding what precisely was going on in Jimi Hendrix's head in the final phase of his career, his attitude toward jazz might be the hardest to pin down. Some critics insist that he was a jazzman at heart longing to burst free of the shackles of rock'n'roll, or at least that he would have moved into jazz had he lived longer. But despite numerous reports and rumours of jams and planned proper recording sessions, Hendrix actually recorded little in his lifetime that could be considered jazz, or even considered more jazz than rock.

As far back as early 1967, Hendrix was declaring his affection for free-form jazz in interviews, singling out **Roland Kirk** (most noted for his uncanny ability to play several instruments at once) as a particular favourite. Jimi even got to jam with him in London in the late 1960s, but it wasn't until the Experience broke up that he recorded jams with major jazz players in the studio. The most renowned of these was a March 1969 session with **John McLaughlin** and bassist **Dave Holland**, as well as Buddy Miles. As with many jams, however, the consensus seems to be that while everybody had a good time, it wasn't worth immortalizing on record. McLaughlin himself didn't think the music was all that great, and hasn't authorized official release of the tapes, although producer Alan Douglas told Keith Shadwick (in *Jimi Hendrix: Musician*) that "if they had developed a rapport and spent time together they could have done incredible things together".

In an autobiography co-written by Quincy Troupe, Miles Davis claimed that "Jimi liked what I had done on *Kind of Blue* and some other stuff and wanted to add more jazz elements to what he was doing." In part for financial reasons, however, the proposed collaboration seemed hard to organize and the much anticipated meeting of musical minds never took place. Less well known is the fact that Jimi also considered playing on the *Gula Matari* album by Quincy Jones, famous for producing Michael Jackson's *Thriller*, but in his earlier career more noted as a top jazz producer and arranger. "Jimi always wanted to play jazz", Jones told Steven Roby in *Black Gold: The Lost Archives of Jimi Hendrix*. "He said his dream was to play with Miles." But when the time came to actually work on something with Jones in the studio, he didn't show up – perhaps through nerves, Jones suggested.

For the most part, then, what these collaborations might have sounded like can only be imagined. What's not imaginary, however, are the many props paid to Hendrix by jazz musicians after his death, manifesting themselves not only in tribute albums (and even a tribute concert titled The Hendrix Project in New York's Town Hall in December 1989), but in the audible influence Jimi exerted on the edgier jazz-rock fusion guitarists, such as James Blood Ulmer, Miles Davis sideman Pete Cosey and John McLaughlin himself.

Jimi would have plunged into jazz if the opportunity had arisen, or at least if he had lived longer. Since relatively little has emerged from the jam sessions in question and the Davis-Hendrix collaboration didn't take place, however, this notion – sometimes advanced, it must be said, by highbrow critics who seem to feel that playing mere rock'n'roll wasn't good enough for Jimi – remains tenuous.

It's not certain whether Hendrix wanted the trio to be a long-term project, or (as is more likely) something like a stop-gap as he marshalled his resources and figured out what to do next. For the time being, and perhaps to further differentiate this group from the Experience, the outfit was christened **Band of Gypsys**. The name was appropriate enough, considering that Hendrix had been leading a nomadic lifestyle for as long as he could remember, and that one of the songs from his most recent album was titled "Gypsy Eyes". It's been suggested, on the other hand, that the choice of Cox and Miles as the rhythm section was at least in part a concession to those African-Americans urging Jimi to embrace his black heritage, and not work with white musicians. Hendrix's band was now all-black, and blacker in sound as well as appearance – not that he had forgotten his blues and R&B roots, even in his wildest psychedelic excursions.

Possibly there was a more practical reason for Hendrix to get a band together in fairly short order. As part of his settlement with his ex-producer, all of the profits from his next album would go to Ed Chalpin. The record would not be issued by a label he was signed to in the US or other territories, but by Capitol Records, the same company that had issued the Curtis Knight–Jimi Hendrix LP *Get That Feeling* in late 1967. Even for an artist more concerned than most with the integrity of his product, there was little incentive for Jimi to go all out to make the album a commercial or artistic success.

This may be, again at least in part, why the album Hendrix subsequently cut with the Band of Gypsys was a live recording, although he had done stacks of studio recordings over the past year from which at least a few basic tracks could surely have been used. This may also explain why the LP would feature relatively little in the way of new material, and not even feature Jimi as singer or songwriter on every selection. While far from being a perfect compromise, the approach Hendrix adopted would enable him to fulfil his legal obligations, provide reasonable value for the many fans certain to buy his next album regardless of its contents, and save the best of his as-yet-unissued songs for the studio LP he truly wanted to make.

Before a concert could be staged and recorded, however, Jimi still needed to stand trial for his May drugs bust in Toronto, on 8 December. How exactly the heroin in particular got in his baggage will never be explained, but it's worth noting that although Hendrix certainly took his fair share of drugs, he's usually not considered to have been a frequent heroin user, and certainly not a heroin addict. It's also worth noting that for all his partying, his drug habits were fairly typical of late-1960s rock stars and far from being the heaviest of his peers. Assuming that he was set up, theories range from the substances being planted on him by over-zealous customs officers looking to make a mark (as they often were with travelling rock musicians), to the goods having been inserted into his belongings by someone he knew. It's not clear how an imprisoned Jimi Hendrix could have been worth more than a free one, but there are even those who think that someone with a financial interest in the musician wanted to scare him so that he didn't

The Final Year

Acquitted in Toronto

become too independent. As an added complication, Hendrix was arrested for drug possession yet again at Toronto airport on his return to Canada, spending a night in jail before the charges were dropped.

In the event, Hendrix's defence successfully contended that Jimi wasn't aware of what was in his luggage. Hendrix himself testified that the vial of heroin had been given to him by a fan in Los Angeles, Jimi (thinking it was Bromo-Seltzer) forgetting to even open it after putting it in his bag. After eight hours of deliberation, the jury declared him not guilty, lifting the threat of a jail sentence and leaving him free to resume his musical career.

Thus liberated, Hendrix and the Band of Gypsys performed four shows at New York's Fillmore East, on New Year's Eve and 1 January 1970. In retrospect, it was asking a lot even of seasoned musicians to come up with an album based on their first-ever live performances as a group. Perhaps it was another sign that, regardless of the possible impact on the band itself, the LP was considered something to get in the can as quickly as possible.

Response to the shows, at least in comparison with what Hendrix had become accustomed to, was fairly muted. Part of the reaction was no doubt due to the disappointment of those expecting a recreation of the Experience, but part was also down to the undoubted inferiority of some of the material. Rock promoter and Fillmore operator Bill Graham, no small legend himself, even scolded Jimi for putting crowd-pleasing showmanship ahead of musicianship after his first show, supposedly resulting in a much improved subsequent performance, though even here opinions differ. At least Hendrix, under all this stress, had the sense of humour to play "Auld Lang Syne" to greet the New Year at midnight.

A mere six songs, all performed on New Year's Day, were selected for April release on what might be termed Jimi Hendrix's contractual obligation album, *Band of Gypsys*. Moreover two of the tunes, "Changes" and "We Gotta Live Together", were written and sung by Miles, not Hendrix, Buddy's secondary vocals featuring strongly on another track, "Who Knows". By far the most funk-tinged of Jimi's albums, it did well enough on the mar-

Touching bottom: Band of Gypsys play the Winter Festival for Peace benefit at Madison Square Garden

ketplace, rising to number five, but left fans feeling as though it was something of a mildly disappointing diversion, if hardly a throwaway. Nevertheless, it did include, almost as a reassurance that Jimi wasn't holding everything back, one of his best-loved songs – **Machine Gun**, which demonstrated that he hadn't lost his knack for devastating riffs or intriguing lyrics, which in this case seemed to combine references to a sexual relationship with what most construed as decidedly anti-war commentary. That suspicion was heightened by his spoken intro to the track on the LP (repeated with variations at other concerts in 1970), in which he

dedicated the number to "all the soldiers that are in fighting in Chicago and Milwaukee and New York… Oh yes, and all the soldiers fighting in Vietnam" – a dedication that also made clear that Hendrix was aware of the violence taking place at home as well as abroad.

The Band of Gypsys did some studio recording over the next few weeks, resulting in a rare single, **Stepping Stone/Izabella**, issued briefly by Hendrix's primary US label Reprise in April before Capitol demanded its almost instant withdrawal. But the next Band of Gypsys show – hard as it is to believe considering how much effort had gone into the project – would be their last. On 28 January, they played as part of a Winter Festival for Peace benefit at Madison Square Garden, itself an indication that Hendrix was becoming more willing to lend his voice to the anti-war movement. Midway through the second song, Jimi simply stopped playing, bringing the set sputtering to a chaotic close.

Most insiders believe that Hendrix was simply in no condition to play, due to something he had ingested before going onstage. Again, theories abound, with some speculating that Mike Jeffery was responsible for giving Jimi some bad acid, in the hope of ruining the performance of a group with whom Jeffery wasn't keen on Hendrix continuing to work. Whatever the cause, most agree it was the worst, most disappointing performance Jimi ever gave, and one that alarmed some fans into thinking that their hero might be having serious problems behind the scenes. Shortly after – lending credence to the theory that he didn't want Hendrix playing with the Band of Gypsys, if not that he was willing to sabotage a high-profile concert in order to do so – Jeffery fired **Buddy Miles**, who was a little too independent for his liking anyway. With Billy Cox following him, the Band of Gypsys had ended almost as soon as they had begun.

With the passage of time, the Band of Gypsys phase of Hendrix's career is viewed a little more kindly than it was back in 1970, when fans were expecting or at least hoping for another giant leap forward along the lines of *Electric Ladyland*. Viewed in the context of his work as a whole, it can be appreciated as an interesting, if not wholly successful, experiment in giving his music a more pronounced R&B slant. In the CD/DVD era, the commercial availability of much more material recorded at the Fillmore shows (on *Live at the Fillmore East*), as well as some video footage taken of the concerts, also helps to flesh out the group's embryonic vision and reveals a somewhat wider scope to their abilities than the relatively truncated original *Band of Gypsys* LP could.

Electric Lady Studios and the Return of Mitch Mitchell

With the heroin bust no longer an issue and his contractual obligation album now out of the way, it might have seemed as though it was finally possible, for the first time in almost a year, for Hendrix to concentrate on music and that all-important, much-delayed next studio LP. Unfortunately, he continued to face obstacles on all fronts. The building of his much-anticipated **Electric Lady Studios** contin-ued to be troubled, work stopping due to lack of funds around the time the Band of Gypsys folded. Hendrix and Jeffery had to take a loan of $300,000 from Warner Bros., Reprise's parent label, to get construction to resume, adding stress to the already strained state of their finances. Money wasn't the only problem impeding the studio's completion: after some flooding, it was discovered that a tributary of an underground river ran underneath, necessitating extra soundproofing against the noise of the flowing water.

"It was funded hand-to-mouth as the earnings came in", Jim Marron, president of the company formed to build the studio, told *Guitar World*. "Jimi would go out and do a coliseum date, in San Diego, say, and come back with $100,000 in his pocket. So he'd peel off $50,000, hand it to me and say, 'OK, start it up again'… and we'd go until the money ran out again."

Worse, when *Band of Gypsys* was delivered to Capitol Records, Ed Chalpin considered it a breach of contract, claiming the settlement specified that it had to be a Jimi Hendrix Experience album produced by himself. Capitol Records' acceptance of the LP nonetheless seemed to clear up Hendrix's problems with Chalpin in North America, but his ex-producer continued to fight for money that he felt he was due for overseas sales. Even the most ardent Hendrix fan might have acknowledged that Chalpin was entitled to some compensation for Jimi's initial breach of contract. But by this time, Chalpin was pursuing damages so extreme that few could sympathize with his actions, which were clearly obstructing the career of a man for whose contract he had paid the princely sum of $1.

Possibly in an attempt to put Hendrix's career back on a stable footing, and possibly because this is what he was manoeuvring for all along, Jeffery orchestrated a brief "reunion" of the original Experience right on the heels of the Band of Gypsys' split. Interviews were

even undertaken in which all three bravely presented a united front for the benefit of the press. Hendrix, however, never really wanted Noel Redding back in the band, although Noel was probably willing to give it a go after Fat Mattress had failed to sell many records. Despite Redding flying to New York to start rehearsing with Hendrix and Mitch Mitchell in early March, the trio never did play together again, Redding not even getting told by Jimi that Billy Cox was going to come back into the group after all (although Jack Bruce and Jack Casady of Jefferson Airplane were apparently also considered, as was the addition of a horn section). Of all the messy, unpleasant incidents dotting the last couple of years of Hendrix's life, this quasi-reunion was the most farcical.

Subsequently, Hendrix defended his decision not to use Redding to Keith Altham in *Melody Maker*: "It's nothing personal against Noel but we finished what we were doing with the Experience and Billy's style of playing suits the new group better. The Experience got into a cul-de-sac: we played for three years and had reached the stage where we were just repeating ourselves."

Some Hendrix biographers have suggested that Jimi's failure to release a fully realized studio album after *Electric Ladyland*, and the sputtering momentum of his career in general, can be attributed mostly or wholly to the cold-blooded business demands that were being made on him. Although there may be a measure of truth in this, it can't be ignored that, whether for circumstantial reasons or from lack of inspiration, Hendrix simply wasn't

Jimi Hendrix, Mitch Mitchell, Billy Cox – performing live onstage at Cal Expo, Sacramento

coming up with new songs to match the ones he had written before. No matter how proficient his playing, or how adventurously he might have been exploiting new technological possibilities in the studio, he wasn't going to get very far without first-class material to work on.

For the last half-year or so of his life, however, Hendrix did seem to gain some focus and

clarity in his songwriting, starting to polish and record material that promised to be the basis of a strong LP, if not one as ground-breaking as *Are You Experienced?* or *Electric Ladyland*. For all the seeming unproductivity of the Band of Gypsys' studio sessions, some of these songs, such as **Room Full of Mirrors**, "Izabella", "Stepping Stone" and **Ezy Ryder**, had actually started to take shape during this time; if for no other reason than giving Jimi a chance to begin working on them, these sessions must be considered to have had some purpose after all. The newer songs he was starting to compose had a somewhat more optimistic, ebullient feel than much of what he had been playing around with over the past year and a half or so.

Still, not much was done with them in the studio before the newly constituted trio of Hendrix, Cox and Mitchell – who had played in Jack Bruce and Friends with Larry Coryell in the gap between his stints with Jimi – kicked off another American tour at the Forum in Los Angeles on 25 April. The trio continued to play fairly regularly throughout the US in May and June, although the dates slowed to a relative trickle in July. Most audiences and critics seemed to agree that the shows by this new version of the Experience (as they were billed) marked a return to form for Hendrix, or were at least the best that he had played on a consistent basis for a year or so. In an encouraging sign of a re-emergence of both his self-confidence and creative spirit, a good half or so of his set featured songs that had yet to be released, as well as two highlights ("Machine Gun" and "Message to Love") from the new *Band of Gypsys* LP.

Of special note were two 30 May 1970 concerts at the **Berkeley Community Theater**, footage of which eventually served as the basis for the 1971 movie *Jimi Plays Berkeley*. Although some critics didn't appreciate the fact that performance clips were interspersed with scenes of student unrest and protest which had little or nothing to do with Hendrix, it was the first

full-length film built around Jimi's music, and much less of a headache to the star of the show than another movie in which he was to figure shortly after. But as at some other gigs Hendrix did that year, crowd unrest clouded the performances, fans without tickets trying to force their way in, while – in the strange spirit of the day's countercultural politics – others demonstrated against the $3.50 movie tickets for the *Woodstock* film.

By this time, however, Jimi was suffering frustrations in live performance which hadn't been so much of a concern when he had first risen to fame. He was tired of playing his most popular numbers over and over again – even if they were just three or so years old – and fed up of the stage gimmicks (such as playing behind his back, with his teeth and so on) which many in the audience expected at a Jimi Hendrix concert. Hendrix might have been underestimating his audience a little in this respect. Rock concert-goers were generally older and more sophisticated in their tastes than they had been in 1967, and many might have reacted favourably if Jimi had taken some more chances onstage with both his material and presentation. Perhaps the lukewarm reception given to the Band of Gypsys had something to do with his reluctance to make too much of a break with the tried-and-tested, so while he did play some new songs that were likely contenders for his next album, standbys like "Foxy Lady" and "Purple Haze" remained in his set.

Sometime around late spring 1970, Hendrix was finally able to start recording at Electric Lady Studios, working on sessions there before

The Story

Devon Wilson: The Real-Life Dolly Dagger

Of the several women with whom Hendrix had serious romantic relationships, none – Monika Dannemann, Kathy Etchingham, Faye Pridgeon or even his high-school sweetheart Betty Jean Morgan – remains as mysterious as **Devon Wilson**, a frequent companion of Jimi's during the last year and a half or so of his life. Born Ida Mae Wilson, she was reported to have begun a life in prostitution at the age of fifteen, and by the time she started hanging out with Jimi, she was usually described as a groupie. Hendrix biographies do not generally paint a flattering picture of Wilson, often concluding that she was at least partly responsible for Jimi's escalating drug use and that she was angling for a position of power in the semi-harem he was keeping in his latter days.

Wilson, however, is also thought to have provided the lyrical inspiration for one of the best songs Hendrix recorded in 1970, **Dolly Dagger**. This, apparently, had its origin in an incident at a party she and Hendrix attended in late 1969, in which Devon sucked the blood from an injured **Mick Jagger**'s finger and subsequently went off with him – hence

the song's key image of Dolly drinking blood from a "jagged" edge (geddit?). Not that either Hendrix or Jagger were particularly monogamous themselves, but it was a little payback for the much earlier incident in which Jimi had tried, with Mick sitting at the same table, to pick up Jagger's then-girlfriend Marianne Faithfull. On a metaphorical level, Hendrix seemed to be depicting Wilson as a vampire-like force sucking the blood out of her conquests, one of numerous slightly fearful-critical portrayals of women lurking below the surface in some of Jimi's songs.

Although Wilson was in London at the time of Hendrix's death, she escaped the fate of her rival Monika Dannemann, who had to live with both the memory of discovering Hendrix's body and being blamed, fairly or unfairly, for not doing more to save him. But Wilson, as it turned out, didn't have much longer to live than Jimi did. She died in February 1971 after falling out of a window in New York's infamous bohemian haunt, the Chelsea Hotel. It's still unknown whether it was suicide, murder or a drug-related accident.

the set-up was finally completed. In fact, the official opening party wasn't held until late August, by which time Jimi had been cutting tracks there for about two months, although he was occasionally frustrated when he couldn't get into his own studio to record because other musicians had booked it – a financial necessity if it was to have any hope of being profitable. Helped by a slackening tour schedule, the presence of long-time trusted engineer Eddie Kramer and an environment created to his own specifications, these

were nevertheless his most productive recording dates since the days of *Electric Ladyland*. Jimi, in fact, thought he had enough suitable material for a double album, which he was planning to call *First Rays of the New Rising Sun*.

It was during this period that many tracks that were doubtless destined for the album were recorded, some of which saw Jimi getting more in touch with his tender and poetic side than he had been for a while. Foremost among these were the transcendentally yearning **Angel** and the gently contemplative **Drifting**. Some songs proved he hadn't lost his goofy sense of cosmic philosophizing ("Belly Button Window") and humour ("Astro Man"), and others found him verging on more or less straight-ahead blues, the Hendrixian twists supplied mostly by his agile guitar lines, which often projected a serenity missing from much of his recent work. **Dolly Dagger**, inspired by his mischievous girlfriend **Devon Wilson**, also showed him rediscovering his facility for swaggering bluesy riff-driven rockers – and, along with "Angel", is ultimately the only song from this batch that ranks among Hendrix's more popular tracks.

Some concert dates continued to be fitted in around the sessions, the most notorious of them being a 17 July appearance at the **New York Pop festival** at Randalls Island. Like many rock festivals of the time, the socio-political turmoil of the era was spilling over into and even threatening the staging of the event itself. Radical groups called for donations to their causes and free admission, somehow feeling – as they would at the Isle of Wight festival Hendrix would play the following month – that rock acts and their promoters were capitalist sell-outs if they were paid for appearing. In keeping with the disorganization afflicting many such events, Hendrix didn't appear until 4am, and his sound was plagued (as in the scene in *This Is Spinal Tap*) by radio transmissions picked up and broadcast by the PA system. Festivals would become somewhat more professional as the rock circuit itself became more of a big business, and politically charged crowd unruliness would dissipate within a year or two. Back in the summer of 1970, however, nobody knew this, and one imagines that such chaos must have made Jimi feel even more fed up with touring, since festivals had become major venues for the audiences that his kind of music attracted.

Rainbow Bridge and the Final Tour

In late July, Hendrix's recording sessions broke off for what ended up being something of a working vacation in Hawaii. On the way, Jimi fitted in a return show at Sicks's Stadium in Seattle, almost cancelled when a rainstorm put him in danger of being electrocuted, and marking the final time he saw his family and the friends he had grown up with. Although the Experience did play a show in Honolulu on 1 August which ended up being Jimi's final US concert, the Hawaiian trip seems to have been largely arranged so that the band could appear in a film for which Mike Jeffery was serving as executive producer, the Chuck Wein-directed *Rainbow Bridge*.

Even in comparison with some of the more ill-judged schemes in which Jeffery involved Hendrix, the movie was pretty much of a fiasco, being based around a mostly plotless scenario of young hippies working toward communal bliss in Maui. Why Jeffery was so determined to invest in the project isn't clear, but apparently it had something to do with his belated attempt to dive into the hippie lifestyle and the drugs that accompanied it. The prospect of a soundtrack album featuring Hendrix's music couldn't have hurt either. Although Jimi was probably a reluctant participant, as he had hoped for an uninterrupted three-week Hawaiian vacation before Jeffery insisted he participate in the film, the performance the Experience staged especially for the occasion, shot in an open field high in the Maui hills, is the undoubted highlight of the movie. While he also managed to squeeze in some relatively undisturbed rest and recreation in Hawaii, getting pressured into rescuing an ill-conceived film project that he had had no role in originating probably increased his disgust with Jeffery, although he seemed unable to make decisive moves to end their business relationship.

Hendrix resumed work on his new album as soon as he returned to New York, but in a familiar pattern, it was interrupted by touring commitments for the Experience in the late summer, this time in Europe. With Electric Lady now open for business – it remains, in fact, a world-class studio to this day – Jimi would have much rather focused his energies on completing *First Rays of the New Rising Sun*, the gap since his most recent studio release now approaching two years. While an album of this title was eventually (re)constructed in the CD era (and is discussed in the section of this book dealing with compilation recordings), it should be emphasized that it was *not* finished, or even all but finished, by the time Hendrix left for Europe, although much of the remaining work would probably have involved mixing or overdubs.

It also needs to be said that although Jimi's use of studio time had become more efficient of late, the perfectionist tendencies which had dogged him in the past had not disappeared. While not perhaps in the same league as the endless fussing of Brian Wilson, which led to the shelving of the Beach Boys' legendary *Smile* album, in hindsight the suspicion remains that if he had been left to his own devices, Hendrix might have taken virtually forever to finish the tracks, especially as he was working in a studio without the usual authority figures looking over his shoulder or otherwise inhibiting his tinkering.

The first date of the Experience's **European tour** was one of their more celebrated ones, since they were one of the key acts at the **Isle of Wight festival** at the end of August – a show that would turn out to be Hendrix's last major performance, though no one knew it at the time. Although not as well remembered as Woodstock, the list of performers was nearly as impressive, including Leonard Cohen, Miles Davis, Donovan, The Doors, Free, Joni Mitchell and The Who. Doubtless the festival would have had more impact if the film of the event, directed by Murray Lerner, hadn't taken about a quarter-century to come out. The movie naturally included part of Hendrix's performance, and eventually both a full-length CD and DVD of his Isle of Wight set were issued, although it doesn't capture him at the peak of his form. Frustrated by some technical problems with the equipment, Hendrix thanked the audience for their patience after the last song ended, dropping his guitar onstage in apparent disgust as he exited.

The tour quickly turned sour, however, when a bad dose of acid in Sweden turned the normally placid Billy Cox into a barely functional headcase. Hendrix himself wasn't doing much better, and in an incident somewhat reminiscent of his Madison Square Garden concert early in the year, walked offstage in Aarhus, Denmark, after playing just a few songs. Indeed, for every account of Jimi's brightening mood as he spent the summer working on his new album at Electric Lady, there's an equally sobering one remarking on how dispirited he seemed in these final weeks, the strain showing not only in his music but in his actual appearance, his hair already starting to grey.

On this particular jaunt, the worst was saved for last when Hendrix played his final concert on 6 September 1970 at the Isle of Fehmarn in Germany, at an event billed as a love and peace festival. Like some other such festivals of the era, alas, it turned out to be quite violent, the first bad omen coming when poor weather delayed the Experience's performance for a day. During their set, a group of European Hell's Angels broke into the box office and stole the entire takings for the event; according to Hendrix's road manager Gerry Stickells, Hell's Angels were also responsible for burning down the stage right after the band's equipment was taken off. With Cox showing no sign of recovery after a week, there was little choice but to cancel the rest of the tour, Billy being sent home from London to recuperate with his parents.

Final Days and Death in London

As eager as he had been to finish *First Rays of the New Rising Sun* before setting off to Europe, Hendrix lingered in London for the next ten days. Not being in such great shape himself, it could be that he wanted a chance to rest and reacquaint himself with friends in the city where he had launched his solo career, but in which he had spent relatively little time since the end of 1967. Since there were the usual problems waiting for him back in the US – including difficulties with Mike Jeffery that he was loathe to confront, but also a much less publicized paternity suit – it's been speculated that he was hiding out for a bit. But even the great distance that he was putting between himself and New York wasn't a guarantee of immunity – Jeffery unsuccessfully tried to find him in London, and Jimi simply didn't show up for meetings relating to settling Ed Chalpin's persistent claims for a cut of Hendrix's overseas income.

A request to Eddie Kramer to bring tapes over to London so that Jimi could work on them there has been seen as another indication that Hendrix wanted to avoid New York for some reason, especially as it seems odd that he wouldn't want to work in Electric Lady, the studios that had been set up to cater to his requirements. Hendrix finally agreed, however – reluctantly in Kramer's recollection – to go back to New York to work with Eddie by 21 September.

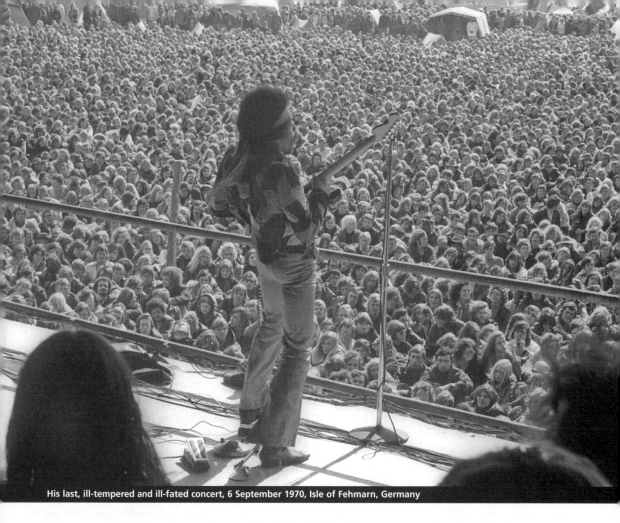

His last, ill-tempered and ill-fated concert, 6 September 1970, Isle of Fehmarn, Germany

Accounts of Jimi's actions and state of mind during the final week of his life vary so widely that it's difficult to know what to believe. Some felt that he was actually in relatively good spirits, eager to implement some of the new ideas he had for his music and recording. He still hadn't abandoned hopes of having an Otis Redding-type R&B band with a horn section, as he told now ex-Monkee Mike Nesmith at a London party, although Nesmith gently tried to persuade Hendrix that he should continue along the path he had already blazed. In another unexpected development, leading jazz composer/arranger/conductor **Gil Evans** later said that he was due to meet with Jimi in New York on 21 September – the same Monday that Hendrix was supposed to start resuming work on his next album with Eddie Kramer – to discuss doing a recording session with entirely new material, for an album to be titled *The Voodoo Child Plays the Blues*. And Hendrix told British music journalist Roy Carr that he was "still supposed to be making an album with Miles Davis. ... Like Miles, I want to invent a new kind of music, a new kind of jazz."

One of his last interviews, published on 5 September in *Melody Maker*, found Jimi expatiating as restlessly as ever on the new horizons he was eager to explore, although his remarks could also be taken as evidence of his continued inability to work out or even articulate exactly what he wanted to do in terms that could be grasped by mere mortals. He wanted a big band, he told Roy Hollingworth, to "paint pictures of earth and space, so that the listener can be taken somewhere". He didn't want to be playing as much guitar, showing concern for developing his songwriting in a context where other musicians could play his material. "I won't be doing many live gigs, because I'm going to develop the sound, and then put a film out with it", he added. "It's so exciting, it's going to be an audiovisual thing that you sit down and plug in to, and really take in through your ears and eyes."

Yet others around him in his final month felt that Jimi's life-force, which had burned so brightly for the last four years, was audibly and visibly fading, with Hendrix apparently burnt out by his struggles with the music business and the itinerant chaos of his personal life. Subsequent statements by some of his professional and personal associates are so much at odds that it seems likely that not all of them could be true representations of the incidents/ conversations they refer to, or at least that some of them could have been misremembered or exaggerated with the passage of time.

One of the most interesting of these is **Chas Chandler**'s memory of Hendrix approaching his ex-manager with a view to having Chas produce him again; it's sometimes reported too that Jimi also wanted Chandler to return as his manager, this time with Jeffery out of the picture. On the face of it, this seems like a reasonable course of action. Chas had served Jimi well (as Hendrix had Chandler), and Jeffery had proved himself untrustworthy in numerous ways since assuming sole management responsibilities. But with all the changes that Hendrix had gone through since Chandler walked out of the *Electric Ladyland* sessions, could the pair really have gone back to working together as before? Some of the problems that had driven Chandler out of the producer's chair to begin with were still there, especially Hendrix's obsessive studio perfectionism and difficulty with making artistic decisions. If they had resumed their alliance, it would probably have been only a matter of time before they butted heads again, especially with Jimi having become more used to getting his own way in the studio in the intervening years.

Another face from the recent past that popped up at this time was **Alan Douglas**, then visiting London with his wife and Hendrix's girlfriend

Devon Wilson. According to Douglas, he and Hendrix had discussions about restructuring Jimi's management so that Jeffery, though not cut off from a financial piece of the pie so as not to incur his wrath, would be effectively shunted to the side. Douglas also had ideas for cutting back on Hendrix's live dates by filming four concerts a year to satisfy demand for those who wanted to see him play, leaving Jimi free to concentrate on the creative side of music-making that was energizing him the most. Chandler, however, dampened any retroactive enthusiasm that might have been ascribed to Hendrix when he claimed that Jimi told him that Douglas could be involved with the changeover, but that Jimi didn't want Alan to have anything to do with his music. Perhaps the memories of the largely unproductive sessions with which Douglas had been involved were still fresh. (More improbably, Ed Chalpin has said that Hendrix asked him to help out with Jimi's business problems during this week, notwithstanding the fact that many of those problems had been caused by Chalpin himself.)

The differing motivations ascribed to Hendrix at this time, however, might have been not so much incorrect memories of what happened as a reflection of the indecisiveness Jimi brought to many business and personal decisions. There might have been an element of Hendrix telling different people what they wanted to hear, even if what he was telling one person contradicted what he was claiming to the next. "Perhaps Jimi's biggest weakness was his inability to say no to anybody – to his fans, to his business advisors, to his peers, to political activ-

ists", John Morthland suggests in his essay on Hendrix in *The Rolling Stone Illustrated History of Rock & Roll*. As Morthland also points out, some of those who knew Hendrix have gone on record directly contradicting each other "about Jimi's drug habits, his sexual appetite, his feelings about blackness, his attitude toward his managers."

In addition to pursuing (or being pursued for) several management and recording options at once, Hendrix was continuing to pursue (or to be pursued by) several women at once. His romantic life, to quote from one of his song titles, was walking an even narrower tightrope than usual between love and confusion. Devon Wilson was over in London; he'd had a brief and intense fling with Danish model Kirsten Nefer during the Experience's European tour; and he had even met up with Kathy Etchingham again. There was also the reappearance of **Monika Dannemann**, the German ice skater he had met back in January 1969. Dannemann would subsequently claim that the pair had made marriage plans early that year, but some doubt that she and Jimi could have been as serious as she always maintained. At the very least, Hendrix's busy schedule – which took him out of Europe for the most part in 1969 and 1970 – would have made it hard for them to see much of each other, and it's known that Jimi was also seeing a number of other women during this period.

It was Dannemann, nevertheless, that Hendrix linked up with in London. Perhaps she sought him out more than he did her, and maybe Jimi holed up with her in the London residential hotel where she was staying as a way of getting

Monika Dannemann: Fiancée or *Femme Fatale*?

Monika Dannemann's story is not nearly as obscure as that of Devon Wilson's, or indeed some of the other women that Jimi Hendrix had relationships with out of the public eye, such as **Diane Carpenter** (who initiated a paternity suit against him after their pre-fame affair in New York) and **Eva Sundquist** (the Swedish student whose son James was recognized as Jimi's heir by a Swedish court, and who eventually received a large settlement from Hendrix's estate). This is mostly because she had the bad fortune to be at Jimi's side when he died. In part, however, it's because she did her part to promote Hendrix's legacy and tell her side of the story for many years after, to the displeasure of some who disagreed with her version of events.

Dannemann was an ice-skating teacher when she met Hendrix on 13 January 1969 at a hotel bar in Düsseldorf, Germany, the morning after his concert there. According to her, Jimi immediately probed her in detail about her life and asked her to be his girlfriend, after which she accompanied him to the next stop on his European tour, meeting up with him in London after it had concluded. Some might find it out of character for the shy Hendrix to proposition anyone so blatantly and boldly, especially considering that by 1969, he could have had his pick of an infinite number of willing partners. Nonetheless, according to her belated 1995 memoir *The Inner World of Jimi Hendrix*, by March she and Jimi were exchanging rings at a King's Road jeweller in London, Hendrix telling her that he wanted them to signify their engagement. That night, she added, her boyfriend led her from table to table at the restaurant in the in-crowd Speakeasy club, declaring to everyone that the pair had just become engaged.

Although Dannemann would deny it vehemently, it may well have been a love-at-first-sight line of sorts he used with other women as well, such as Kirsten Nefer, to whom he actually proposed marriage after less than a week's acquaintance – and only a couple of weeks or so before he died in Dannemann's hotel room. Other observers have since expressed puzzlement as to what drove Hendrix to get to know Dannemann in the first place, for whatever length of time. As Joe Boyd (esteemed record producer and director of the first Jimi Hendrix documentary) writes in his memoir *White Bicycles* of interviewing her for the movie: "We couldn't see what had drawn Jimi to the gloomy, self-justifying, rather plain German ex-figure skater."

Some inconsistencies were later discovered in Dannemann's accounts of Hendrix's death, namely her assertion that Jimi was still alive when the ambulance came and died on the way to the hospital. Although it seems doubtful that she did anything to directly cause or hasten his death, some of Hendrix's friends felt that she did not call for help, or discover or recognize his perilous state, soon enough. Also disagreeable to many were the strange, disquieting, quasi-mystical oil paintings she did of her ex-lover, many of which are used as illustrations in *The Inner World of Jimi Hendrix*. (A less well-known artistic sideline of hers was writing some songs with – and providing some album cover-art for – a subsequent boyfriend, ex-Scorpions guitarist Uli Jon Roth.) Shortly after the book's publication, however, she ran into heavy-duty trouble of her own when she was found guilty of breaching a British court order prohibiting her from repeating allegations of untruthfulness against another of Jimi's ex-girlfriends, Kathy Etchingham. Two days later, Dannemann was found dead in a car near her home in southern England, presumed to have gassed herself to death.

away from people he might have been trying to avoid. Still, Hendrix didn't disappear entirely, jamming with his old friend Eric Burdon (now fronting War) at Ronnie Scott's club. Hendrix and Dannemann certainly spent a lot of time together on 17 September, although not in the best of moods. When a young man pulled up beside them in the street and invited them to his home that afternoon, Monika reluctantly followed Jimi, a lengthy argument breaking out between them around 10pm. Yet later that evening, Hendrix went to another party alone, only for Dannemann to start another argument when she came to pick him up shortly afterward. The pair finally headed back to the Samarkand Hotel at around 3am.

Exactly what happened in the next eight hours is unclear. What is certain is that eventually Hendrix and Dannemann fell asleep, and that Dannemann could not rouse him the following morning. Between 11am and noon on 18 September 1970, an ambulance was called and Hendrix taken from the hotel room to the hospital, where he was officially pronounced dead at 12.45pm.

Again, accounts of the exact circumstances of the tragedy have varied, and Dannemann was the only one who was with Jimi in the hours leading up to his death. What seems fairly certain is that he took a bunch of sleeping pills early that morning. In combination with some alcohol in his system, it probably caused him to vomit in his sleep, in effect suffocating him. The inquest labelled the cause of death as "inhalation of vomit due to barbiturate intoxication".

Different theories have been advanced as to what and/or who might have been responsible for Hendrix's death. There have been dark suggestions of a conspiracy by someone wanting Jimi out of the way. More mundanely, some have found holes in Dannemann's version of the events, and even intimated that she bore some responsibility for the death, not getting help as quickly or efficiently as she should have. The fact remains, however, that Hendrix took an excessive number of pills, even a few of which were unwise to combine with the wine he had drunk. In this sense, the immediate responsibility for Hendrix's death probably lies with Jimi himself, although it was almost certainly an accident rather than suicide. Considering that he was already prone to mixing alcohol and liberal quantities of various substances, it could easily have happened before, without Dannemann present.

Paradoxically, although Hendrix's death undoubtedly came as a shock, it wasn't altogether a surprise. Certainly Jimi was immediately mourned by millions of fans in many countries, most of whom understandably had no idea of the conflicts he was wrestling with and were impatiently waiting for his next album and tour. And Hendrix wasn't someone who, like Jim Morrison and Brian Jones – or for that matter, a quarter of a century later, fellow Washington State native Kurt Cobain – had gone through a much more public and visible period of physical and psychic deterioration. Hendrix, for all most admirers knew, was a young man just a couple of months short of his twenty-eighth birthday, still at the peak of his artistic powers and without any obvious health or psychiatric problems that might have cut him down in his prime. What made it all the more galling was that Hendrix, for all his problems, obviously had so much more to offer, and, given his appetite for experimentation and keeping up with the latest technological advances, seemed likely to unveil some exciting surprises.

Yet at the same time, it was an era when several major rock icons were dying prematurely under sordid, mysterious circumstances, at least in part because of the excesses of their lifestyles. Hendrix, his old friend **Brian Jones** (who had drowned in his own swimming pool in July 1969), **Janis Joplin** (who would succumb to a drug overdose just a couple of weeks after Jimi's death), and Doors singer **Jim Morrison** (dead of an apparent heart attack in a Paris hotel in July 1971, in the most mysterious circumstances of all), departed in such rapid succession that it seemed like an epidemic was sweeping through rock's top ranks. Given that Hendrix, like the others, led a particularly flamboyant and adventurous lifestyle, some might have felt that it was only a matter of time before he fell off the high wire. On the other hand, many who skirted such serious trouble came out of the era alive and perform to this day, such as one of Jimi's original inspirations, Bob Dylan, and one of his first rock star friends, Eric Clapton. Hendrix's death might have been an unintended consequence of the way he lived, but it was by no means inevitable.

The oft-posed question of what Hendrix would have done next had he lived is impos-

Dannemann leaving her flat in Lansdowne Crescent, Notting Hill, 18 September 1970

sible to answer. Sometimes, as with his life, there's the feeling that associates and critics are projecting their own wishes and preferences upon Jimi, without objectively assessing the big picture. Some feel that he would or should have gone into **jazz**, improvising, composing and recording with cutting-edge players of both guitars and other instruments, although it's difficult to imagine pure jazz leaving much space for the lyrics Hendrix clearly enjoyed crafting. Others think he would have drifted back into a purer blues bag, a suggestion given some weight by the somewhat greater emphasis Jimi placed on blues-rock material in the post-Experience days, although such efforts never came to define or dominate his work.

There's also speculation that Hendrix would have immersed himself in futuristic technology, particularly the **synthesizers** that would be developed shortly after his death. Hendrix was usually not one to exploit technology or the novel sounds it could produce simply for its own sake, however, and it's hard to imagine him ever devoting much of his attention to an instrument other than the electric guitar, which seems to have meant more to him than anything (or anyone) else. And finally, the possibility can't be dismissed that – like some other 1960s rock greats – his music wouldn't have notably progressed or even maintained its high quality, but have become more diluted, uninspired, and irrelevant as time went on. That's especially possible considering the progressively erratic nature of his songwriting shortly before his death, and his difficulties in seeing his ambitious schemes and studio recordings through to completion.

Since Hendrix's future courses of action were impossible to predict when he was alive, however, it's doubtful whether he would have set off in one definite or predictable direction. Besides, Hendrix, like many towering figures of contemporary popular music, was an eclectic, not attached to any one musical style (or, indeed, to associating with or being influenced by any one race of people). Blues, soul, pop, avant-garde electronics, jazz, folk-rock, the British Invasion, even 1950s rock'n'roll and hoary standards like "The Star Spangled Banner" and "Auld Lang Syne" – all had a place in Hendrix's universe. His genius was not in mastering particular forms, but in combining them to produce some of the most enduring and innovative rock music of his and our time.

Fortunately, Hendrix crammed an amazing amount of not just high-flying living, but also recording in his four short years as a solo artist. This meant there was much unheard music in the vault to be released, and to some degree exploited – so much so that much of it is still emerging. The way it was made officially available and its revenue distributed, however, has been the cause of great dispute over the last few decades, starting almost from the moment Jimi was laid to rest.

The Legacy
1970–Present

"... all you're doing is getting rid of that old body."

Hendrix reflecting on death

The Legacy
1970–Present

When Jimi Hendrix died on the morning of 18 September 1970, he was – despite not having released an album of new studio material in about two years – still one of the hottest properties in the music business. And for quite a while afterward, he was *still* one of the hottest properties in the music business. This wasn't solely due to the ghoulish sales boost any major artist experiences after their death, especially when the death was sensational and unexpected. It was also the by-product of all the time Hendrix spent – and according to some of his associates, often wasted – in the studio. For there were still small mountains of unissued Jimi Hendrix tapes for the public to hear, and for many in the music industry to exploit, in addition to a relatively small but significant back catalogue – the relentless mining of which continues even as of the writing of this book.

Posthumous Jimi Hendrix Albums, Phase I

The first controversy in which Jimi was unable to have a voice was the decision over where to bury him. According to the wishes of his father Al, he was laid to rest in Seattle (actually a little outside of the city itself in the suburb of Renton), although he had spent little time there in his last decade. Attending the funeral on 1 October were most of his key musical and business associates, including Mitch Mitchell, Noel Redding, Buddy Miles, Mike Jeffery, Eddie Kramer and Alan Douglas; paramour Devon Wilson; and a number of musicians with less direct connections to Jimi's work, among them Miles Davis, John Hammond and Johnny Winter. Also in the several hundred-strong crowd were many family members and friends who had rarely seen Hendrix since he enlisted in the army, including his brother (or half-brother, depending upon who you believe) Leon, who had to obtain special permission to attend as he was currently serving a jail sentence. One family friend read the lyrics to Jimi's "Angel", which, like many of the songs he had been working on, would never benefit from his final polish before it was released. Afterwards Mitchell, Redding, Miles, Winter and others played a memorial jam of sorts at the Seattle Arena, although it's doubtful there could have been much joy at this particular wake.

Jazz trumpeter Miles Davis and his singer wife Betty Mabry (left) arriving at the funeral

In the view of some of Hendrix's more sensitive associates, the vultures started to circle around what Jimi had left behind even before he was buried. Rumours that he might have killed himself were fanned by suggestions in an Eric Burdon interview a few days after Hendrix's death, leading Warner Bros. to worry that their large insurance payout would be nullified. Track Records were quick to issue **Voodoo Child (Slight Return)** as a single in the UK, where it topped the charts just a couple of months after Jimi's passing, marking his only number one single in the country. It's also been reported that it wasn't long before some of Hendrix's tapes, guitars and other possessions were taken from his apartment by employees of Mike Jeffery, many of them never to be recovered.

In addition, the stage was being set for protracted tug-of-wars over Hendrix's estate, which was already worth a considerable sum, though ultimately worth far more than anyone envisioned. As Jimi had died without a will, his father was named sole beneficiary, although Jeffery obviously still had a large stake in Hendrix's estate, especially the expensive and just-completed Electric Lady Studios. Because of the chaotic state of his son's finances, only $20,000 cash was immediately available for Al Hendrix, although he undoubtedly expected much more. Some further money materialized when Jeffery bought out Hendrix's interest in Electric Lady. But the precarious state of the manager's own affairs – especially with the *Rainbow Bridge* film in which he had invested yet to be completed – would have made him determined to dip his own hand as deeply into the future earnings of Jimi's estate as he could.

The most valuable items in Hendrix's estate, obviously, were the many unreleased tapes he had made, particularly the ones he had been working on just prior to his death for a projected double-LP set. Millions of fans, probably most of whom had no idea of the business wheels spinning behind the scenes, had been eagerly awaiting the next Hendrix studio release for two years. With his sudden death, they were even more impatient for more material than they might have been otherwise. With this in mind, Jeffery got Eddie Kramer – ultimately, the most trusted associate of Jimi's on the studio/engineering side – to select the best of the tapes for what would become the first posthumous Hendrix album.

No such project could be ideal, first and foremost because although many songs had been laid down in a state of near-completion, there's no telling what Jimi might have added, erased, or otherwise changed, especially bearing in mind his perfectionist nature. In a slightly contentious move, it was determined to add some percussion overdubs to recordings that were judged unfinished. At least in this instance, however, the overdubbing was done by Hendrix's most noted musical sideman, Mitch Mitchell, and overseen by Jimi's most qualified

Hendrix's casket is followed from the church by members of his family and childhood friends

studio technician, Kramer (with Buzzy Linhart also adding a vibes part to "Drifting"). If it might not have been exactly how it would have turned out under Hendrix's own supervision, it was at least as close as possible to such a thing under the tragic circumstances.

"I have no doubt that he would have scrapped quite a lot of the stuff that was there and started some things all over again", admitted Mitchell in his memoir *Jimi Hendrix: Inside the Experience*. "Basically I tried to think of

Alan Douglas: Hendrix Producer, Posthumously

Although he's not as reviled a figure as Mike Jeffery, **Alan Douglas** is nonetheless viewed with suspicion for what many see as his dubious handling of Hendrix's recorded legacy from the mid-1970s through to the mid-1990s. As with Jeffery, however, it's important to note that for all his questionable decisions on Jimi's behalf, Douglas did have some qualities that could be seen as beneficial to Hendrix in some respects.

First, although he might not have been the best-qualified person to assume the role of overseeing Hendrix's musical estate, Douglas's track record cannot be dismissed. In the early 1960s, he had headed the jazz department of a sizeable label, United Artists, where he produced world-class musicians such as

Art Blakey, Duke Ellington, Charles Mingus and Cecil Taylor. In the mid-1960s, his FM label recorded a pre-Mamas-and-Papas Cass Elliot (as part of The Big Three) and avant-garde jazzman Eric Dolphy. His subsequent Douglas Records label issued material by Allen Ginsberg, Timothy Leary and comedian Lenny Bruce, as well as The Last Poets, now recognized as important proto-rappers. As major as these figures now appear to be in the cultural landscape, their socio-political radicalism was such that Douglas Records could hardly be accused of being a solely commercial enterprise.

It's also clear that Douglas made a lot of effort to get involved in finding releasable unissued Hendrix recordings at a time when, apparently, few producers

what he would have done, or what he would have wanted, which was a very difficult thing to do."

The biggest compromise, however, was the decision to make the record a single disc, rather than the double LP that Hendrix had envisioned. Business considerations probably played a part in this decision, as did the pressure to get a record onto the shelves quickly. For these reasons, the ten-song album issued in March 1971, *The Cry of Love*, can't be considered to be the fourth studio album Hendrix would have released had he survived, whether it would have ended up being called *First Rays of the New Rising Sun* or something else. It did, however, present some of the best work from that project with taste (if a bit of haste), including some songs – such as "Ezy Ryder", "Nightbird Flying", and especially **Angel** – that most listen-

ers would have judged virtually certain to make the cut for whatever record Jimi had in mind. Certainly the LP did about or nearly as well as a new album by a living, breathing Hendrix would have done, reaching number three in the US and number two in the UK.

The Cry of Love wasn't so much the closing of a book, however, as the first page of a new and increasingly scrambled one. To those of Hendrix's associates with even a passing knowledge of what he had been up to in the studio, it was obvious that there had to be a good amount of additional material stockpiled in the cupboard, and not all of it leftovers by any means. "Dolly Dagger", for example, had somehow not been included on *The Cry of Love*, even though Jimi had intended it as the A-side of his next single; nor had one of the better songs he had cut in his final year, "Room with his experience were interested in doing so. This might be a reflection of the unwillingness of others in the industry to deal with Mike Jeffery or – after Jeffery's death in 1973 – the complicated Hendrix estate; it might also be a reflection of the financial gain Douglas hoped to make from mining the Hendrix vaults. Criticism of Douglas, however, has centred not on his possible motivations, but rather on his aesthetic decisions – particularly the use of overdubbing by outside musicians of little note and erasing some of Hendrix's original parts.

Perhaps Douglas made such decisions partly because he was feeling under pressure to come up with something that would be considered commercial and marketable. But he didn't help his image when he made comments indicating that the original rhythm sections Jimi had recorded with weren't up to par, or arguing that – as John Morthland reported in *The Rolling Stone Illustrated History of Rock & Roll* – "what Hendrix himself would have added to the tapes was implicit in the way Jimi played his parts". Serious Hendrix scholars would argue that not only should the tapes have remained untouched, but that the mixing should have been in the hands of someone more sympathetic to the original vibe, such as engineer Eddie Kramer – who has, indeed, exerted a strong hand in the remastering and mixing of Jimi's catalogue since it's been taken over by Experience Hendrix.

Full of Mirrors". Suspicions that some goodies were being held in reserve were confirmed by the appearance in late 1971 of the *Rainbow Bridge* album, which despite its title was not a soundtrack to the film of the same name. Instead, it was a rather hodgepodge compilation of 1968–1970 studio material (and one live track) from various sources, including but hardly limited to tracks in the running for *First Rays of the New Rising Sun*, among them the aforementioned "Dolly Dagger" and "Room Full of Mirrors".

Undoubtedly clouded by an exploitative tinge missing from *The Cry of Love*, sales of *Rainbow Bridge* suffered accordingly, with the album reaching number fifteen in the US and one slot lower in the UK. But if it wasn't as huge a seller as *The Cry of Love* or the Experience albums, it certainly sold *well* and

was very profitable – enough to make the prospect of a series of such LPs (which in truth were compilations) viable. Yet the market was already being crowded with so much Hendrix material that he was, little more than a year after his death, in danger of being both overexposed and subject to a lack of quality control, leading to releases that Jimi would not have felt were up to standard. In particular, Mike Jeffery had arranged for the release, just a month after the *Rainbow Bridge* LP, of erratic live recordings from Hendrix's 1970 Isle of Wight show (unimaginatively titled *Isle of Wight*) in the UK and Europe.

In addition, two non-US releases of live February 1969 Albert Hall recordings were issued around the same time. And on top of that, there were two 1971 films – *Rainbow Bridge* itself, and *Jimi Plays Berkeley* – that

The Story

were both built around live Hendrix performances, neither of which were really substantial enough to merit the theatrical releases bestowed upon them. Even for the devoted Hendrix lover, this was simply too much product to digest at once, none of it (with the possible exception of *The Cry of Love*) as consistent or revelatory as his 1966–1970 releases had been. And soon enough, Jeffery was embroiled in a lawsuit with Steve Gold and Jerry Goldstein, whose production company had been involved in the Albert Hall shows, over rights to the resultant recordings and film footage – not that the average Hendrix fan, already exhausted by the avalanche of new product, would have had much sympathy for any of the parties involved.

There were certainly tracks here and there that were quite nifty, if not on a par with Hendrix's masterworks. You would never put Jimi's live covers of "Blue Suede Shoes", "Johnny B. Goode" or "Sgt. Pepper's Lonely Hearts Club Band", for instance, on the same level as his best originals (or even best interpretations), but they were certainly cool to hear, as you could on one of the better early-1970s anthologies, **Hendrix in the West**, released in 1972 and devoted entirely to in-concert recordings. But by the time of **War Heroes** at the end of that same year, it was obvious that some fairly noteworthy tracks ("Stepping Stone", "Izabella", the B-side "Highway Chile") were being parcelled out as relative gems in the company of cuts that might not have even made the grade as filler on a regular Hendrix LP. Accordingly, it became the first Hendrix album on Reprise/Warner Bros. not to make the top twenty, or even the top forty.

Even Eddie Kramer abandoned ship after *War Heroes*, unhappy with the record's quality and unconvinced that more worthwhile stuff could be excavated from the archives.

One cause of this deluge of Hendrix material was Mike Jeffery's appetite – which some have recalled more as desperation – for squeezing more albums out of Jimi's cache, even after Hendrix's contract with Warner Bros. expired in 1972. His role, though not the deluge, was brought to an abrupt end on 5 March 1973, when Jeffery died along with several dozen other passengers in a mid-air collision between two planes on a flight to Majorca. There have been suspicions floated from time to time that Jeffery somehow managed to fake his death, as he was noted both for making multiple flight reservations and for a background in intelligence that supposedly could have prepared him to pull off that sort of thing. Such trickery would certainly have enabled him to elude the many financial and legal problems chasing him, although it would almost certainly have cut him off from the lucrative benefits he still stood a chance of gaining from Hendrix's catalogue. Most signs, however, point to his having perished on that flight, never again to wield a direct hand in the affairs of the Hendrix estate.

In the midst of these never-ending additions to Hendrix's catalogue, it's important to note that his larger status as both a musical and cultural icon was never threatened. Indeed, his early death had ensured an extra layer of mythical status, as it had for two other legends who had also recently died at the age of 27,

Jim Morrison and Janis Joplin. One of the first major steps taken to commemorate his life (as opposed to merely exploiting his music) was the almost embarrassingly literally titled 1973 documentary *A Film About Jimi Hendrix*, co-directed/produced by respected record producer Joe Boyd. If its combination of concert footage and talking heads looks a little raw and primitive by today's standards, it was nonetheless one of the very first major rock documentaries. And in an age before Hendrix biographies had been written, it gave many fans some insights into aspects of his history that had previously been fairly hidden, especially via interviewees such as Mitch Mitchell, Pete Townshend, Eddie Kramer and Eric Clapton. Admittedly, it also gave Warner Bros. the opportunity to cash in further by issuing a double-LP sound-track of live recordings which spanned most of Hendrix's brief solo career.

Meanwhile the flood of Hendrix marginalia continued, beginning with a project that Jeffery had initiated, the aptly titled 1974 collection *Loose Ends* (not issued in North America). Apart from the early B-side "The Stars That Play with Laughing Sam's Dice", the inferior nature of its jams and demos, as well as its shoddy packaging, was starting to make even the less discriminating and astute Hendrix fans be wary of "new" LPs bearing his name and image. The situation was compounded by the continued proliferation of numerous pre-fame sideman recordings that were billed as Hendrix LPs, a syndrome that had never really stopped since the appearance of the first of these, *Get That Feeling*, in 1967.

Posthumous Jimi Hendrix Albums, Phase II

It was around this time that **Alan Douglas**, who had been involved in Hendrix's career relatively briefly as a producer of sorts, came back onto the scene. With Eddie Kramer no longer being involved in raking through the Hendrix library, Douglas now assumed a similar position, although he had only jams, demos and scraps with which to work. Decades later, much such material by many major (and even minor) artists circulates on bootlegs – and, to a not insignificant degree, even on officially sanctioned releases, though often as bonus CD tracks or collections clearly packaged as special-interest fan-only items. Back in the mid-1970s, however, it was relatively rare for such obviously incomplete exercises by a major rock artist to be issued. Feeling that extra work – not just mixing, editing and miscellaneous reconstruction, but substantial overdubbing of new parts, for which some original performances were erased to make room – was necessary to make even the best of the tapes releasable, Douglas enlisted **session musicians** for the purpose. Nor were they session musicians with whom Hendrix had played; instead, they were relatively anonymous instrumentalists, some of whom even added guitar lines to the skeletal tracks.

Perhaps it had something to do with the absence of fresh Hendrix product in the States for a couple of years or so, but the first such Douglas-administered compilation, early 1975's *Crash Landing*, actually sold quite well, reaching number five in the US. It also could have had something to do with the relative lack of excitement in contemporary rock music at the time, punk and new wave still being a couple of years away on the horizon. Nonetheless, for a package of previously unissued material by an artist who had been dead for nearly five years to reach the top five spoke volumes about the durability of his appeal, if not of the merits of the specific album that managed this feat. Critical reaction ranged from mixed to harshly negative, however, and the failure of the next instalment – *Midnight Lightning* in late 1975 – to even make the top forty seemed to put Douglas's approach on ice for the time being.

The hunger for more Hendrix was evidence of just how hard it was to replicate what Jimi had done on guitar, let alone with as much imagination or in combination with his talents for songwriting, singing and overall flash. In spite of increasingly elaborate and technologically sophisticated gadgets for both the guitar and studio recording, Hendrix was – even within five years of his death – simply proving inimitable. His influence was most blatantly felt, somewhat discouragingly, not in the most creative rock (whether mainstream or underground), but in the legions of hard rock and heavy metal guitarists who sought to capture Jimi's phallic presence without holding a candle to his inventive musicianship, let alone displaying any of his sensitive lyricism.

Hendrix had actually influenced some notable soul-funk artists (such as Parliament-Funkadelic, Stevie Wonder, and Sly and the Family Stone) who took some inspiration from Jimi with far more subtlety and taste, as well as some fiery jazz-fusion pioneers – like Larry Coryell, John McLaughlin and one-time Miles Davis guitarist Pete Cosey – working in a primarily instrumental framework. Such was the demand for even a facsimile of the real thing, however, that by the late 1970s, the still-active Hendrix imitator **Randy Hansen** was making a good living as a tribute act – this long before there were "tribute" or "cover" bands for dozens of rock superstars (and sometimes dozens of such bands for one specific act).

Alan Douglas made one more attempt to raid the vaults with the 1980 compilation *Nine to the Universe*, which in fact consisted of five extended, unfinished instrumental jams. In hindsight it offers at least something of interest to hardcore Hendrix fans, and wasn't defamed by posthumous instrumental overdubs. But its poor sales performance – it failed to even crack the US top 100 – seemed to finally put the lid on attempts to excavate the studio vaults.

The next Douglas-produced compilation of previously unreleased Hendrix recordings, *Jimi Hendrix Concerts* in 1982, signalled a sensible shift from studio to live material in the ongoing raid on the archives. Fortunately, there were quite a few well-recorded Hendrix gigs around. There seemed no temptation to overdub these with inappropriate, long-after-the-fact embellishments, and arguments as to whether the music was what Jimi intended were redundant, as the performances, if sometimes imperfect, simply were what they were.

Even here, however, Douglas couldn't escape criticism, as the actual quality of the discs that followed in the 1980s was distinctly erratic. Some were sublime: it was great, for example, to have Hendrix's entire Monterey set available (on both record and video), as well as many of his BBC sessions on *Radio One*. Others were more questionable ragbags, like *Band of Gypsys 2*, which despite its title was only half-devoted to actual Band of Gypsys tracks. Others again tested the limits of Hendrix fanaticism – you'd have to be at least slightly mad to sit through the seven consecutive versions of "Red House" on *Red House: Variations on a Theme*. The decision to take the box-set compilation *Lifelines* directly from a radio programme also drew some ire, although the anthology that followed, *Stages*, won back some goodwill by simply presenting a concert apiece from 1967, 1968, 1969 and 1970.

Experience Hendrix

By the time the last of these releases appeared in the early 1990s, conflicts were beginning to brew over the administration of the Hendrix estate, which would eventually result in its transfer to different caretakers. As with the tangled business/legal affairs of some other great rock acts in the aftermath of their deaths and splits – from Elvis Presley and Buddy Holly to The Beatles, Pink Floyd, and The Sex Pistols – ploughing through the fine points of these disputes makes for an often depressing and tedious exercise, especially coming in the aftermaths of careers that were fascinating from almost every angle while the performers were active. In Hendrix's case in particular, it's made yet more difficult by the absence of any especially sympathetic or likeable figure on any side of the disputes. Nonetheless, it's important to at least outline the key events in this transfer of power, as it's likely to affect the nature and availability of Jimi's creative output for some time to come.

Back in the mid-1970s, primary control of the Hendrix estate had fallen to Alan Douglas and attorney Leo Branton, who had been appointed by Jimi's father Al. For many years Al Hendrix received $50,000 annually, as well as some other payments, which was probably far more than he had ever expected to receive in his middle and old age. Yet neither he nor anyone else had expected the Hendrix catalogue to not only maintain its value two decades later, but just keep growing in worth, especially as the compact disc and video era exponentially expanded the market for vintage and reissued music. In 1993, Al filed a suit against Branton and Douglas in the hope of getting control of the estate. Even with the assets he had accumulated over the previous 25 years, he would have had a hard time meeting the considerable legal costs if not for a $4.1 million loan from Microsoft co-founder Paul Allen. By the 1990s, Seattle native Allen was one of the richest men in the world, and

Experience Hendrix

The **Experience Hendrix** organization has attracted mainstream media attention because of the legal battles which first restored control of Jimi's estate to his family and then contested control of that estate within the family itself. Yet it shouldn't be overlooked that Experience Hendrix has done much to restore some semblance of order and dignity to a catalogue that was in many respects disorganized and overexploited, although it can't stop the countless shoddy packages of some of his more peripheral work which continue to crop up. The Experience Hendrix imprint has issued worthwhile, if not always flawless, live performances from Woodstock, the Fillmore East, and the Isle of Wight festival. It's also done the best reconstruction to date of what Jimi might have put on his fourth album, *First Rays of the New Rising Sun*, and involved Eddie Kramer and Hendrix authority/biogra-

pher John McDermott in key roles in the preparation of its releases.

Its Dagger subsidiary, meanwhile, has made less stellar, more specialized live material officially available for the hardcore fanatic. There are also, at the time of writing, no fewer than nine officially available videos, encompassing not only live and television performances, but also documentaries. A less celebrated aspect of its programme includes DVD releases of vintage performances by blues musicians other than Hendrix, as well as projects featuring his sidemen Billy Cox, Buddy Miles and Noel Redding – all releases that more likely than not would have met with Jimi's approval.

Details of the Experience Hendrix catalogue, as well as news updates about the other activities in which the organization is involved, can be found on its website, *jimihendrix.com*.

using much of his fortune to bolster numerous regional enterprises, including Seattle's professional sports franchises and the rock history museum that would eventually take shape as the Experience Music Project.

In June 1995, Al Hendrix won back control of Jimi's estate in a legal settlement, although the victory didn't come without some financial bloodshed, as Branton and Douglas received $9 million. Soon afterward, the **Experience Hendrix** company was formed to oversee the empire. Al was its nominal head, but for most practical purposes it was run by his stepdaughter, **Janie Hendrix**, with another close relative, nephew Bob Hendrix, also taking a key role as vice president. Experience Hendrix continues

to run the estate to this day, not only looking after the considerable revenues it generates, but also assuming a very active role in both the packaging of Jimi's existing catalogue and the generation of new titles and anthologies from his vaults.

The establishment of Experience Hendrix has not been universally popular among Jimi's fans. While his family would seem like his most logical heirs if anyone deserved those positions, it can be fairly pointed out that Jimi wasn't all that close to his father, who didn't give him all that much encouragement in his artistic aspirations and barely saw him after 1960 – although he did care enough to save some of the postcards and letters his son would send him during his wayward travels. If theirs wasn't the closest father-son relationship, Jimi was far more of a stranger to Janie, whom he met just four times – all while passing through Seattle as a super-star, when she was just a young child. Some would argue that close professional associates of Hendrix – such as Noel Redding and Mitch Mitchell, who had benefited as little from the income from Jimi's catalogue as Al Hendrix had – were equally or more deserving of some of the cash coming the estate's way.

Yet at the same time, it's almost universally agreed that Experience Hendrix *has* substantially improved the packaging of Jimi's music, which remains his real legacy to the rest of the world. Even as late as 1995, as his lawsuit with Al Hendrix was still going on, Alan Douglas still couldn't resist the temptation to tamper with Jimi's recordings: *Voodoo Soup*, a mis-begotten attempt to approximate what might have been his fourth studio album, was even subjected to drum overdubs by, of all people, Bruce Gary (most famous for his membership in passing late-1970s pop-rock superstars The Knack). Experience Hendrix put a stop to such tomfoolery, apparently for good, as well as assembling anthologies of unreleased material more clearly marked out for (and marketed to) serious fans, rather than getting passed off as discs on a par with his official releases.

Two people who were close to Jimi Hendrix, however, most definitely did not feel that Experience Hendrix was fairly distributing its funds. When he died on 17 April 2002 at the age of 82, Al Hendrix left virtually nothing to Jimi's brother (or half-brother) Leon,

the relative with whom the guitarist had been closest in his childhood and adolescence. Four months later, Leon sued Janie Hendrix and Bob Hendrix, getting joined by several other relatives who felt they had been undercompensated by Al's will. Meanwhile, Noel Redding – who, far more than Mitch Mitchell or others who had made vital contributions to Jimi's music, felt severely wronged by deals he had made long ago limiting his cut of the pie – was preparing to begin legal proceedings against Experience Hendrix. Redding died in May 2003, however, before he could even file a case.

Leon Hendrix's lawsuit came to court in 2004, and although the ruling left his father's will intact – amid allegations that Leon's battles with drugs and periodic imprisonment disqualified him as a beneficiary – it did remove Janie Hendrix and Bob Hendrix from their financial roles in Experience Hendrix, replacing them with trustees. Appeals and battles between Leon and Experience Hendrix continued over the next two years, and will probably continue in the future. At the time of writing, Janie remains CEO of Experience Hendrix, and Leon has yet to gain any share of Hendrix's estate, valued at the time of Al Hendrix's death at $80 million. Periodic news items also continue to appear about Experience Hendrix's involvement in some or other business/financial dispute, whether it's trying to stop other companies from putting out vintage recordings of questionable legality, or suing a company attempting to use Jimi's likeness on its vodka.

It's likely that the average Hendrix fan – even the average *serious* Hendrix fan – cares little about such niggling battles. From one viewpoint, there has never been a better time to be such a fan, at least if your yardstick is the number of Hendrix titles on sale. Never have so many Hendrix recordings and video/DVD compilations been so readily available. No doubt Jimi himself would not have approved of the release of at least some (and possibly most) of them, but they allow an examination of his four amazing years as a true solo artist which is more in-depth than that of almost any other comparable artist of his era. The real tragedy is that, if a few events during his lifetime had gone the other way and he had avoided a premature death, the Hendrix catalogue could have been much, much larger, with far more than three truly finished albums.

As another testament to Hendrix's enduring legacy, the last thirty years – like the decade immediately following his death – have found his influence continuing to hover over much popular music, without his essence ever getting reproduced or matched in quality. At the extreme left, his sheer outrageous volume was echoed in noisy punk and post-punk outfits like Black Flag, Sonic Youth and My Bloody Valentine. In the mainstream, guitar virtuosos like Steve Vai and Joe Satriani owed some of their vocabulary to Jimi, as did of course uncounted heavy metal bands. African-American acts such as Prince and Living Colour created some similar crossover rock-R&B and appealed to both black and white audiences, while blues-rockers like Stevie Ray Vaughan took more than a little from Hendrix's bluesier side. But nobody has blended incredible instrumental innovation with first-rate songwriting, stylistic eclecticism, cosmic vision and – above all – pure heart and soul in the way that Jimi Hendrix did. He remains a unique figure in the annals of twentieth-century music, often idolized, but never replicated.

Part 2:
The Music

Studio Albums

In spite of his superstar status and enduring fame – and despite the hundreds of releases that have been available at one time or another – Hendrix made only three records that can be considered proper studio albums, conceived and completed as such with substantial input from Jimi at every stage.

Among rock supernovas who burned briefly and brightly, there are very few acts whose discography rests upon such a small core, even taking into consideration that one of those three albums was a double LP. What Hendrix's catalogue of studio albums lacks in quantity, however, it makes up in quality, with each of the three records continuing to be hailed as a major work and continuing to sell steadily into the twenty-first century.

Because there is so much Hendrix material – and so much of note, although selective weeding is necessary – on recordings other than these three studio albums, this book will use three separate categories in examining his discography. This initial section will deal with his three bona fide studio LPs (these days all available on CD); the second will cover his live releases, all but one of which appeared after his death; and the third will look at the numerous compilation albums (again most of them posthumous) his catalogue has generated, whether based on previously issued material, studio outtakes, live performances, or a mixture of these.

Are You Experienced?

PURPLE HAZE/MANIC DEPRESSION/HEY JOE/LOVE OR CONFUSION/MAY THIS BE LOVE/I DON'T LIVE TODAY/THE WIND CRIES MARY/FIRE/THIRD STONE FROM THE SUN/ FOXY LADY/ARE YOU EXPERIENCED?/STONE FREE/51ST ANNIVERSARY/HIGHWAY CHILE/CAN YOU SEE ME/ REMEMBER/RED HOUSE
MCA/Experience Hendrix CD, April 1997 (original LP released in 1967).

Unlike the other two albums by The Jimi Hendrix Experience, the sessions that eventually led to the material compiled for their *Are You Experienced?* debut LP don't always seem to have been done with a long-playing release in mind. When Hendrix and producer Chas Chandler first entered the recording studio in London in late 1966, the idea was very much to make the hit single they desperately needed to establish the Experience as a viable act. Initially, they didn't even have the resources to record a B-side, let alone think about working towards an LP.

Even so, laying down the tracks that would be assembled for *Are You Experienced?* was in some ways a surprisingly scattershot, piece-

The Music

The original UK design for *Are You Experienced?* had a rather ordinary group shot, but its North American counterpart was bolder and more psychedelic.

meal affair. Sessions had to be squeezed into the group's hectic touring schedule over several months; three different studios were used; and tracks had to be completed with far more haste than they would within a year or two, when Hendrix was already becoming somewhat notorious for the long hours he would take to lay down and polish his recordings. Nor did it seem certain which cuts would be reserved for singles and which kept for the LP, a confusion amplified by the different track selections for the UK and US versions, the latter of which included some songs that were only available on 45 in Britain.

What's remarkable is that, despite the chaotic way in which its component parts were made, *Are You Experienced?* – no matter which version you're listening to – never sounds like a slapdash production. The playing is honed and purposeful; the sound clean and balanced; the songwriting consistently strong. Most impressively, the music heads off into unexplored sonic territory on a variety of fronts without (with the possible exception of "Third Stone

from the Sun") lapsing into self-indulgence or novelty. The songs bristle with tightly wound tension, great guitar and bass riffs, penetrating lyrics and passionate singing which complement and accentuate Hendrix's arsenal of stunning guitar effects, rather than being obscured by them. In the summer of 1967, it was breathtaking in both its sheer power and mapping of new ground unprecedented in rock music; more than forty years later, it sounds scarcely less fresh and exciting.

Crucially, Hendrix's first three singles, "Hey Joe", "Purple Haze" and "The Wind Cries Mary", were all omitted from the UK version (which appeared first, in May 1967) but included on the US counterpart (issued three months later) at the expense of "Can You See Me", "Remember" and "Red House". (The three singles appeared on LP in the UK soon enough when they were included on the British version of the *Smash Hits* album in April 1968.) For a good quarter century, then, one's perception of this monumental debut varied substantially depending upon where you lived. This even applied to the cover, which in the UK was a relatively straightforward and serious photo of the trio by Bruce Fleming. North Americans, however, got a far more interesting and psychedelic fish-eye photo of the band in London's Kew Gardens by Karl Ferris, with suitably wavy accompanying lettering.

As the CD reissues that have been available since the early 1990s include all fourteen of the tracks used on the original UK and US LPs – as well as the three British B-sides to the first three 45s – it makes most sense to discuss

Are You Experienced? in its current seventeen-track format. While some might find it heretical to do so, considering that Hendrix probably had the original eleven-track UK version in mind as the music that should be considered as the definitive *Are You Experienced?*, the fact is that all seventeen of the tracks on the CD were cut at around the same time with a similar vibe and mindset. Even more importantly, the seventeen-track CD version simply has substantially more great music, and it now seems inconceivable to evaluate this great work without including "Hey Joe", "Purple Haze" and "The Wind Cries Mary", which were not only the three hit singles that first established his reputation (at least in the UK), but also core classics of Hendrix's early repertoire.

More even than Hendrix's explosive solos and effects, what first stands out about *Are You Experienced?* are the indelible hard-rock riffs. The roving Curtis Mayfield lines that introduce "Hey Joe"; the insanely dissonant march that kicks off "Purple Haze", giving way to lines of take-no-prisoners-insistence; the edgy up-and-down patterns of "Manic Depression"; the ridiculously catchy chorus of "Fire"; the sweetly ascending chords of "The Wind Cries Mary"; the relentless bump-and-grind of "Foxy Lady"; the ominous intro of "I Don't Live Today"; even the anthemic soar of the more coherent melodies in "Third Stone from the Sun"... the list goes on. Some of these riffs, like the one at the start of "Purple Haze", have become a permanent part of rock's vocabulary. Regardless of their familiarity, they're unceasingly nervy, and often skin-crawling in their intensity, though sometimes quite delicately introspective in their beauty.

Also striking about *Are You Experienced?* are both the variety of sounds Jimi coaxes from his axe, and how well the trio gels as a unit, even if Hendrix is indisputably the main attraction. The solos are piercing in their distortion and full-bodied in their shock-wave roar, but – perhaps in a tribute to Chas Chandler's eye for economy – never overstay their welcome. Well, almost never... After a wonderful cluster of incandescent jazzy strums opens "Third Stone from the Sun" and gives way to a trumpeting theme, the track almost drowns in excessive and somewhat directionless howls and distorted, slowed-down voices. Yet even some of the boldest reinventions of the electric guitar, like the flutters of "Foxy Lady" and the ultra-high squeals of "Purple Haze", are used to heighten the song's power, not overwhelm the songs themselves. And throughout the proceedings, Hendrix is pushed at almost every turn by Mitch Mitchell's restless drumming and Noel Redding's bulging bass – itself capable of memorable riffs, as in "Manic Depression" and "Fire".

More than anything else, *Are You Experienced?* is made into much more than a showcase for virtuoso playing by Hendrix's versatile, thoughtful songwriting and underrated, committed but often playful vocals. Few psychedelic stars could project cosmic dislocation as enticingly as he did in "Purple Haze", or put over pure sexual lust as convincingly as he did in "Foxy Lady" and "Fire". Those attributes are understandably the ones for which he's most renowned as a songwriter, but he also proved to have a fine touch for

The Music

roller-coaster rockers reflecting the dizzying disorientation of the changing times ("Manic Depression", the undervalued "Can You See Me" and "Love or Confusion"); the euphoria of what was, most likely, the psychedelic drug experience ("Are You Experienced?", now sometimes cited as a pre-hip-hop song of sorts for the backward effects that uncannily pre-date turntable "scratching"); and the vulnerable romanticism behind all this bravado ("The Wind Cries Mary", and less strikingly in "May This Be Love"). As reminders of his chitlin' circuit roots, "Remember" could almost pass for a straightforward soul number. Far more memorably, "Red House" was a showcase for his skills as a straight blues guitarist. The exclusion of "Red House" from the US version was most likely the alteration that Jimi found most objectionable, especially as he played it in concert for American audiences before the song finally found belated Stateside release.

These days, no discussion of *Are You Experienced?* can be complete without noting the three B-sides added to the CD version. The swaggering "Stone Free", far from being the throwaway that might be expected given that it was written virtually overnight when Chas Chandler demanded that Hendrix should start writing his own material, is as strong as all but the best cuts that made the grade for one or the other editions of the LPs. "Highway Chile" (the UK B-side of "The Wind Cries Mary") isn't quite up to that level, but is nonetheless a quite acceptable down-home bluesy rocker with yet another of the naggingly declarative riffs so common to Hendrix's early tunes, as

well as yet more of the "can't tie me down" ethos flavouring much of that material. "51st Anniversary" might be the least essential of the trio, but there's still some fun to be had from its scampering tempo changes and Hendrix's amused vocal.

Some critics feel that *Electric Ladyland* should be judged as the summit of Hendrix's recorded achievements, especially as it was an album over which he exerted much more artistic control as regards its recording and mixing from start to finish. Yet even if it's somewhat less refined, and certainly subject to odd variations in packaging, *Are You Experienced?* is truly his most consistent, enjoyable and ground-breaking album, with more of the songs for which he'll be most remembered than either of its two successors.

AXIS: BOLD AS LOVE

EXP/UP FROM THE SKIES/SPANISH CASTLE MAGIC/WAIT UNTIL TOMORROW/AIN'T NO TELLING/LITTLE WING/IF SIX WAS NINE/YOU GOT ME FLOATIN'/CASTLES MADE OF SAND/ SHE'S SO FINE/ONE RAINY WISH/LITTLE MISS LOVER/BOLD AS LOVE
Track UK, December 1967; Reprise US, January 1968; available on CD.

Axis: Bold as Love is usually considered to be the weakest of the Experience's three studio albums. That's not to say that the record was weak per se, and certainly not that it was perceived as anything other than a commercial or artistic success at its time of release and in the following decades. Once again it was packaged as a very of-its-age psychedelic album, superimposing a Roger Law painting of the group

More distinctive psychedelia adorned *Axis*: a painting by Roger Law blended with a photo by Karl Ferris that incorporates all the trio Hindu-style.

(based on a photo by Karl Ferris, who had taken the shot used on the US *Are You Experienced?* cover) on a poster of a Hindu painting showing the many forms of the supreme being Vishnu.

It's undeniable, however, that it simply didn't pack the punch or surprises of *Are You Experienced?* and *Electric Ladyland*. While the other two records routinely show up on many surveys of the best rock albums of all time, *Axis* seldom does. It didn't even sell as well, although its failure was relative, since it actually charted higher than its predecessor in the US, though it didn't stay on the chart for nearly as long.

In part this is probably because *Axis: Bold as Love* doesn't have nearly as many songs that are judged Hendrix classics as its two companions do. Only two or three of its thirteen tracks – certainly "Little Wing", and probably "If Six Was Nine" and "Spanish Castle Magic" – are among the more familiar of Jimi's staples to the general public. That's not to say that *Axis* isn't a song-oriented album, or more given to guitar pyrotechnics: in fact, just one of its cuts breaks the five-minute mark, and then only just. It simply doesn't boast as many striking riffs as the records that bookend it, although certainly it shows Hendrix refining his craft in

numerous notable ways as songwriter, singer, guitarist and studio musician.

Certainly Hendrix was able to take appreciably more time and care over the recording and preparation of *Axis* than he had with *Are You Experienced?* This time around, he knew that he was working toward a follow-up album from around mid-1967 onward, as opposed to the slightly fraught progression of *Are You Experienced?*, which took shape in fits and starts between sessions targeted toward making hit singles. The entire focus of the Experience, in line with much of the hip rock community around 1967, might have been shifting toward albums rather than 45s. Jimi's fourth single, "The Burning of the Midnight Lamp" (not included on *Axis*), had done relatively unimpressively compared to his earlier ones, barely slipping inside the British top twenty even as *Are You Experienced?* continued to perch near the top of the album charts. In the US, the Experience's debut LP was doing much to prove that it was possible to have hit albums that didn't ride on the backs of hit singles, which might have affected the approach that was taken to the follow-up.

Partly because there was more dedication to making a standalone album, but maybe even more due to Hendrix's huge clout as a new superstar, the Experience were able to take a somewhat more measured approach to recording this time around. Chandler was a little more relaxed about giving the group more time to develop the material in the studio, as well as giving them (and Jimi especially) more input into the mixing. Everything was done

The Music

Three of a kind. The original inner of *Axis* was very much a group portrait with Jimi at the centre of things. The caption included the words "Jimi Hendrix is the man in the middle with the curly hair and broken face (because of the fold in the sleeve) ...". The design is by David King and Roger Law, the latter of whom went on to find fame as the co-creator of UK TV satirical puppet show *Spitting Image*.

at Olympic Studios in London with the same engineering staff, headed by Eddie Kramer.

By modern standards, nonetheless, the recording schedule was rather rushed, in part because the group's record companies were so eager for a follow-up to *Are You Experienced?*, by Christmas if possible. Although a little recording had been done in mid-1967, most of *Axis: Bold as Love* was recorded in October, and much of that in hurried sessions in the last week of the month. Such was the importance of getting the LP finished that half the record had to be remixed on Halloween after Hendrix somehow managed to take the masters out of the studio to a party he was attending, losing some of them in the taxi on the way back. *Axis* was ready – just – for the Christmas market in the UK when it was issued on 1 December, but was held back to 10 January in the US to avoid sales suffering from competition with the infamous Curtis Knight/ Jimi Hendrix *Get That Feeling* LP.

As with *Are You Experienced?*, however, there's no sense when listening to *Axis: Bold as Love* that the record was rushed in either

conception or execution. It's evident that Hendrix is moving his sound somewhat away from the flash guitar wizardry so prevalent on his earlier work, and guiding his songwriting toward a somewhat more R&B-soul-oriented feel. In this respect, Hendrix was quite brave, as much of his audience would no doubt have lapped up a record that put even more weight on his solos and freakouts. Instead, they got something altogether more thoughtful, although there was enough way-out weirdness at points to satisfy the freaks, especially on "If Six Was Nine".

The album's most enduring numbers tend to be the ones that find Hendrix exploring his more lyrical, gentle and personal side. "Little Wing" is the obvious standout in this regard, and one almost gets the feeling that Jimi was determined to prove, as with "The Wind Cries Mary", that there was more to him than loud licks and flipped-out musings. Although few would have known enough about his background to detect this at the time, "Spanish Castle Magic" and "Castles Made of Sand" showed Hendrix looking beyond the psyche-delic milieu of the times and within himself, drawing upon his pre-fame life with references to the people and places of his boyhood.

For those attracted to Jimi Hendrix more for how he sounds than what he sings, there are still plenty of sonic delights on *Axis*, some of which finds him tinkering with new electronic devices and effects. "Spanish Castle Magic" itself has a glorious clamour of slashing guitar riffs much like a musical traffic jam, fore-shadowing *Electric Ladyland*'s "Crosstown Traffic". Wah-wah guitar comes to the fore on "Up from the Skies", though its then-novel texture doesn't get in the way of what's a sur-prisingly sweet'n'jazzy soulful groover. Reprise judged it sufficiently appealing to issue it as a single in the US, though its lacklustre chart performance (it peaked at number 82) might have reinforced the feeling that Hendrix was now an albums rather than a singles artist.

To be frank, however, some of the similarly upbeat soul-flavoured songs on *Axis* are more pleasant than compelling. "You've Got Me Floatin'", never a favourite of Chandler's, does benefit from energetic background harmonies. "Wait until Tomorrow" again makes obvious Hendrix's debt to Curtis Mayfield, perhaps the most under-acknowledged major influence on Jimi as a guitarist and songwriter. "Ain't No Telling" and "Little Miss Lover" take a more avowedly blues-rock direction which is closer to the sound and attitude with which Hendrix first rose to fame, but without the immediately arresting hooks of his earlier tunes. And Noel Redding's rather Who-ish "She's So Fine" can't

be heard as anything other than a concession to keep the peace within the band as the bass-ist became more frustrated by his inability to place his own material on Experience releases.

When Hendrix reached for the outer limits on *Axis: Bold as Love*, he did so with vari-able results. Though the opening cut "EXP" has its admirers, it might be more dated than any other track on the first three Experience albums, mostly owing to its reliance on speed-ed-up voices jabbering about extraterrestrial life in not-so-funny patter that yields to almost *musique concrète*-like blasts of white noise guitar. Hendrix didn't need gimmicks to sound like he was tapping into the heavens: here, it seems almost as though he's donning a self-conscious billboard announcing his far-out-ness. The tastier soulful ballad "Bold as Love" uses liberal phasing on its extended outro, which was a novelty back in 1967, but doesn't sound nearly as exotic today. "If Six Was Nine" makes for a far more entrancing expres-sion of Hendrix's most psychedelic side, its devastatingly crunchy power riffs gliding into thrilling spiralling free-falls, driven along by some of Hendrix's most likeably goofy (and, in his putdown of a "white-collar conservative", most anti-Establishment) wordplay. Even this highlight, however, suffers from something of a free-jazzish meandering lack of direction as it stumbles toward the end, anticipating some of the problems Hendrix would have editing his ideas in the future.

To Hendrix neophytes, one of the most enduring mysteries about *Axis: Bold as Love* is the phrase that gives the album its title, even

The Music

though it's used (more or less) in the song "Bold as Love" itself. Hendrix's own explanation, as quoted by Michael Fairchild in the liner notes to one of the CD reissues of the album, was as follows: "The axis changes the face of the Earth and it only takes about a quarter of a day. The same with love; it can turn your world upside-down, it's that powerful, that bold." But as he accurately added: "The way I can explain myself thoroughly is through songs."

ELECTRIC LADYLAND

AND THE GODS MADE LOVE/HAVE YOU EVER BEEN (TO ELECTRIC LADYLAND)/CROSSTOWN TRAFFIC/VOODOO CHILE/LITTLE MISS STRANGE/LONG HOT SUMMER NIGHT/ COME ON (PART 1)/GYPSY EYES/THE BURNING OF THE MIDNIGHT LAMP/RAINY DAY, DREAM AWAY/1983... (A MERMAN I SHOULD TURN TO BE)/MOON, TURN THE TIDES ...GENTLY, GENTLY AWAY/STILL RAINING, STILL DREAMING/ HOUSE BURNING DOWN/ALL ALONG THE WATCHTOWER/ VOODOO CHILD (SLIGHT RETURN)
Reprise US, October 1968; Track UK, October 1968; available on CD.

It's now well known that the recording of *Electric Ladyland* was a much more protracted and painstaking affair than either *Are You Experienced?* or *Axis: Bold as Love*, and not just because it was a double LP. Although some recording had been done as early as December 1967 in London, the bulk of the sessions stretched out over a period of around half a year, mostly in New York's Record Plant studios. For Chas Chandler and Noel Redding in particular, the sessions were not just painstaking but painful, each of them getting fed up with Hendrix's laborious perfectionism and multiple retakes,

as well as the growing crowds of hangers-on who weren't serving any musical purpose. Part-way through the sessions, Chandler would quit as the group's producer, a role in which he had served since its inception; he would resign as Hendrix's co-manager shortly afterward. Redding would stick it out, but his resentment at the worsening atmosphere, and Hendrix's occasional use of other musicians to play bass (and playing of some of the bass parts himself), helped sow the seeds of discontent that led to the Experience's split in mid-1969.

The cover of *Electric Ladyland* also led to its fair share of controversy. Although Hendrix had wanted to use a photo by Linda Eastman (soon to marry Paul McCartney) of the group posing around a statue with kids in New York's Central Park, in the US a grainy photo of Jimi bathed in red light (by Karl Ferris, who had taken photos used for the covers of both of the Experience's previous albums) was chosen. In the UK, Track Records upset Hendrix considerably more by using a David Montgomery photo of a group of naked women which covered the entire outer gatefold.

For all the travails that went into its creation, however, it should be emphasized that such problems weren't unique to *Electric Ladyland* among the front-line rock releases of 1968. The Beatles' *White Album*, the other major double LP of the year, was another drawn-out marathon with more than its share of frayed nerves, blown tempers, and artistic disputes, even leading to the temporary resignation of Ringo Starr in the middle of the sessions. Big Brother and the Holding Company's *Cheap*

Red House Burning Down: Hendrix's Studio Albums on CD

In 1993, *Are You Experienced?*, *Axis: Bold as Love*, and *Electric Ladyland* were packaged in what seemed to be definitive CD editions by MCA. Confusingly even to longtime fans, all of these albums were reissued on CD with different packaging again by MCA (this time in conjunction with Experience Hendrix) a mere four years later.

Although the differences aren't nearly as radical (or interesting) as those between the original US and UK editions of these LPs, a few might be worth noting to serious fans. While the 1993 and 1997 versions have identical tracks, the liner notes are entirely different – and, in the case of the 1993 editions, quite a bit more thorough and detailed. And whereas the 1993 versions use frankly ugly, garishly coloured front covers (though at least the original US front cover art is contained in the booklet), the 1997 editions restore the original US front sleeves. The sound on the 1997 editions might possibly be considered more faithful to Hendrix's intentions, as his original studio engineer Eddie Kramer was involved with the remastering, but frankly most people won't notice much of a difference.

One little-noted variation between the CDs and the original LP that Hendrix aficionados should be aware of, however, is that the US CD versions of *Are You Experienced?* do *not* use the version of "Red House" that appeared on the original 1967 UK LP, substituting a different one first used on the 1969 American *Smash Hits* collection. US listeners who want to hear the original "Red House" can find it on the *Jimi Hendrix: Blues* compilation.

Thrills was pieced together from an aborted attempt at a live concert recording and troubled studio sessions which saw tension between the band and producer John Simon nearly reach breaking point; lead singer Janis Joplin would leave the group shortly afterward. But for all their troubled incubations, these are the three albums that, with the exception of two weeks, would hold down the number one spot on the US charts from 12 October 1968 until 7 March 1969. Such was their musical brilliance that both at the time and decades later, most listeners would never guess that these classic albums were so troubled behind the scenes.

Yet on each of these albums, you *can* tell that they're not exactly the most cohesive works

– a tribute to their eclecticism and versatility, but also a reflection of sky-high ambitions that couldn't always be fulfilled, musical differences between the players, and different ideas about how the music should be produced. The risks and tension could help drive the sounds to new heights, but also result in an unevenness guaranteeing that at least some of each record would probably not be to any given listener's taste. Such is the case with *Electric Ladyland*, a record that contains some of virtually every Hendrix fan's most treasured tracks, but also tries the patience of all but his most fervent admirers for at least some of its 75-minute running time.

To a somewhat lesser degree than *The White Album*, *Electric Ladyland* displays several dif-

The Music

The Music

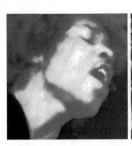

Whereas the US sleeve for *Electric Ladyland* featured a garishly lit picture of Hendrix, the UK counterpart was shocking for its time, assembling a veritable harem of naked young women in David Montgomery's photo. Hendrix did not approve.

ferent aspects of creative genius, to the point where the juxtapositions can be a little jarring. Some of the tracks count among the most recklessly experimental Hendrix ever

waxed. Others, by contrast, sound like dandy hit singles; some of them, in fact, were (and one of them, oddly enough, had already been released as a single more than a year before the album). Some of it verges on free jazz; other cuts dip into the purest blues. Some of the lyrics are among Hendrix's flightiest; others are some of his earthiest and angriest. Some of the songs aren't even by Hendrix. If this zigzag is part of the frustration of listening to *Electric Ladyland*, it's also much of its reward. No other Hendrix release shows him taking so many chances in so many areas – and much more often than not, succeeding.

Electric Ladyland's two most popular songs are perhaps its least characteristic. "Crosstown Traffic", the earliest recording, is the great

The Lost Fourth Album

Much confusion continues to hover over what Jimi Hendrix would have issued as his fourth studio album, and indeed over what it would have even been called. As early as a January 1969 BBC interview, he announced two albums that were in the pipeline, one to be called *Little Band of Gypsys* (presumably the origin of the name of his Band of Gypsys group in late 1969) and the other *First Rays of the New Rising Sun*. "The Americans are looking for a leader in their music", he declared. "*First Rays of the New Rising Sun* will be about what we have seen. If you give deeper thoughts in your music then the masses will buy them." By contrast, *Little Band of Gypsys*, he told *NME*, would be a "jam-type" affair.

Although it's thought that the fourth album would have most likely been a double LP, in fact Hendrix had

enough material by the summer of 1970 to consider a three-disc set. Typical of his mindset in his final days, however, he couldn't decide on either which songs to include or the size of the release. Even the title was uncertain, with *People, Hell and Angels* and *Straight Ahead* also under consideration.

While an album titled ***First Rays of the New Rising Sun*** was assembled from these sessions and released on CD in 1997, it's important to note that this was *not* a ready-to-go record that Hendrix had finished, but an approximation of what it might have sounded like and which songs would have been selected. For that reason, it will be covered in the section on Hendrix compilations, rather than discussed with his studio albums.

Even more confusingly, during this period Hendrix was also working on an apparently unrelated, alto-

Hendrix hit single that somehow never was, and sounds as though it might even have been recorded with the 45 format in mind. This is Hendrix's brand of soul-rock at its most listener-friendly, with a giddily infectious chorus, carefree backing harmonies, steamhammer-force riffs, and a superbly confident vocal. With "All Along the Watchtower", Jimi achieves the impossible feat of not only delivering a credible Dylan cover, but pulling off one of the greatest Dylan covers of all time, as well as landing a hit single on both sides of the Atlantic. Both of these cuts overshadow another single on *Electric Ladyland*, "Burning of the Midnight Lamp", which had first been issued on a British 45, but was peculiarly retrieved for inclusion on the LP more than a year later.

More typical of *Electric Ladyland*, however, are longer tracks – sometimes *much* longer – that give Jimi a chance to stretch out in the studio more than he ever had before, though he'd done so with some frequency in live performance. This took the shape not only of extended solos and jam-like passages, but also showcases for some almost siren-like tones for his guitar, as well as some distortion that was still largely uncharted territory in 1968. Here there starts to be a division of opinion among fans, even among some Hendrix enthusiasts. Some find such passages – particularly the suite-like opus "Rainy Day, Dream Away"/"1983... (A Merman I Should Turn to Be)"/"Moon, Turn the Tides... Gently Gently Away"/"Still Raining, Still Dreaming" – simply too sprawl-

gether less serious project titled **Black Gold**, described by Keith Shadwick in *Jimi Hendrix: Musician* as a "suite named after a fictional hero – a not even thinly disguised and often humorous idealization of himself. In late April [1969] he had made a cassette tape as a personal aide-memoire that collected apartment recordings of the complete *Black Gold* suite into a coherent whole ... a suite conceived using something like a cartoon technique telling the story."

In December 1969, Hendrix himself described the project so incoherently for the book *Superstars – In Their Own Words* that one wonders how it could have formed a suite or concept album of any sort. There was someone called Black Gold, there was someone else called Captain Coconut, and some other unspecified people too. Hendrix was apparently all these people

before going home and becoming a little boy from Seattle once again... before then setting off once more as the titular Black Gold. "That's my life until something else comes about", he put it, rather enigmatically to say the least.

Black Gold, like some other legendary Hendrix works (such as his fabled jam with John McLaughlin), remains unissued and is probably more intriguing on paper than on tape. For some more interesting speculation as to how Hendrix's fourth album might have taken shape, check out Lewis Shiner's excellent fantasy fiction novel *Glimpses*, where the music-freak protagonist transcends space and time to intervene in and facilitate the completion of legendary unreleased recordings by Hendrix, The Beatles, The Doors and The Beach Boys.

ing to keep their attention, and at times so noisy as to be grating. At the other extreme, some maintain that it's only at this point that Hendrix found his true voice, untethered by such white-collar conservative niceties as song structures and commercial appeal. Yet no matter what one's preferences, almost everyone likes the more tuneful and cogent part of these epics, like the almost cinematic way the lead guitar soars in "1983", and the interplay between wah-wah guitar and organ on "Still Raining, Still Dreaming".

Also on *Electric Ladyland*, Hendrix manages the difficult feat of both expanding his music and diving deeper into his rootsier influences. In one respect, the fifteen-minute "Voodoo Chile" is Jimi jamming at greater length than he ever had before on record, with musicians (Steve Winwood and Jack Casady) from outside the Experience, no less. In another, it's Hendrix reaching back to the earliest blues he'd been exposed to as a child, albeit moulding it into an almost avant-garde form. The merely five-minute "Voodoo Child (Slight Return)" does so in a much more concise form, its commercial appeal belatedly recognized when it became a number one hit single in the UK shortly after his death.

Elsewhere, as befitting a double album, there's a mixed bag of items whose appeal would vary according to the idiosyncrasies of specific listeners' tastes. "House Burning Down" (one of the relatively few instances in which Hendrix's songwriting reflected – if obliquely – the social and racial angst of the late 1960s), "Long Hot Summer Night" (one of the record's less remarkable tracks – basic funky blues-rock that verges on soul, especially in its high vocal harmonies) and "Gypsy Eyes" (one of several songs thought by some to be inspired by his late mother) are more interesting for what they try to do than what they achieve. The effects-laden "And the Gods Made Love" makes, like "EXP" on *Axis: Bold as Love*, for an arguably unnecessarily gimmicky opening to a record whose futurism should be allowed to speak for itself instead of virtually getting announced in a grandstanding fashion. Yet more Curtis Mayfield influence pops up, especially in the vocals, on "Have You Ever Been (To Electric Ladyland)", and Noel Redding is granted another incongruous power-pop-tinged ditty in "Little Miss Strange". Perhaps strangest of all, at least in the midst of music straining so hard to forge new horizons, is a cover of "Come On (Let the Good Times Roll)", an obscure 1960 single by bluesman Earl King.

Incidentally, although Hendrix had much more control over the production of *Electric Ladyland* than he'd been allowed on his first two albums, he wasn't quite happy with how it came out on vinyl, feeling that record labels couldn't quite handle the subtleties of what he was pioneering. "When it came time for them to press it, quite naturally they screwed it up, because they didn't know what we wanted", he griped to *Hullaballoo*. "There's 3-D sound being used on there that you can't even appreciate because they didn't know how to cut it properly. They thought it was out of phase."

The credit of the album's production to Hendrix did not sit well with Chas Chandler, who had been particularly vital to Hendrix's career, and had indeed produced some of the tracks on the record. Chandler was especially dismayed to see the words "produced and directed by Jimi Hendrix" on the sleeve with no acknowledgement of his own contribution, although he blamed that on Mike Jeffery – who assumed full control over Jimi's management shortly after Chas left the Hendrix camp – rather than on Hendrix himself. If Chandler had stuck it out as producer, *Electric Ladyland* would no doubt have sounded different in the end, and if he had ever resumed his production duties, he might have been the only one who could have shepherded another studio album out of Jimi before Hendrix's death. Yet if Chandler *had* stayed on, *Electric Ladyland* would also quite possibly have been less adventurous and, ultimately, less worthy of the undeniably classic status it has retained over the last four decades.

The Music

Live Albums

It's often said that many of the great rock acts have never been properly served by studio recordings and that they could only be properly appreciated in live performance. This is certainly the case with Jimi Hendrix, who only had to walk down a street to cut a striking figure. Onstage, he added a host of visuals – gyrations, humps, wild arm-waves and heroic poses – to high-volume performances that could never be faithfully reproduced on vinyl (or even CD), as well as a host of covers, improvisations and jams that would not be included on the studio releases issued during his lifetime. If you didn't see him live, proclaim some veterans of the 1960s guitar wars, you never really heard Hendrix – albeit sometimes with the smug satisfaction of those who have experienced something that, often simply because they were born too late, many others never will.

As usual, there's both some truth and falsehood in the myth. Like many great live acts, Hendrix was frankly prone to excess and self-indulgence in concert, and actually made more enduring *recorded* music – and certainly gave more finely honed, more focused and sonically clearer performances – in the studio, where he was every bit the innovator that he was onstage. The extended arrangements and improvised solos he devised in live settings could be thrilling, but also tedious, or at least seem far less impressive when heard out of their original context. And as for getting a fuller sense of the Hendrix concert experience, you might be better off with some of the extensive live footage of Jimi in action, much of which has been made officially available (and is covered in a separate section).

For all Hendrix's prowess as a live act, just one live album, *Band of Gypsys*, was issued before his death (though one LP side of his Monterey Pop performances came out just before his passing, as did a few songs from his Woodstock gig on the first volume of live material from that festival). Fortunately, Jimi's concerts were often recorded in highly professional sound quality, whether with an eye for possible release, use for a film soundtrack, or by venue staff or crew who simply wanted to preserve a show for posterity. These came in handy after his premature passing, both from the standpoint of fans hungry for more and, more cold-bloodedly, record labels and keepers of the estate in need of more product to satiate that hunger.

As a consequence, there is, even considering the zeal with which his archives have been mined, a surprising abundance – some would say over-abundance – of live Hendrix albums on the market. You would have to be pretty fanatical to want all of them, even if you were limiting yourself to those with acceptable fidelity, owing to the repetition of so many songs on different sets – as good as "Purple Haze" is, for instance, do you really want or need to hear ten or so versions? For quite a few Hendrix fans, the answer is a resounding "yes!" For many other genuine enthusiasts, however, at least some selectivity is advisable.

Bearing this in mind, the following listings will concentrate on the most notable releases in his live catalogue, with an eye to presenting a chronological range that doesn't heavily oversample from any given era. While *Band of Gypsys* is listed first as the only live album to gain official release before Hendrix's death, the other discs are presented in more or less the order in which they were recorded. Regardless of their somewhat uneven quality, it's indisputable that at least some are necessary to gain a full appreciation of Hendrix's scope as both a musician and an entertainer.

BAND OF GYPSYS

WHO KNOWS/MACHINE GUN/CHANGES/POWER OF SOUL/
MESSAGE TO LOVE/WE GOTTA LIVE TOGETHER
Capitol US, March 1970; Track UK, June 1970;
available on CD.

Critics, fans and even the participating musicians seem doomed to be at perpetual odds about the merits of this troubled release – the only proper live album to be issued during

Jimi Hendrix's lifetime, and indeed one of only four major LP releases before his death. Some musical and social critics who feel that Hendrix's African-American identity was suppressed to some degree by the circumstances under which he became a pop star

An uncharacteristically downbeat Hendrix, eyes cast down, looking seriously grim on the *Band of Gypsys* cover.

view it as a gem of his catalogue, one in which his R&B/funk influences are allowed to fully bloom. More often, it's seen as a flawed and somewhat disappointing excursion into that territory at the head of a trio that simply wasn't as good as the original Experience, or at least one that didn't have enough time to gel before this material was recorded at the Fillmore East on 1 January 1970. Hendrix himself doesn't look too pleased on the album's cover, which captures him in a rather grim downward-looking pose.

One of the chief disappointments, both to listeners in 1970 eagerly buying a "new" Hendrix album after a year-and-a-half gap and latter-day fans coming to the record for the first time, is that there are only six tracks, and that two of the songs were written and sung by drummer Buddy Miles (although one, "Changes", was Miles's best – and best-known – original). But on the whole, the songs were slight and undeveloped by Hendrix's very high standards, the playing powerful but not as

The Music

imaginative or combustible as Jimi at his best. Elemental but less than compelling blues-rock riffs drive much of the material, and the constant basic lyrical urges toward love and brotherhood, admirable as they are in principle, get a little wearisome even over the course of a half-dozen song album.

However, all was redeemed, more or less, by the inclusion of **Machine Gun,** which was not only one of Hendrix's most impressive later songs, but also contained some of his most startling guitar work. Two additional versions of that classic are on the two-CD *Live at the Fillmore East* (reviewed later in this section), which gives a fuller representation of the Band of Gypsys' repertoire at their four shows at the venue on 31 December 1969 and 1 January 1970.

LIVE AT MONTEREY

KILLING FLOOR/FOXY LADY/LIKE A ROLLING STONE/ROCK ME BABY/HEY JOE/CAN YOU SEE ME/THE WIND CRIES MARY/ PURPLE HAZE/WILD THING
MCA/Experience Hendrix, October 2007; released on CD.

By the time this set was recorded on 18 June 1967, The Jimi Hendrix Experience had been playing together for about eight months. Hendrix himself had led a live band in New York in the summer of 1966, and, of course, he had been playing onstage as a sideman for years before that. There are even a few live pre-Monterey UK and European Experience performances that have dribbled out officially and unofficially, but this truly represents the first widely available full-length Hendrix

concert. (Although an LP side of recordings from the show came out on a compilation in 1970 – the other side was devoted to part of Otis Redding's performance at the same event – the material wasn't issued in its entirety until the 1986 release *Jimi Plays Monterey*. Reissued under the title *Live at Monterey*, the CD's cover photo shows Jimi setting fire to his guitar at the climax of his act – possibly the most iconic pose he ever struck.)

Jimi Hendrix at his most iconic, burning his guitar *Live at Monterey* and sacrificing "something" he really loved.

For this reason alone – and for capturing the Experience's very first American show, one that was instrumental in breaking them in the US – the album is of huge historical importance. And while it might seem a bit rawer and less adventurous than much of what was subsequently taped at Jimi's live gigs, that's part of its considerable appeal. For this is the Experience on the verge of their international breakthrough. They're lean, hungry, and not about to let their Stateside obscurity stop them from making just as indelible a mark as the most celebrated of Monterey's superstars. Nor – with the notable exception of the finale – do they launch into any extraneous noise-mongering. It's the Experience at their most versatile and song-oriented, and if some might deride it as being a relic of the band at their poppiest, this is certainly some of the heaviest pop of that or any other time.

Perhaps because he was unknown to the Monterey audience, Hendrix might have played it a bit safe in terms of song selection, devoting half of his set to covers. Still, what you hear here isn't all that different from the set lists the Experience had recently presented in the UK and Europe. More importantly, the presence of those covers actually makes it more interesting in a sense, as several of them weren't included on his studio releases of the time. Particularly galvanizing in this respect is the hyperkinetic charge of the opening track, Howlin' Wolf's **Killing Floor**, which in the Experience's hands becomes a *rock* rather than a blues song. The amiable ramble through "Like a Rolling Stone" shows Jimi's skills as an interpreter; B.B. King's "Rock Me Baby" revisits his blues roots; and the closing **Wild Thing** testifies to his capacity for sheer outrageousness. All of his previous major UK hit singles are here too, although it's a little surprising he didn't play "Fire", considering that it was a staple of his live act throughout his career.

As exciting as "Wild Thing" is to see in the *Monterey Pop* film, however, the extended squalling at the end doesn't make for very entertaining listening without the visuals of Jimi setting fire to his guitar. Fortunately, the set was also filmed, and can now be seen on DVD (reviewed in the video section) if you want the whole "experience" of the Experience on this historic occasion.

BBC SESSIONS

FOXY LADY/CAN YOU PLEASE CRAWL OUT YOUR WINDOW?/ (I'M YOUR) HOOCHIE COOCHIE MAN/DRIVING SOUTH/FIRE/ LITTLE MISS LOVER/THE BURNING OF THE MIDNIGHT LAMP/ CATFISH BLUES/STONE FREE/LOVE OR CONFUSION/HEY JOE/ HOUND DOG/DRIVING SOUTH/HEAR MY TRAIN A COMIN'/ PURPLE HAZE/KILLING FLOOR/WAIT UNTIL TOMORROW/ DAY TRIPPER/SPANISH CASTLE MAGIC/JAMMIN'/I WAS MADE TO LOVE HER/FOXY LADY/HEY JOE/MANIC DEPRESSION/ DRIVING SOUTH/HEAR MY TRAIN A COMIN'/VOODOO CHILD (SLIGHT RETURN)/HEY JOE/SUNSHINE OF YOUR LOVE MCA/Experience Hendrix, June 1998; released on CD.

Is it live, or is it studio? That might depend upon who you ask – BBC radio sessions are recorded in a studio environment, but commonly played live or nearly live. For the purposes of this book, this two-CD compilation of Jimi Hendrix Experience BBC sessions – mostly taken from five radio sessions the group did in 1967 – will be classified as a "live" album, since it certainly wasn't recorded under his usual studio conditions or with initial intentions of commercially releasing the material. And while there may not have been an audience, Jimi was certainly playing with at least some of the same lack of inhibition he brought to his onstage performances. The very existence of these BBC recordings, incidentally, is yet another unexpected benefit of Hendrix's decision to base himself in Britain for much of his career. Even if he had managed to become a star in his native US, he would have had few if any opportunities to engage in regular radio sessions back home, where such recordings were not common practice.

As with virtually all the major rock acts who recorded frequently for the BBC in the 1960s, from The Beatles on down, the differences between this body of work and official studio material range from slight to major, usually depending very much on the song being performed. In Hendrix's case, it's safe to say that many average listeners will find the renditions of familiar tunes relatively inessential, both because they're usually not too different from the more well-known studio versions, and because they're lacking the edge and audience feedback of genuinely live concert tapes. But there's still an engaging looseness to standbys like "Stone Free", "Fire" and "Foxy Lady" that the more committed Hendrix fan will appreciate, even if they're not as finely tuned and penetrating as their studio counterparts.

The chief pleasure – again, as with BBC compilations by The Beatles and others – is the presence of many songs Hendrix didn't put on his studio releases or even attempt in the studio, especially cover versions of classics from several of his heroes. Highlights here include a romp through Elvis Presley's "Hound Dog"; a high-spirited take on The Beatles' "Day Tripper"; and a homage to Dylan via a rendition of Bob's relatively obscure mid-1960s single "Can You Please Crawl Out Your Window?" There's also some hardcore blues on Muddy Waters' "(I'm Your) Hoochie Coochie Man", Howlin' Wolf's "Killing Floor" and, more unexpect-

The cover photo of *BBC Sessions* shows the Experience with the wildest Afros they ever sported.

edly, three versions of the burning instrumental "Driving South", a relic from his days in Curtis Knight and the Squires. There's even a rudimentary instrumental cover of Stevie Wonder's "I Was Made to Love Her", with Wonder himself (who just happened to be waiting to be interviewed for the BBC on the same day) on drums. The presence of incidental BBC announcer introductions, chatter and even a Radio One jingle specially recorded by the Experience adds to the period fun.

Although some of the BBC sessions first came out on the *Radio One* compilation in the late 1980s, this double CD is a genuine upgrade. It adds some more songs, including the audio tracks to one April 1967 and three January 1969 BBC television performances, most notably their famous off-the-cuff version of "Sunshine of Your Love", which caused so much consternation when the Experience launched into it without warning on Lulu's variety show. Probably unintentionally, the casualness the Experience brought to these performances – not being under pressure to either deliver studio tracks for the ages or a crowd-pleasing concert – also reflects what seems to be a happier frame of mind than the live recordings Hendrix made as a superstar stadium attraction. It's a shame no session logs are reproduced in the liner notes, but the cover photo does show the Experience with the wildest Afros they ever sported.

LIVE AT WINTERLAND

FIRE/MANIC DEPRESSION/SUNSHINE OF YOUR LOVE/SPANISH CASTLE MAGIC/RED HOUSE/KILLING FLOOR/TAX FREE/FOXY LADY/HEY JOE/PURPLE HAZE/WILD THING
Rykodisc US, May 1987; released on CD.

Considering how many Hendrix live albums have appeared over the years, the absolute peak of the original Experience's run as an upper-echelon international draw – which covers approximately the last year and a half of their existence, from the beginning of 1968 to mid-1969 – is surprisingly lightly represented in the official discography. It's also a little surprising that this 71-minute disc – culled from three concerts at San Francisco's **Winterland** from 10–12 October 1968 – has been allowed to go out of print. Perhaps Alan Douglas's role as co-producer has something to do with Experience Hendrix failing to make it available as part of its current catalogue. It's still pretty easy to pick up used, however, and is easily identified by a cheapish, perfunctorily psychedelic design using an inset of a picture of a smiling Jimi. It might be the best official live representation of the band during this period, although interesting concerts (and excerpts of concerts) of varying quality have shown up on other discs, often on compilations or Experience Hendrix's collector-targeted Dagger label.

For all the oft-justified criticism of many of Douglas's archival projects, the sound on this CD seems to have preserved Hendrix's power without resorting to any unnecessary tampering. Some aficionados might be mildly disappointed at the absence of much post-*Are You Experienced?* materi-

Live at Winterland: a smiling Jimi amidst a rather perfunctory modicum of psychedelia-on-the-cheap adorns the cover.

al. But these are pretty satisfyingly high-voltage, even occasionally raw, versions of standbys like "Foxy Lady" and "Purple Haze", with "Fire" given an almost punk-like speeded-up arrangement. Jimi also stretches out on these old chestnuts at least a little, lengthening them (especially "Hey Joe", here lasting almost seven minutes) without quite going overboard.

For those in search of something a little more exotic, there's a cover of Cream's then-recent blockbuster "Sunshine of Your Love", Jimi observing in his typically rambling intro that the Experience will do it their own way, like an "instrumental jam scene"; a very heavy "Spanish Castle Magic" (the only item from *Axis: Bold as Love*); an eight-minute "Killing Floor", with Jefferson Airplane's Jack Casady guesting on bass; and an eleven-minute "Red House" – which, as Jimi notes, had yet to be issued on vinyl in the US. The cover of Hansson and Karlsson's "Tax Free" (learned from a Swedish act who supported him in Copenhagen in early 1968), anticipates, alas, some of the turgid jamming that would often cloud Hendrix's final two years. Overall, though, it's a reasonable snapshot of how the Experience were giving their repertoire a harder rock slant in concert by late 1968 – and how, in terms of song selection, they were in some ways surprisingly conservative. (A hard-to-find 1992 special edition of this release added three bonus tracks on a CD single: "Are You Experienced?", "Voodoo Child (Slight Return)" and "Like a Rolling Stone".)

LIVE AT WOODSTOCK

MESSAGE TO LOVE/HEAR MY TRAIN A COMIN'/SPANISH CASTLE MAGIC/RED HOUSE/LOVER MAN/FOXY LADY/JAM BACK AT THE HOUSE/IZABELLA/FIRE/VOODOO CHILD (SLIGHT RETURN)/ STAR SPANGLED BANNER/PURPLE HAZE/WOODSTOCK IMPROVISATION/VILLANOVA JUNCTION/HEY JOE
MCA/Experience Hendrix, July 1999; released on CD.

The earliest of the major post-Experience-break-up live performances to be given official release is Hendrix's festival-closing set at Woodstock on 18 August 1969. Although it forms a significant part of his legend, it's not Jimi at his best, due less to the quality of his own playing and singing than the band with which he was playing and the uncertainty over his future direction. It's just as well that the cover shows only Jimi, and not the unwieldy group he was leading on this occasion.

This was the highest-profile gig of the few shows mounted by the ad hoc ensemble Hendrix dubbed Gypsy Sun and Rainbows, although frankly it's difficult to hear anyone but Jimi and drummer Mitch Mitchell, with the rhythm guitarist (Larry Lee) and percussionists (Juma Sultan and Jerry Velez) hardly audible. This isn't so much a problem on the straight songs, where you're essentially listening to the Hendrix-Mitchell-Billy Cox trio that

became Jimi's last stable band in 1970, although they're a little rhythmically ragged, perhaps feeling overwhelmed by the task of trying to coordinate with three less experienced (even superfluous) players.

Minus the band: *Live at Woodstock's* cover shows only Jimi and not the unwieldy band assembled for the occasion.

The three instrumental jams, however, are largely lacking in even rudimentary melody, meandering as if Hendrix was trying to cover up the absence of a roadmap by simply jamming in heaps of notes, effects and volume. Although he did play a few songs he had yet to put on record ("Message to Love", "Lover Man" and "Izabella"), even these were too flashy and drawn-out. From the let's-get-this-over-with way he speeds through "Fire", there's also a sense of frustration at revisiting crowd-pleasing classics, although Jimi didn't seem to have yet come up with an alternative that would satisfy both himself and his fans. This is, however, where Hendrix gave his most famous performance of "The Star Spangled Banner", transcending the problematic setup to deliver a rendition unencumbered by the under-rehearsed accompanists.

Although MCA put out a single-disc collection of Woodstock material in 1994, the double-CD 1999 edition containing the whole set – apart from a couple of songs featuring temporary second guitarist Lee on vocals – is the preferred alternative, even if the sprawl of its execution can be downright tiring for those who don't hang on every phrase of Hendrix's guitar soloing. Better still, for that matter, is the two-DVD set with footage of virtually the entire concert, reviewed in the video section.

LIVE AT THE FILLMORE EAST

STONE FREE/POWER OF SOUL/HEAR MY TRAIN A COMIN'/
IZABELLA/MACHINE GUN/VOODOO CHILD (SLIGHT
RETURN)/WE GOTTA LIVE TOGETHER/AULD LANG SYNE/
WHO KNOWS/CHANGES/MACHINE GUN/STEPPING STONE/
STOP/EARTH BLUES/BURNING DESIRE/WILD THING
MCA/Experience Hendrix, February 1999; released on CD.

Like *Band of Gypsys*, this two-CD set was recorded during this short-lived band's four shows over two consecutive nights at the **Fillmore East**, beginning on New Year's Eve 1969. But it's *not* an expanded version of the *Band of Gypsys* album, although you may well come across several reviews describing it as such. In fact, there is just one track here ("We Gotta Live Together") that also appears on *Band of Gypsys*, though there it was presented in an edited mix. The other five songs from *Band of Gypsys* are represented here by entirely different performances recorded over the course of the four concerts, embellished by a bunch of tunes that didn't make it onto *Band of Gypsys* in any form.

Does it represent an improvement? Yes, in the sense that there's more music – and, at the risk of being unkind, a higher proportion of Jimi Hendrix and a correspondingly lower

Stage presence: *Live at the Fillmore East's* cover captures some of the amazing physical showmanship of a live Hendrix performance.

proportion of Buddy Miles. There are also some notable then-new songs (**Izabella, Stepping Stone**) not on *Band of Gypsys*. A glowing high-voltage instrumental mauling of "Auld Lang Syne" is a nice bonus, as is a cover photo of a squatting Jimi concentrating intently as his guitar neck points to the heavens. As for the songs that appear in different versions on *Band of Gypsys*, although the performances selected for the 1970 LP are overall the best ones, it's also cool to have two additional renditions of "Machine Gun", as well as some additional funk-bluesy workouts in "Earth Blues" and "Burning Desire". However, the basic problem with *Band of Gypsys* remains – it's not the format to which Hendrix is most suited, and the trio could probably have done with more time to tighten up musically and develop more material before getting thrown into the lion's den by making a live recording. And almost inevitably, the new group's versions of popular Experience songs such as "Stone Free" and "Voodoo Child (Slight Return)" begged unfavourable comparisons with the originals.

Although it's historically valuable, *Live at the Fillmore East* nonetheless doesn't quite represent the last word on the music played at these four shows. Most of the performances

The Music

The Best of the Rest ... and the Worst

Although this chapter focuses on the best live recordings of Jimi Hendrix that – with the exception of *Live at Winterland* – are currently available, inevitably a lot of other live material has been issued. Much of it is of secondary interest, or at least mostly of value to collectors and specialists, simply because the lower (at times downright poor) sound quality make them more of historical interest than something you'd be likely to play often for pleasure. If you're determined to dig yet deeper into Hendrix's live catalogue, however, some of them are definitely to be preferred above others.

The four-CD *Stages* box set doesn't have great sound, but at least it documents (after a fashion) Jimi's development as a live performer by including one complete concert from each year between 1967 and 1970. *The Jimi Hendrix Concerts*, originally issued as a double LP in 1982 and later reissued on CD, is a decent enough sampler of 1968–70 performances, although all but one song has appeared on other CD releases. Also be aware that many Hendrix anthologies mix studio and live recordings. Some of the most interesting of these are covered in the section on compilation discs, such as *Lifelines*,

which devotes an entire CD to a decent, good-sounding 26 April 1969 live show at the Los Angeles Forum.

Described (by the organization itself) as an "official bootleg label", Experience Hendrix's collector-targeted **Dagger** imprint has issued numerous live recordings that are probably too lo-fi for general release; further details can be found at the website *daggerrecords .com*. Of these, the most interesting may be *Paris 1967/San Francisco 1968*, if only for the relative scarcity of live Experience recordings from 1967.

As for the worst – or at least the most embarrassing – Jimi Hendrix live recording, there's really no contest. It has to be the lo-fi March 1968 jam at New York's Scene club, in which a foul-mouthed Jim Morrison clambered onstage to drunkenly curse and make noise, doubtless to the annoyance of everyone else present. For many years it's been widely available on bootlegs or "grey-area" releases that have even found their way into high street/chain stores. Numerous titles have been used, but by far the most notorious of these is *Woke Up This Morning and Found Myself Dead*, which set a new benchmark of tastelessness even in the world of bootlegs.

from the first two sets, and some of the ones from the subsequent two, still haven't been issued (though a version of "Foxy Lady" was available on a poorly conceived vinyl compilation LP misleadingly titled *Band of Gypsys 2*). Since serious Hendrix scholars aren't wholly satisfied by any of the packages of recordings from these concerts, it's probably time to put out all the surviving tracks from the four shows in their entirety and be done

with it, although technical problems affecting the sound quality at some points might help to explain their failure to appear. If you want yet more in the meantime, rehearsals for the concerts are available via Experience Hendrix's Dagger imprint on *The Baggy's Rehearsal Sessions*, highlighted by the best version (in terms of the performance, though not the sound quality) of "Ezy Ryder" available anywhere.

The Music

LIVE AT BERKELEY

PASS IT ON (STRAIGHT AHEAD)/HEY BABY (NEW RISING SUN)/
LOVER MAN/STONE FREE/HEY JOE/I DON'T LIVE TODAY/
MACHINE GUN/FOXY LADY/STAR SPANGLED BANNER/PURPLE
HAZE/VOODOO CHILD (SLIGHT RETURN)
MCA/Experience Hendrix, September 2003; released on CD.

When Jimi Hendrix was filmed at the two Berkeley, California, concerts from which footage was featured in the movie *Jimi Plays Berkeley*, he was naturally also recorded. This CD features the entirety of the second set on 30 May 1970, by which time the Experience – as Jimi's band was again now billed – had Hendrix flanked by Mitch Mitchell and Billy Cox. The cover doesn't, however, show a still from the film, as you might expect, but opts instead for a reproduction of the poster for the gig.

To be blunt, this new line-up wasn't as exciting as the "other" Experience, but clearly by this time the trio was becoming more comfortable playing together, and Jimi more at ease mixing new material with the crowd-pleasers like "Hey Joe", "Foxy Lady", "Purple Haze" and the set-closing "Voodoo Child (Slight Return)". The new material may not be as strong as these relative oldies, but at least this gives you the chance to hear some fairly underexposed tunes, such as the tight blues-rock of "Lover Man" (even if it sounded like a hybrid of his old stage faves "Killing Floor" and "Rock Me Baby"), the rather muddled blues-rock of "Pass It On (Straight Ahead)", and the jazzy quest-ing-toward-who-knows-what "Hey Baby

(New Rising Sun)". There's also a welcome appearance of "I Don't Live Today" ("I know for goddamned sure I don't live today", he exclaims at one point).

If this were the only Hendrix live album available, his genius would be evident. One has to concede, however, that in the company of so many others, quite a few of which contain more memorable versions of some of the same songs, it's not the first or second place to turn to for a Hendrix concert document. Note, incidentally, that the music is *not* identical to that heard in the *Jimi Plays Berkeley* movie, which also contains some material from his first set (including some songs not on the CD, most notably a cover of Chuck Berry's classic "Johnny B. Goode") and doesn't include some of the songs from the second set in any form. The DVD release of *Jimi Plays Berkeley*, however, does contain all of the music from the *Live at Berkeley* CD as an audio-only bonus, in 5.1 surround sound if you've got the appropriate equipment.

BLUE WILD ANGEL: JIMI HENDRIX LIVE AT THE ISLE OF WIGHT

GOD SAVE THE QUEEN/SGT. PEPPER'S LONELY HEARTS
CLUB BAND/SPANISH CASTLE MAGIC/ALL ALONG THE
WATCHTOWER/MACHINE GUN/LOVER MAN/FREEDOM/RED
HOUSE/DOLLY DAGGER/MIDNIGHT LIGHTNING/FOXY LADY/
MESSAGE TO LOVE/HEY BABY (NEW RISING SUN)/EZY RYDER/
HEY JOE/PURPLE HAZE/VOODOO CHILD (SLIGHT RETURN)/
IN FROM THE STORM
MCA/Experience Hendrix, November 2002; released on CD.

The Music

When Hendrix was filmed – which happened increasingly often over the last year or so of his life – full albums and videos of the performances weren't necessarily what he and his management had in mind. The fact that so many audio and video recordings were made, however, meant that in the wake of his death, fans had more Jimi on film and disc than they'd ever imagined possible. His record labels and his estate not only had more product to issue, but could sometimes release material from the same (or essentially the same) source in both CD and DVD form, each reinforcing sales of the other. Such was the case with his set at the **Isle of Wight festival** on 30 August 1970, which represents the last time he was captured on both tape and celluloid in decent professional quality.

Some critics feel that Hendrix was in somewhat tired and uninspired form at this event, and if you compare these cuts to his best performances, there's some validity to such claims. But if you disregard the tense and sometimes depressing circumstances of this final tour, it's really not that bad at all. If Jimi is less ebullient than he was back in the original Experience days, the Hendrix-Mitchell-Cox trio still plays with reasonable power. The over-the-top soloing has been reined in to some degree, and isn't as wearying here as it is on some of his other later live recordings. Most notably, Jimi was final-

ly spicing up his set with some new material and items from his official releases that hadn't been done to death in concert. "Dolly Dagger" and "Freedom" were highlights among the songs that wouldn't have been familiar to the audience from

Blue Wild Angel: for once on a Hendrix cover Jimi is singing as well as playing.

discs. It's also good to hear "All Along the Watchtower", which was featured far less in concert than one would expect, although the version here is rather unpolished, while "Machine Gun" is marred by what sound like security announcements through walkie-talkies.

This, then, is Hendrix just weeks before his premature demise – not progressing as fast as some critics might have liked in hindsight, but still moving forward with his music, if a bit haltingly, and still capable of delivering the goods only he could come up with. Note that the Isle of Wight performance is available in both complete form on two CDs and as a shorter one-CD set that omits seven songs. Also note that the DVD isn't quite complete either, missing a couple of tracks present on the full CD version.

Compilation Albums

Are You Experienced? hadn't even been out a year before the first official Jimi Hendrix compilation album, *Smash Hits*, was issued in the UK in April 1968. (If the Hendrix-Curtis Knight exploitation LP *Get That Feeling* from late 1967 is considered a ragtag anthology of pre-fame recordings, then the first Hendrix compilation dates from even earlier.) *Smash Hits*, which found release in an altered form in the US in 1969, would be the only true Hendrix compilation on the market while Jimi was alive. His death in September 1970, of course, almost immediately triggered a rush of anthologies as managers and labels scurried to exploit his vaults via both collections of previously released material and newly assembled aggregations of unissued live and studio performances. These sometimes combined released, unreleased, live and studio tracks, often in a haphazard and illogical manner. The stampede continues to this day, on product ranging from fully authorized, thoughtfully conceived and packaged CDs to shoddy rip-offs of highly dubious legality.

It's a massive mess to weed through, made even more confusing for the unseasoned enthusiast by the different themes under which separate compilations are (sometimes very tenuously) gathered. Some are straightforward (or more-or-less straightforward) best-ofs. Others concentrate on a specific style or era. Still others seem to have no theme in mind other than offering a wide assortment of material spanning several years and sources while incorporating enough rarities to persuade hardcore fans to lay out their cash. And quite a few seem to follow no particular rhyme or reason at all, other than getting naïve fans and/or completist collectors to part with their money.

For all these reasons, this section, like the previous chapter on live recordings, will concentrate on the most notable and most widely available Hendrix compilations. And make no mistake, these *are* notable releases, and not just for the more casual Hendrix admirer who will settle for greatest hits collections. Some of them contain very fine music, and one in particular, *First Rays of the New Rising Sun*, almost (but not quite) amounts to his fourth studio album. If only for this reason, no Hendrix listener can ignore the discs in this section. For most Hendrix fans, at least a few of the other discs detailed here will contain much music unavailable on his proper studio albums and live-only releases that will both entertain and enlighten.

The Music

SMASH HITS

*PURPLE HAZE/FIRE/THE WIND CRIES MARY/CAN YOU
SEE ME/51ST ANNIVERSARY/HEY JOE/STONE FREE/THE
STARS THAT PLAY WITH LAUGHING SAM'S DICE/MANIC
DEPRESSION/HIGHWAY CHILE/THE BURNING OF THE
MIDNIGHT LAMP/FOXY LADY*
Track UK, April 1968

*PURPLE HAZE/FIRE/THE WIND CRIES MARY/CAN YOU SEE
ME/HEY JOE/ALL ALONG THE WATCHTOWER/STONE FREE/
CROSSTOWN TRAFFIC/MANIC DEPRESSION/REMEMBER/RED
HOUSE/FOXY LADY*
Reprise US, July 1969

Both reissued on CD, with sometimes varying track listings.

The first and still, for all its imperfections,
most beloved Jimi Hendrix best-of compilation
was a bit premature when it was issued in the
UK in the spring of 1968, though it did have
the benefit of including a bunch of A-sides
and B-sides that had yet to appear on British
LPs at the time. The US version the following
year was logically geared toward the American
market, adding his two most popular post-
Are You Experienced? tracks ("All Along the
Watchtower" and "Crosstown Traffic"), as
well as the three songs from the UK debut
LP that hadn't yet appeared Stateside ("Red
House", "Remember", and "Can You See
Me"). Three B-sides and "The Burning of the
Midnight Lamp" were lost in the transition,
but musically the US mutation actually made
for a stronger collection.

Smash Hits, with its distinctive cover of
three overlapping photos of Hendrix under
rainbow-coloured lettering, seems to be technically out of print at this writing – certainly
it's not listed on the otherwise comprehensive

selection of Hendrix
product available
through *experience-
hendrix.com* – but
it's very easily find-
able in used and
sometimes even new
bins, as well as via
resellers online. It's
hard to keep up with
all the CD versions
that have appeared
in the US and UK,
of which there are at least four, with at
least three varying track listings. The UK
1985 edition is one to avoid owing to its
substandard sound quality, and in any case
the most crucial tracks are on the more comprehensive greatest hits anthology *Experience
Hendrix: The Best of Jimi Hendrix* (see
below).

The main attraction: *Smash
Hits* bore three overlapping
photos of Hendrix under
rainbow-coloured lettering.

EXPERIENCE HENDRIX: THE
BEST OF JIMI HENDRIX

*PURPLE HAZE/FIRE/THE WIND CRIES MARY/HEY JOE/ALL
ALONG THE WATCHTOWER/STONE FREE/CROSSTOWN
TRAFFIC/MANIC DEPRESSION/LITTLE WING/IF 6 WAS 9/
FOXY LADY/BOLD AS LOVE/CASTLES MADE OF SAND/RED
HOUSE/VOODOO CHILD (SLIGHT RETURN)/FREEDOM/
NIGHT BIRD FLYING/ANGEL/DOLLY DAGGER/THE STAR
SPANGLED BANNER*
MCA/Experience Hendrix UK, September 1997; MCA/
Experience Hendrix US, November 1998; released on CD.

An improvement on *Smash Hits* in both
length and chronological breadth, *Experience*

The Music

Hendrix: The Best of Jimi Hendrix is the best of the Hendrix best-ofs, even if it has one of the blandest covers of any major Hendrix release. A few selections ("Night Bird Flying") and omissions ("Spanish Castle Magic", "Machine Gun") might be questionable. But almost everyone would agree that this is a fine summary of his career highlights, although owing to space limitations, it lacks any of the long tracks from *Electric Ladyland*. Ultimately it serves well as either an introduction to Jimi or a sound choice for those who want just one Hendrix disc in their collection. The concise track-by-track annotation in the liner notes also gives a good basic history of the songs and recordings.

A 1993 MCA compilation, *The Ultimate Experience*, has many of the same tracks and can still be easily found second-hand, but the song selection isn't as solid. And while *Voodoo Child: The Jimi Hendrix Collection* appears at first glance to be a two-CD best-of – a worthy project for those who want a lot of Hendrix, but not a complete run of his core discography – it's not quite that, as some of the tracks are alternate takes and live performances rather than the most familiar versions, and the second disc consists entirely of live material.

Experience Hendrix: a good selection but one of the blandest covers of any major Hendrix release.

FIRST RAYS OF THE NEW RISING SUN

FREEDOM/IZABELLA/NIGHT BIRD FLYING/ANGEL/ROOM FULL OF MIRRORS/DOLLY DAGGER/EZY RYDER/DRIFTING/ BEGINNINGS/STEPPING STONE/MY FRIEND/STRAIGHT AHEAD/HEY BABY (NEW RISING SUN)/EARTH BLUES/ASTRO MAN/IN FROM THE STORM/BELLY BUTTON WINDOW MCA/Experience Hendrix, April 1997; released on CD.

Some Hendrix fans might take issue with *First Rays of the New Rising Sun* being classified as a compilation, rather than as a studio album, consisting as it does solely of studio recordings, most of them cut and/or polished shortly before his death in September 1970. Certainly it contains the bulk of the material that was in the running for what would have been his fourth studio LP, if not all of it. The cover probably isn't similar to whatever Hendrix would have come up with, however, apparently depicting a pensive Jimi gazing down from the heavens.

Yet when all is said and done, *First Rays of the New Rising Sun* is *not* what Hendrix would have issued as his fourth album. No such record could be posthumously compiled, as nobody knows with absolute certainty what songs he would have included, and what additional production work he might have done on the ones he had laid down in the studio, no matter how complete they might have seemed to others.

As a collection of the material that Hendrix was working on at the time, however, *First Rays of the New Rising Sun* is undoubtedly the best that has yet been produced. At 68

The Music

Perhaps marking its status as a posthumous approximation of Hendrix's fourth album, the cover of *First Rays of the New Rising Sun* seems to show a pensive Jimi gazing down from the heavens.

minutes, it's considerably longer than the ten-track LP from March 1971, *The Cry of Love*, which represented the first attempt to make something of these sessions. *First Rays of the New Rising Sun* has all ten of the songs heard on *The Cry of Love* and adds seven more, including a few of Jimi's more notable compositions from this era, such as **Room Full of Mirrors, Dolly Dagger, Stepping Stone** and **Izabella.** And even more than *The Cry of Love*, it's certainly preferable to the similarly intended 1995 CD *Voodoo Soup*, which had fewer songs and new overdubs by Knack drummer Bruce Gary on a couple of tracks.

More important than the packaging and speculation as to what Hendrix was up to, however, is the music. And although it inevitably doesn't hang together as well as his three actual studio albums, or contain material of quite the same standard, *First Rays of the New Rising Sun* does offer what for the most part are decent songs with imaginative production, often with a more upbeat mood than you would expect given the reports of Jimi's internal anguish in his final days. **Angel** and **Dolly Dagger** are the standouts, but there's some welcome cosmic humour and wistfulness in **Astro Man** and

Belly Button Window, and a generally pleasing uplifting spiritual quality to some of the rest. A number of the tracks may skirt nondescript blues-rock or riffs that haven't quite fully developed into songs, but in hindsight this collection suggests that Hendrix was gradually rediscovering his songwriting skills without abandoning his technological wizardry.

First Rays isn't a complete overview of the songs Jimi was working on post-*Electric Ladyland*, missing, for instance, "Message to Love", which he was featuring in concert. Even if it's considered as an approximation of his fourth album, there's also a slight sense of letdown, in that there isn't nearly the same sense of creative advancement as there had been with each of the LPs he made with the original Experience. But it's ultimately a highly worthwhile encapsulation of his final group of studio outings, with – as is the case on numerous Experience Hendrix-sanctioned CDs – highly informative liner notes from Hendrix authority John McDermott.

BLUES

HEAR MY TRAIN A COMIN' (ACOUSTIC)/BORN UNDER A BAD SIGN/RED HOUSE/CATFISH BLUES/VOODOO CHILE BLUES/ MANNISH BOY/ONCE I HAD A WOMAN/BLEEDING HEART/ JELLY 292/ELECTRIC CHURCH RED HOUSE/HEAR MY TRAIN A COMIN' (ELECTRIC)
MCA/Experience Hendrix, April 1994; released on CD.

For those who regarded Jimi Hendrix as a bluesman at heart – and even for some who didn't – *Blues* was a welcome addition to the Hendrix catalogue. Naturally there was a fair

Too Many Comps in the Kitchen

There are a shed-load of other Jimi Hendrix compilations besides the ones given individual reviews in this section, ranging from other attempts at best-ofs and collections of his singles (never mind that he was mostly an album-oriented artist) to trashy samplings of his pre-fame recordings as a sideman and the infamous Alan Douglas-produced mid-1970s LPs that added new overdubs. Considering the quantity, there's shockingly little in this sea of discs that's very interesting, but there are a few items that the die-hards might find more interesting than others.

Nine to the Universe, a 1980 LP that represented the last of the three Alan Douglas-produced dives into the vaults, does *not* have overdubs, instead presenting five unadorned jams from 1969. This is at least of historical interest, both as evidence of his jam persona and the presence of jazz organist Larry Young on one cut. Never issued on CD, it's now more or less available on a non-Experience Hendrix-authorized disc called *Message to the Universe,* which not only presents longer unedited versions of the five tracks, but adds five others with a similar mindset from the same era; it's discussed in this book's "Oddities" chapter.

Lifelines, a four-CD set from 1990, irritated at least as many fans as it stimulated, despite the inclusion of live and studio rarities, as well as interviews with Hendrix and other musicians. Most of the rarities were presented as incomplete fragments, and were sometimes obscured by voiceover narration from the original US radio special on which they were broadcast. It does at least feature, as the fourth disc, most of a 26 April 1969 show at the Los Angeles Forum. The continued surplus of copies in the used racks testifies to its low level of public esteem, though this does mean that it shouldn't be hard to pick up for a reasonable price.

Finally, if you're determined to hear the largely mediocre music Hendrix recorded with Curtis Knight from 1965–67, the 2000 six-CD (!) set *The Complete PPX Studio Recordings* has more of it in one place than any other package (though some of it's actually live, not studio). Typically, however, this poorly annotated set is ultimately no more responsibly presented than other Knight/Hendrix compilations, and it remains uncertain which of its tracks are original performances, and which might have undergone post-1967 surgery in the form of overdubs and edits.

amount of blues material in his repertoire, and quite a few songs that were more or less straight-ahead blues in structure, though these never dominated the programme. *Blues,* however, wasn't just any old excuse to regurgitate stray cuts tied to a loose theme in new packaging, as eight of the eleven tracks were previously unreleased. Its cover literally wore Jimi's major blues influences on its sleeve, overlaying an image of Hendrix with

postage-stamp-sized pics of a couple of dozen major bluesmen.

Heard in one sitting, this group of cuts testified to Hendrix's skills as a blues player and singer, with the influence of Muddy Waters in particular coming through strongly on originals like "Voodoo Chile Blues", the traditional "Catfish Blues" and the funky cover of Muddy's own "Mannish Boy". This is also the only release on which the ver-

The Music

The cover of *Blues* literally wore Jimi's major blues influences on its sleeve, overlaying an image of Hendrix with postage-stamp-sized pics of a couple of dozen major bluesmen.

sion of "Red House" that appeared on the original UK edition of *Are You Experienced?* can be found in the US. The downside is that, even with Jimi unpredictably twisting the blues template with his frenzied riffing, there's far less variety here than on the average Hendrix disc. Expressive range is a hallmark of all great artists, and hearing Hendrix do only blues is as limiting in its way as a Beatles anthology that only features love ballads, or a Scott Walker compilation with nothing but Jacques Brel covers. And although one wishes he had performed more acoustic blues in the style of the opening version of "Hear My Train A Comin'", the guitar on that track certainly seems imperfectly tuned.

Examining a similar theme, in a manner that some might find more accessible, is the 2003 collection *Martin Scorsese Presents the Blues: Jimi Hendrix*, released as part of the series issued in conjunction with the seven-part TV documentary *The Blues*. This, however, offered just two previously unreleased cuts, the rest (including the relatively well-known "Red House" and "Voodoo Chile") being selected from studio albums and compilations reviewed elsewhere in this book.

THE JIMI HENDRIX EXPERIENCE

PURPLE HAZE/KILLING FLOOR/HEY JOE/FOXY LADY/HIGHWAY CHILE/HEY JOE/TITLE #3/THIRD STONE FROM THE SUN/ TAKING CARE OF NO BUSINESS/HERE HE COMES (LOVER MAN)/ BURNING OF THE MIDNIGHT LAMP/IF 6 WAS 9/ROCK ME BABY/ LIKE A ROLLING STONE/SGT. PEPPER'S LONELY HEARTS CLUB BAND/BURNING OF THE MIDNIGHT LAMP/LITTLE WING/ LITTLE MISS LOVER/THE WIND CRIES MARY/CATFISH BLUES/ BOLD AS LOVE/SWEET ANGEL/FIRE/SOMEWHERE/(HAVE YOU EVER BEEN TO) ELECTRIC LADYLAND/GYPSY EYES/ROOM FULL OF MIRRORS/GLORIA/IT'S TOO BAD/STAR SPANGLED BANNER/STONE FREE/SPANISH CASTLE MAGIC/HEAR MY TRAIN A COMIN'/ROOM FULL OF MIRRORS/I DON'T LIVE TODAY/ LITTLE WING/RED HOUSE/PURPLE HAZE/VOODOO CHILD (SLIGHT RETURN)/IZABELLA/MESSAGE TO LOVE/EARTH BLUES/ ASTRO MAN/COUNTRY BLUE/FREEDOM/JOHNNY B. GOODE/ LOVER MAN/BLUE SUEDE SHOES/CHEROKEE MIST/COME DOWN HARD ON ME/HEY BABY/IN FROM THE STORM/EZY RYDER/NIGHT BIRD FLYING/ALL ALONG THE WATCHTOWER/ IN FROM THE STORM/SLOW BLUES
MCA/Experience Hendrix, September 2000; released on CD.

From a casual inspection of its contents, this four-CD box set looks like a gargantuan anthology offering relatively little that can't be found elsewhere. Further investigation, however, reveals that much of the material is previously unreleased, the familiar titles being represented by unfamiliar live recordings and alternate takes. It's true that the definition of "previously unreleased" in this context depends a little on the ear of the listener: some collectors and critics claimed that some of these supposed rarities differed from already-available cuts only by virtue of having different mixes. It's also true that the dedicated collector might well have some of the unreleased material on bootlegs, raising the question of whether the yield of

The blue-velvet cover of the box seems ready for proud display on the collector's mantelpiece.

genuinely new material on this 56-track extravaganza justifies the substantial cash investment necessary to acquire it.

For the average Hendrix fan, however – and even for the average avid Hendrix fan – the unimaginatively titled *The Jimi Hendrix Experience* is a fine trawl through much of the cream of his rare and unreleased material. As such, it's both educational and enjoyable, especially if the standard versions of these songs are so familiar to you that you've pretty much committed them to heart. Heavy on songs and light on jams, it's also – unlike the numerous Hendrix bootlegs which concentrate on lengthy instrumental improvisations – highly listenable from start to finish, providing a detailed look at his artistic evolution, albeit one that takes a different route from most of the Hendrix product on the market.

There are so many interesting variations contained in this package that there isn't space to detail all of them here. Some of the niftier highlights and surprises, however, include a take of "Hey Joe" that's much heavier on the haunting female background vocals; unexpectedly well-recorded performances of "Hey Joe" and "Killing Floor" from one of the Experience's very earliest shows on 18 October 1966; a heavy live performance of "Sgt. Pepper's Lonely Hearts Club Band"; an instrumental version of "Little Wing"; a demo of "Angel" (here titled "Sweet Angel") dating way back to late 1967; a wistful country-bluesish demo of "Room Full of Mirrors"; a nine-minute version of Them/Van Morrison's garage-rock classic "Gloria" with X-rated improvised spoken banter; and a weirdly ornate studio version of "Star Spangled Banner" that predates the Woodstock showcase by five months. And that's just on the first two discs.

The second half of the programme is less impressive, not so much because of the shift in direction in Hendrix's music over the last couple of years of his career, as because there are fewer eyebrow-raising discoveries. Nevertheless, it has unissued and rare (albeit previously available) live performances of high-calibre songs like "Voodoo Child (Slight Return)", "I Don't Live Today" and "Spanish Castle Magic"; Band of Gypsys studio outtakes, including versions of "Message to Love" and "Astro Man"; a storming live cover of "Johnny B. Goode" and a sound-check of "Blue Suede Shoes" from the May 1970 Berkeley concerts (neither of which is on the *Live at Berkeley* CD); and excerpts from the performances Jimi gave in Maui in the summer of 1970 as part of the trip to film *Rainbow Bridge*.

A large box set of a major artist that concentrates on less easy-to-find material will almost by definition fail to please many hardcore collectors, who will often complain about the omission of stellar items, the choice of inferior alternate versions and so on. *The Jimi Hendrix Experience* anthology is no exception, and undoubtedly

The Music

The Music

much similar stuff of worth that *could* have been selected remains out of official circulation. But by most objective standards, it's a smartly chosen and annotated sampler – if that's the right word for such a huge box – of the "alternate" recorded output of Jimi Hendrix for committed fans, whether or not they're determined to track down every last note he played.

SOUTH SATURN DELTA

LOOK OVER YONDER/LITTLE WING/HERE HE COMES (LOVER MAN)/SOUTH SATURN DELTA/POWER OF SOUL/MESSAGE TO THE UNIVERSE (MESSAGE TO LOVE)/TAX FREE/ALL ALONG THE WATCHTOWER/THE STARS THAT PLAY WITH LAUGHING SAM'S DICE/MIDNIGHT/SWEET ANGEL (ANGEL)/BLEEDING HEART/PALI GAP/DRIFTER'S ESCAPE/MIDNIGHT LIGHTNING
MCA/Experience Hendrix, October 1997; released on CD.

Something of the runt of the litter in the current catalogue, *South Saturn Delta* isn't tied to any particular era, style or concert. Instead, it's a round-up of outtakes, jams and live performances that haven't found a home elsewhere, especially as Experience Hendrix hasn't gone down the route of adding bonus tracks to reissues of the canonical albums (or releasing "special editions" that add one or more discs of extras to the same). You'll read about many of these songs in books about Hendrix, as these are largely numbers he considered as serious contenders for his albums, rather than the usual throwaway improvisations. Yet you'll rarely hear them played on the radio, with the exception of a few classics ("Little Wing", "All Along the Watchtower" and "Angel") represented here by alternate versions. You'll also rarely see Hendrix dressed the way he is on the cover, where he looks more like

a Hell's Angel than a hippie.

So yes, *South Saturn Delta* is weak compared to the other in-print Hendrix CDs in his standard discography. That doesn't mean, however, that it's not worth owning for those whose interest goes beyond the usual trio of studio

With no guitar Hendrix looks more like a Hell's Angel than a musician on *South Saturn Delta*'s cover.

LPs and best live concerts and compilations. Here's the place to find the weird 1967 psychedelic B-side "The Stars That Play with Laughing Sam's Dice" and his most elusive Bob Dylan cover, "Drifter's Escape" (actually a different version from the one first available on the *Loose Ends* LP). Here also are early demos of "Angel" (of which the track titled "Little Wing" is actually an instrumental version) and a Band of Gypsys studio recording of "Power of Soul". And the instrumental title track, recorded with a horn section, might be as close as Hendrix came to credibly meshing rock and jazz.

True, there are also rather average blues-rock numbers like "Look over Yonder" and "Here He Comes (Lover Man)", and instrumentals that are more like sketches than fully formed compositions. But that goes with the territory when you dig a little deeper into Jimi Hendrix's catalogue than his classic repertoire – a liability that most fans now accept, rather than wishing such material would somehow be more than what it is.

30 Great Jimi Hendrix Songs

All songs written by Jimi Hendrix unless otherwise indicated

1. Hey Joe
(Billy Roberts)
First released as A-side UK single 16 December 1966; available on *Are You Experienced?* CD

Although "Hey Joe" was not a traditional song, such was the archetypal nature of its tale of infidelity and bloody revenge that it sounded like a murder ballad which had been handed down through the generations. By the time Jimi Hendrix recorded it for his debut single in late 1966, it had certainly been covered by enough rock acts for it to *seem* like a folk song that was undergoing a popular revival. The Byrds and Love had already released versions; The Leaves, another Los Angeles folk-rock band, had actually taken it into the US top forty with a maniacal garage-rock treatment; and Tim Rose had used an altogether slower-burning arrangement on the single which caught producer Chas Chandler's and, most likely, Jimi Hendrix's ears.

Compared with the follow-up single "Purple Haze" and the *Are You Experienced?* album, "Hey Joe" is actually pretty restrained. Maybe Chandler didn't want to get *too* outlandish with the Experience's maiden offering; maybe the band's music simply hadn't developed into something as loud and outrageous as it would be a mere few months later. Nevertheless, it still sounded advanced for late 1966, especially in its screeching guitar solo. Otherwise Jimi's playing is relatively mild, though assured and fluid. The opening figure shows that he had assimilated the influence of Curtis Mayfield in particular, its roving riffs aptly reflecting the wandering ways of the song's protagonist – a wholly unsympathetic fugitive, incidentally, on his way to Mexico after shooting his two-timing woman.

Although Hendrix would end up writing most of his material, "Hey Joe" testifies to his first-rate talents as an interpreter, able to reinvent a familiar song and make it his own. His singing is already hip, sly, and knowing, if rather more sober than would be his wont. His guitar also does much of the talking, punctuating the drama almost as if it's offering an ominous Greek-chorus commentary on this deadpan murder ballad. Although the sighing female backing vocals by The Breakaways have been criticized as an unnecessary concession to pop, in fact they subtly amplify the song's simmering tension.

2. Stone Free

First released as B-side UK single 16 December 1966;
available on *Are You Experienced?* CD

Just as important and impressive in retrospect as "Hey Joe", the flip side "Stone Free" was Hendrix's first proper recorded composition. According to most accounts, he was pretty much cornered into writing it – and writing his own material in general – by Chas Chandler, but if so, Jimi seems to have taken to it like the proverbial duck to water. From the first bars, "Stone Free" bursts with urgent energy, its fuzzy chords and grinding riffs almost hailing the birth of hard rock guitar itself. Mitch Mitchell ups the ante with his insistent cowbell, and the trio sound as though they can barely keep a lid on the proceedings, which come to the boil with an explosive guitar solo. A nice bonus is the brief coda, which suddenly shifts to a higher key and altogether jazzier rhythm, Jimi's guitar taking on a zonked-out disappearing-in-the-distance tone with equal suddenness on the fade.

Lyrically, "Stone Free" unveils much of the persona that would come to be expected from Hendrix's songs. Nowadays, the resentment it expresses towards women who try to tie a man down might seem to smack of sexism. More than a macho manifesto, however, it's a declaration of intent to be footloose and fancy free, not tied to any one place or existence – certainly not by those who put down the clothes he wears, who "don't realize they're the ones who's square". It's a credo that Hendrix put into practice for much of both his musical and personal life, leading to the highest of highs, but also perhaps contributing to his premature demise.

"Stone Free" was a particular favourite of another great guitarist making his mark in the 1960s, Jeff Beck, who told *Rolling Stone*: "It's got bits of Buddy Guy; it sounds like Les Paul in places. Jimi does every trick in the book and nails it all together so tight that you can't even see the joints." Inexplicably, Hendrix would try to record a new version in April 1969, which failed to match the original on all fronts – another illustration of how, in his final years, he would often try to improve on something that didn't need additional polish in the first place.

3. Purple Haze

First released as A-side UK single 17 March 1967; available on *Are You Experienced?* CD

Perhaps the most famous Hendrix song of all, "Purple Haze" is also probably the one that, over the last few decades, has done the most to cement his image as the ultimate cosmic hippie. This, of course, was just one facet of Hendrix's work, but if it tends to overwhelm some other dimensions of his musical personality, it's a tribute to how utterly convincing Jimi was when he took on the role of benign psychedelic astronaut. "Purple Haze" is a *tour de force* in this respect, mixing druggy free-associative imagery, voodoo menace and the hypnotic spell of sexual desire in a way that makes them all seem of one piece.

The most infamous feature of "Purple Haze" is its weirdly dissonant, jerky up-and-down sequence of opening chords. It wasn't noted by critics at the time, but now it's fairly well known that these are "tritones", considered so jarring that they were lambasted as the devil's music in olden times (in the Middle Ages, they were even banned by the Church). There's lots more going on in "Purple Haze", of course, starting with the only marginally more conventional riffs that take over after the intro. They're penetrating, quizzical, ominous, yet impossibly seductive, like the most thrilling of forbidden pleasures, be they sexual or drug-induced.

In his solos, Jimi really takes off into a new stratosphere of axework with his sustained, Octavia-induced shrieks, as if he were floating up through the clouds of purple haze into an entirely different plane of existence. So incomparable were these to other guitar sounds that when "Purple Haze" was released as a single in the US on 19 June, Warner/Reprise took the precaution of writing "deliberate distortion, do not correct" on the original tape box – not an idle consideration, as a feedback-laden 1965 single by The Who had been initially rejected by a record label in the belief that the tape was actually defective.

Inevitably, "Purple Haze" was assumed by many to be an evocation of an acid trip, but it's more likely the result of Hendrix's early exposure to Chas Chandler's science-fiction books, one of which (Philip Jose Farmer's *Night of Light*) refers to a "purplish haze". Whatever the case, it's a central classic of the psychedelic canon, and not without its wacky sense of humour, most famously when Jimi jubilantly declares "'scuse me while I kiss the sky" – a phrase famously misheard by many as "'scuse me while I kiss this guy".

4. The Wind Cries Mary

First released as A-side UK single 5 May 1967; available on *Are You Experienced?* CD

Coming after the brooding murder ode "Hey Joe" and the psychedelic free-for-all of "Purple Haze", "The Wind Cries Mary" might have been Hendrix's way of demonstrating that there was more to him than flashy flamboyance. This wouldn't have meant much, however, if he hadn't had a great song with which to make his case. And although one doubts whether many fans would include it among their top ten Hendrix tracks, "The Wind Cries Mary" is indeed a great composition, as well as one of his most lyrical and melodic.

With the obvious exception of Bob Dylan, folk-rock is a largely uncredited influence on Hendrix, and along with "Little Wing", "The Wind Cries Mary" is about as close as he got to playing folk-rock on his own records. Musically, this is most evident in the delicate, upward-rising chords that serve as the song's principal hook, while lyrically, Dylan's influence comes through via an oblique tribute to a goddess-like woman that's both wistful and slightly surreal. It's a better pop tune, however, than virtually anything Dylan himself was coming up with in the mid-1960s, and Jimi sings with commendable humility. Humble too are his Curtis Mayfield-esque guitar riffs, smooth and note-jammed, but lilting and restrained, avoiding overplaying or the kind of volume and distortion Hendrix was habitually employing to make his more aggressive points by early 1967.

"The Wind Cries Mary" was written by Hendrix as a sort of olive branch to his then

The Music

girlfriend Kathy Etchingham after a fight between the pair, its gentleness evoking halting steps toward romantic reconciliation. When he sings "a broom is drearily sweeping up the broken pieces of yesterday's life", it's clear that the smashed crockery from their squabble is fresh in his mind. Jimi inadvertently cast doubt on the sincerity of his sentiments, however, when he told Marianne Faithfull, in one of his unsuccessful attempts at seducing the singer, that he had written it for her.

5. Highway Chile
First released as B-side UK single 5 May 1967; available on *Are You Experienced?* CD

The UK B-side to "The Wind Cries Mary", "Highway Chile" has never been among the more renowned Jimi Hendrix tracks, especially in the US, where it didn't find official release until the early 1970s. It's actually a pretty solid rocker that counts among the Experience's most blues-soaked early outings. And of all the riffs that start early Hendrix songs, this is among the most evil-sounding. The lick may not be to everyone's taste, David Stubbs describing it in his book *Voodoo Child: Jimi Hendrix: The Stories Behind Every Song* as being "horribly prescient of Deep Purple at their most weedily portentous". But it's portentous with a purpose, and in any case quickly gets out of the way for Hendrix to deliver what's essentially a rough-and-ready roadhouse rocker, though that insinuating lick reappears in the chorus.

Although Jimi sings this tale of a sort of ne'er-do-well alter ego of Johnny B. Goode in the third person – "his guitar swung across his

back, his dusty boots, and it's his Cadillac" – it's tempting to read quite a few autobiographical elements into it. This "highway chile" left home at seventeen (Jimi was just a year older when he left Seattle), longing to see the world, leaving a girl behind. He hasn't seen a bed in a long time, his long hair is flowing in the wind, and he wanders around with a guitar slung across his back, a child of the highway. Things might not have been quite so bad for some of the time when Hendrix was struggling on the chitlin' circuit and in Harlem, but they were bad enough, and similar enough to the circumstances he outlines here to suspect that this is a bit of a self-portrait.

"Highway Chile" is the relic of an era when major UK acts were still putting some highly worthwhile tracks on non-LP B-sides. Hendrix put a lot into each of his first three B-sides, but seemed to lose his enthusiasm for the exercise by the time of the next one, "The Stars That Play with Laughing Sam's Dice", which is more of a throwaway than virtually anything else he issued as a band leader during his lifetime. Thereafter his emphasis would be wholly on albums, not on stand-alone singles.

6. Foxy Lady
First released on UK version of *Are You Experienced?*, 12 May 1967; available on *Are You Experienced?* CD

Chosen as the opening track for the original (UK) version of the *Are You Experienced?* LP, "Foxy Lady" is about as celebrated – and good – as any Jimi Hendrix track that didn't end up becoming a hit single. The parade of arresting opening riffs that Jimi was seemingly summoning up at will by early 1967 continued at the beginning of this track, which kicks off with a slow fade-in of wiry, fluttering notes, like an insect buzz slowly making its way through your speakers. Then the whole band crashes in like a bunch of Hell's Angels demanding entrance to your party, the stair-climbing licks capped by thick declarative exclamations. Jimi might not be as mean as a gate-crashing Hell's Angel, but he's not going to stand for anybody getting in his way when he eyes his foxy lady either. When he announces his intention to take her home, it's time for those riffs to inexorably go down those same stairs they've mounted, with an inevitability that doesn't have to spell out what's going to happen when they get back to his place.

It sounds pretty macho on paper, but it comes off as pretty ingratiating on disc, and more like the ultimately healthy expression of sexual desire than the urge to subjugate or dominate. It helps a great deal that Hendrix keeps his puckish sense of humour in his vocal delivery, with wordless whoops and pops to drive home just how knocked out he is by this bewitching woman. There's also a sense of humour at work in the stop-restart ending – a trick that surely must have fooled many listeners into thinking the song was over the first couple of times they played it.

It's a measure of just how popular "Foxy Lady" became that, for the last few decades, sexy ladies have been known as "foxes" throughout the English-speaking world. This doesn't explain, however, why the spelling was changed to "Foxey Lady" for the US release,

the song continuing to be spelled that way more often than not to this day.

7. Manic Depression
First released on UK version of *Are You Experienced?* 12 May 1967; available on *Are You Experienced?* CD

Many of Jimi Hendrix's songs are anchored by herky-jerky, up-and-down riffs. "Manic Depression" has the most rollercoaster-like licks of them all, the progressions constantly twisting upward but never resolving themselves. Lots of Hendrix numbers bristle with uneasy restlessness, and true to its title, "Manic Depression" takes that mood to extremes, as usual right from the start, where stuttering rhythms interrupt a six-note glide up the scale.

Like most of the material from this early period, "Manic Depression" has an unstoppable forward thrust. Mitch Mitchell and Noel Redding outdo themselves in their knack for nearly upping the tempo so frenetically that the track threatens to outrace itself, as if the song were barely able to keep pace with the rhythms. Psychological disorder is more than hinted at when Hendrix conjures some desperately squiggly squeals from his guitar, almost like the musical equivalent of an oncoming migraine. The mania comes suitably crashing down in the instrumental section at the end, capped off by a wail of feedback.

For all its bubbly energy, the lyrics of "Manic Depression" are far from uplifting, perhaps reflecting – if only subconsciously – some doubt and frustration as Jimi finally started to get the success he craved, only to find that it brought its own complications. "I know what I want, but I just don't know how to go about getting it", he muses – an anticipation of the problems he would experience in trying to translate his more high-flying ideas from head to tape as his recording career progressed. But at this point at least, an engaging humorous bounce to his vocals mitigated any fear that the "Manic Depression" he sang about could be a serious real-life hindrance.

Hendrix gave an unexpected insight into what he saw as the real subject of "Manic Depression" in his spoken intro to the song at a San Francisco concert in October 1968, as heard on the *Live at Winterland* album. It was, he revealed, "a story about a cat wishing he could make love to music, instead of the same old everyday woman".

8. Red House
First released on UK version of *Are You Experienced?*
12 May 1967; available on *Are You Experienced?* CD

Blues was an undeniably heavy influence on Hendrix throughout his career, and he sometimes paid tribute to the bluesiest of his roots with covers of songs he particularly liked, such as B. B. King's "Rock Me Baby" and Howlin' Wolf's "Killing Floor". Yet he wrote very little in the straight blues idiom, always configuring the form into something rather different and more off-kilter even when blues was the strongest element. Bearing this in mind, "Red House" can be seen as his demonstration that, when the whim took him, he could play traditional-style twelve-bar electric blues just

as well as anyone. Having done so definitively on this *Are You Experienced?* cut, he seemed to find little need to do so again.

This isn't to say that "Red House" doesn't bear Jimi's individual, even idiosyncratic stamp. It's particularly evident in the opening bars, where Jimi's up-down patterns throb with such molten heat that you can almost see the smoke coming out of the amps. The extended solos, by Hendrix standards, are on the conventional side, as if it's B.B. King suddenly playing through different equipment, giving his guitar added volume and blurs around the edges. Hendrix's playing might be busier than King's, but it's similarly tasteful, getting the most out of the limitations of the twelve-bar format and resisting the temptation to bend it (as he often did) into something else entirely. Lyrically, there might be an autobiographical reference to the Seattle community he abandoned when he sings about trying to come home, only to find that his key won't fit the door and his baby's gone. But he still has his guitar to console him as he goes off a-wanderin'...

There are two entirely separate studio recordings of "Red House" from the Experience's early career, one originally found on the UK version of *Are You Experienced?*, the other first issued on the US version of *Smash Hits* in 1969. Hendrix often played "Red House" live, and there are numerous versions floating around on official releases. An entire album of live performances of the song, titled *Red House: Variations on a Theme*, will probably strike all but the most ardent fans as overkill.

The Music

9. Can You See Me

First released on UK version of *Are You Experienced?*
12 May 1967; available on *Are You Experienced?* CD

Undervalued by most Hendrix critics, "Can You See Me" is usually regarded as more or less of a filler track. Reprise Records seemed to see it that way, as it was one of the three tracks from the UK edition of *Are You Experienced?* that they omitted from the US release, making its first Stateside appearance on the 1969 *Smash Hits* LP. Hendrix himself seemed to hold it in higher regard, however, as it was one of just four original songs he chose to perform at his first American concert at the Monterey Pop festival.

If "Can You See Me" is judged an inferior cut, that's only relative to the extremely high standards of the best half or so of the original *Are You Experienced?* album. This might be the early Experience at their poppiest, and indeed it was one of the earliest tracks they laid down in the studio, beginning work on it in late 1966, not long after "Hey Joe". It's driven by another urgent riff, which, as was early Hendrix's wont, alternates licks with upward and downward exclamation marks. For added emphasis, he inserts a questioning, reverberant, plucked bent note just before each verse – a small touch, but a very nifty one.

For that matter, "Can You See Me" itself is a pretty nifty rocker, with space in the middle for Jimi to unleash a burning solo. If only in comparison with much of his subsequent work, lyrically it seems a little on the generic side, basically being a lament over a fox who done him wrong. But as presumably one of the first songs he wrote after "Stone Free", it shows him quickly coming to grips with combining pop and R&B to write something that doesn't sound quite like anything else from late 1966.

10. Love or Confusion

First released on UK version of *Are You Experienced?*
12 May 1967; available on *Are You Experienced?* CD

If there weren't such an embarrassment of somewhat angst-ridden riches on *Are You Experienced?*, "Love or Confusion" would undoubtedly be regarded as more of a standout in the Jimi Hendrix discography. Unlike most of the album's highlights, it doesn't quite put its most gripping riff front and centre, instead starting with a ringing, slightly feedback-flecked chord that sounds a little more like something you might hear on a Who record, followed by patterns that would bring The Byrds to mind if they had been using something heavier than their usual twelve-string electric guitars. It's not until the end of the first verse that you get the killer blow with a circular, devious lick that seems to reflect the mental meltdown of the song's narrator.

Typically, Jimi can't let the song pass without taking most of the opportunities available to pour on some exotic dressing, like the superheated light pulsations on the verses, and the burst of pure static that starts the instrumental break before Mitch Mitchell kicks the tempo into a much faster, jazzier gear. Hendrix's use of fuzztone is clearly getting more advanced than it had been when the Experience first entered the studio, at times approximating a violin-like tone in its thick sustain.

Like some other early Hendrix compositions which seem, on the surface, like good-natured early psychedelia, "Love or Confusion" hints at unrest behind the scenes. If it's love he's feeling, it's pretty painful, its sensations burning, cold and pounding, but not exactly exhilarating. There's a sense of the self-doubt and insecurity – "my mind is so mixed up, goin' round an' round" – that plagued Jimi before and after his mammoth success, although the tension of those struggles undoubtedly seems to have fuelled part of his musical brilliance as well. According to one interview he gave, such was the strength of "Love or Confusion" that it had even been selected as the follow-up single to "Hey Joe" before getting deservedly edged out by "Purple Haze", which he wrote soon afterwards.

11. I Don't Live Today

First released on UK version of *Are You Experienced?*
12 May 1967; available on *Are You Experienced?* CD

Yet another steamroller riff introduces "I Don't Live Today", and if it sounds like the beats are almost emulating American Indians on the warpath, there's a reason for this. In concert, Hendrix himself dedicated the song to their plight, as well as to that of other US minority groups. If it seems a little odd that Jimi should be waving a banner for Native Americans while shying away from African-American militancy, it should be remembered that Hendrix himself had Cherokee ancestry, taking perhaps disproportionate pride in that side of his heritage. And while their hardships didn't get as much attention in the 1960s as those of the African-American population, Native Americans had

With Mitch Mitchell backstage at the Fifth Dimension Club on 15 August 1967 in Ann Arbor, Michigan

also suffered long-standing discrimination at the hands of the white US majority.

Musically "I Don't Live Today" is as strong as all but the very best tracks on *Are You Experienced?*, the vocal complemented at every turn by pounding riffs before transitioning into a proud, glowering chorus which in turn makes an unpredictable switch into double-time. The guitar work has a searing pulse, the track dissolving in the kind of freakout crossfire that would blow minds at Monterey, although it also masks a failure to bring the song to a neat conclusion. There are also some thrilling detours into strangulated low swooping moans, even if it now seems that Jimi was showing off a little too much by cramming all these noisy fireworks into one track.

If it weren't for Hendrix dedicating the song to American Indians, however, "I Don't Live Today" would not be perceived as a political statement. Instead, its lyrics read like a surprisingly downbeat meditation on mortality and outright misery. "No sun coming through my windows, feel like I'm sitting at the bottom of a grave" sounds more like the sort of phrase to be found in goth-rock than psychedelia. Yet as usual in his early (and many of his later) songwriting efforts, it's played and sung with an ebullience that belies the darkness of the lyrics, sounding more like a determination to live life to the fullest than a fear that there might not be too many more days left.

12. Fire

First released on UK version of *Are You Experienced?*
12 May 1967; available on *Are You Experienced?* CD

Although some of the songs on *Are You Experienced?* are not as happy as they seem when the words sink in, "Fire" can't be experienced as anything other than an expression of sheer joy. It might not be as overtly lustful as "Foxy Lady" or as mystical as "Purple Haze", which has caused some critics to view it as somewhat lightweight compared to the strength of "Love or Confusion". But that doesn't make it any less worthwhile, because "Fire" is not only as catchy as any single by the Experience or any other major rock act

of 1967, it also teems with as much energy as anything the group cut, and if it's not quite as carnal as "Foxy Lady", it certainly has more than enough hormonal heat to go around.

While "Fire" boasts Hendrix's usual white-hot riffs, these are – and refreshingly, within the context of the Experience's debut LP – upbeat rather than even slightly ominous, though as urgent as they are in any of their other early classics. It's also a showcase for some of Mitchell and Redding's best work as a rhythm section, and if Mitch and Noel weren't the world's greatest backing singers, the way they egg Jimi on in the chorus can't fail to raise a grin. Hendrix comes through with the usual incendiary (though relatively brief) solo, and also tosses off one of his most likeable asides when he prefaces it with the declaration, "Move over, Rover, and let Jimi take over!" As another aside, the boast provides a further example of the fascinating combination of confidence and diffidence that Hendrix displayed in different areas of his life and art: so unsure of his singing ability that he couldn't bear to have people looking at him when he sang in the studio, he nonetheless seemed to have no trouble improvising supremely assured bragging when thrust into the spotlight.

Great songwriters often take inspiration from the most mundane of scenarios, and so it was with "Fire". The Experience's last gig of 1966 was in Redding's home town of Folkestone, and while at Noel's mother's chilly home, Jimi asked her if he could stand next to the fire – soon the catchphrase for a song in which "fire" took on an entirely different, more sexually charged meaning.

The Music

13. Third Stone from the Sun
First released on UK version of *Are You Experienced?*
12 May 1967; available on *Are You Experienced?* CD

If half a great song counts for the purposes of this survey, "Third Stone from the Sun" meets those qualifications more than any other Jimi Hendrix track. For the first part of this largely instrumental cut is both beautiful and notably different from anything else on *Are You Experienced?* The jazz influence of the early Experience was often down to Mitch Mitchell's drums, but the opening guitar-strums tingle the senses with a fingering virtually unknown in rock, justly compared to some of the ones that jazz-guitar great Wes Montgomery sometimes used to great effect. Heavier, bluesy riffs announce a shift to far more of a standard rock tempo, Jimi then taking the reins with a ringing, gates-of-the-kingdom-opening lick. If much of what Jimi did with the guitar translated the R&B-blues-soul sensibility to the psychedelic age, here he does the same for the kinds of riffs associated with surf music, or perhaps the Northwest combos like The Ventures that had been a key part of his adolescent musical education.

Uncharacteristically, on this occasion Hendrix and producer Chas Chandler couldn't let the strength of the core song speak for itself, instead adding some frankly distracting, grotesquely slowed-down spoken murmuring in the background. Even more questionably, after the stately tempo breaks stride almost halfway into this nearly seven-minute track to return to choppy jazz rhythms, Jimi abandons the quite attractive melody to run through just about every odd fuzz-burst, squeal, and howl he can extract from

his axe. Those alien, Darth Vader-at-16 RPM grumbles – most notably the sardonic "you'll never hear surf music again" – continue more or less unabated, even when Hendrix does briefly return to the grand theme near the song's end

As a showcase for Jimi at his most far-out, this definitely succeeded in one sense, wowing listeners who had never heard anything like this before, even on much else of *Are You Experienced?* But as a song, it's unfortunately dated badly in some respects, not least the forced attempt to re-create a science-fiction spaceship trip of sorts on record – something Hendrix was doing quite ably already, by drawing far more judiciously on lyrical imagery and trippy guitar effects in his more structured compositions.

14. Are You Experienced?
First released on UK version of *Are You Experienced?*
12 May 1967; available on *Are You Experienced?* CD

If "Third Stone from the Sun" can be accused of biting off more than it could chew in its pull-out-the-stops evocation of a psychedelic spaceship, the title track of *Are You Experienced?* can likewise be construed as at least a slightly self-conscious attempt at oh-so-psychedelic grooviness. But "Are You Experienced?" is more of a real *song*, even if it's less conventional than anything else on the album except "Third Stone from the Sun" itself. If the studio effects put to liberal use on the track are somewhat excessive, the song underneath it would have been rather slight and threadbare without them.

There's not much of a tune to "Are You Experienced?", and Hendrix is arguably trying a little too hard to be far-out in his constant questioning of whether we're experienced, as well as arguably a little smug in declaring that, well, *he* is. The real star of the track, however, is not the song, the singing or even the guitar playing, though of course there's much of that in the distorted, just-this-side-of-unhinged solo. The main attractions are the studio effects, especially the backwards ones that produce the scratchy, irregular percussive beats at the beginning and during the choruses. Today it sounds like a remarkable anticipation of the sound of hip-hop turntables being wiggled back and forth, especially when Jimi actually tones down his singing to a near-spoken (if addled) rap during those choruses.

As for the experience Hendrix makes so much of here, it could be sex or it could be drugs, particularly of the psychedelic sort. It could be both, given his own predilection for mixing the two and the counterculture's appetite to hear both subjects addressed more openly in songs than had seemed possible even a year or two previously. And, of course, the song's title is a pretty clever pun on the group's name, put to good use in giving their debut album a title that probably couldn't have been bettered.

15. Wild Thing
(Chip Taylor)

First released on *Historic Performances Recorded at the Monterey International Pop Festival* August 1970; available on *Live at Monterey* CD

Apart from "Hey Joe", every song on *Are You Experienced?* and the Experience's first three singles was a Hendrix original. He continued,

however, to play a good number of covers in concert, and they took up about half of the group's debut set in the US, at the Monterey Pop festival in June 1967. There were songs by Howlin' Wolf ("Killing Floor"), B.B. King ("Rock Me Baby"), Bob Dylan ("Like a Rolling Stone") – and, most famously, "Wild Thing", which not only closed the set, but ended with Jimi setting fire to, then smashing his guitar.

That might be what Hendrix's take on "Wild Thing" is most remembered for today, but it shouldn't overshadow a performance that was one of his very best and most radical interpretations, if not quite on the level of "All Along the Watchtower" and "Hey Joe". In its prior incarnation as a chart-topping hit by The Troggs, "Wild Thing" was a great record, and their own lecherous, caveman-like rendering of the tune remains the definitive one. It's no insult to The Troggs, however, to note that Hendrix turned it into something more blatantly sexual and even threatening, slowing the bump-and-grind tempo even more, adding layers of fuzzy distortion, and peeling off an out-there guitar solo which quoted from Frank Sinatra's hit "Strangers in the Night". And at the end of one of the verses, there was the memorable added aside that was pure Jimi: a cockily demure "Aw shucks, I love ya!"

To be honest, the track goes on too long on disc, dissolving in a welter of headache-inducing feedback and miscellaneous roaring. Live at Monterey, however, the same passage was mind-blowing, accompanied as it was by Hendrix's showmanship and guitar sacrifice. For that reason – and because it was the Hendrix performance featured in the *Monterey*

Pop film, seen long before the track was finally issued on vinyl in August 1970 – it must be considered as Jimi's definitive version.

16. Like a Rolling Stone
(Bob Dylan)
First released on *Historic Performances Recorded at the Monterey International Pop Festival* August 1970; available on *Live at Monterey* CD

"Like a Rolling Stone" was almost certainly a pivotal song in Jimi Hendrix's early growth as a solo artist. It was probably this song, more than any other, that gave him the confidence to sing his own material, even if this was in part due to his realization that such a track could be a huge hit even if sung by someone (Bob Dylan) who didn't have what was usually thought of as a good or pretty voice. Its success probably also fuelled his fascination with and admiration of Dylan in general, whose lyrics and attitude – if not so much his melodies and arrangements – would be a substantial influence on Hendrix's own songwriting. So it was natural for him to pay tribute to Dylan and the song by including it in his set at the Monterey Pop festival, the recording by which most people know Jimi's interpretation of the tune.

Compared to some of Hendrix's other covers – including his far more famous take on another Dylan song, "All Along the Watchtower" – "Like a Rolling Stone" is a little on the sedate and respectful side. Perhaps Jimi was still so much in awe of Dylan in general and this number in particular that he didn't feel entitled to take outrageous liberties with it. Nonetheless, it works well because Hendrix sounds comfortable making it his own, even if the adjustments are more subtle than usual. The tempo is slowed down to a funkier thump, almost recalling the beat Hendrix would give "Wild Thing" in places, though Mitch Mitchell adds busy, jazzy flourishes to help keep things tense. The guitar takes an almost fuzzed-out power-chord approach, steering clearer of overheated leads than usual. Crucially, Jimi sounds very at home inhabiting the song's lyric of alienated dislocation. If Dylan delivered the sentiments with something of a putdown, Hendrix does so with the wise chuckle of someone who's truly been without a home for many years. To paraphrase a key part of the song, he really *knows* how it feels.

17. Up from the Skies
First released on UK version of *Axis: Bold as Love* 1 December 1967; available on *Axis: Bold as Love* CD

After *Axis: Bold as Love* opened with the Martian-like voices and stormy guitar screech'n'scrawl of "EXP", many listeners must have been expecting the album to take off into outer reaches of psychedelic space that might have made the experimentalism of "Are You Experienced?" seem tame. Instead, they got a slinky, soulful groove with a hint of Mose Allison-like hipster lounge jazz, sung by Jimi in one of his sweetest timbres. The only avowedly futuristic feature was Hendrix's wah-wah, though it bends to and fro with a vivacious wink rather than being exploited as a novelty.

"Up from the Skies" is one of the Hendrix songs cited by Chas Chandler as reflecting a science-fiction influence, and although it's sung almost like a sly romantic come-on to a girl that Jimi's eyeing, there could well be some truth to Chandler's claim. Hendrix takes the guise here of a curious, well-meaning alien, descending to Earth to find out more about its peculiar residents. His claim to have lived here before the Ice Age indicates that he's revisiting a planet he once called home, though – typically for Jimi – what he finds doesn't quite live up to what he might have hoped for, with "the stars misplaced and the smell of a world that has burned". Heard early in the twenty-first century, one can't help but take his passing notice of the changing climate as an early warning bell for global warming, a concept barely on the radar when Hendrix recorded this in 1967.

Perhaps because there wasn't an obvious single from *Axis: Bold as Love* – as opposed to its predecessor *Are You Experienced?*, from which about half a dozen singles could have been culled – "Up from the Skies" was chosen as an unlikely 45 for the US market in early 1968. It barely dented the top hundred even as the album from which it was taken invaded the top ten, reinforcing the perception of Hendrix as an album-oriented artist.

18. Spanish Castle Magic

First released on UK version of *Axis: Bold as Love*
1 December 1967; available on *Axis: Bold as Love* CD

Like much of *Axis: Bold as Love*, "Spanish Castle Magic" signalled a move towards less immediately arresting material in terms of the melodies and hooks, but in some ways

towards more subtle areas that could have found Hendrix drawing more on his own emotions and experiences. The song still had plenty going for it in purely musical terms, starting with a tumultuous riff before a crafty change of tempo gave more space to more characteristic stinging, slightly venomous licks. On much of his prior material, some of his more downbeat or at least serious lyrics were somewhat cushioned by a more uplifting verve in the melodies, playing and singing. By contrast, here we have an instance where the tune is considerably more foreboding than the fantasy-laden lyrics, though to good effect.

Like some of his other more colourful songs from "Purple Haze" onward, the inspiration behind "Spanish Castle Magic" turned out to be, if not exactly ordinary, not exactly psychedelic either. It wouldn't be known by many fans for quite some time, but the Spanish Castle was an actual rock'n'roll club in which Hendrix spent time in his Seattle boyhood. It's a groovy place, Jimi still feels, and if taking half a day to get there seems like an exaggeration, it might indeed have taken a long time to get there as a teenager without access to a car.

His Seattle youth might have supplied the spark for "Spanish Castle Magic", but it's not wholly about that club, either. With its images of clouds of cotton candy and travelling by dragonfly, it might well have owed at least as much to his science-fiction reading and drug ingestion. In this respect, it's a reflection not just of his roots, but also of how very far he had travelled from them by late 1967.

The Music

19. Little Wing
First released on UK version of *Axis: Bold as Love*
1 December 1967; available on *Axis: Bold as Love* CD

Perhaps Hendrix's most beloved ballad, "Little Wing" is also the most popular song from *Axis: Bold as Love*, even as its relative lack of volume and ingenious electronics makes it arguably the record's least representative track. In the honourable tradition of "Hey Joe" and "The Wind Cries Mary", the recording gives precedence not to mind-bending ultraviolet electric-guitar rays, but deft melodious picking that could have translated well to acoustic guitar had he been so inclined. In addition, the song has a melody both beguiling and unorthodox, which like "The Wind Cries Mary" is graceful yet imbued with a fragility which suggests the mood would shatter if just an extra ounce of force was exerted. Jimi can't resist adding some of his own electric touches to the guitar work, however, putting it through a Leslie organ speaker to give it an attractively wavering quality. The use of glockenspiel is also crucial to suffusing the cut with a warm glow.

Hendrix's lyrics are uncommonly brief, but memorable for painting one of his most romantic (and some would say idealized) portraits of a woman. She's a woman, though, who might be too good to be true, or at least one so unselfish as to be unlikely to be found in Jimi's real life, giving him a thousand smiles for free and telling him "you can take anything you want from me". There's enough gaudy imagery to satisfy the psychedelic crowd as well, what with her ability to walk through clouds and her "circus mind" full of various visionary fauna.

Very few artists have been able to cover a Jimi Hendrix song so memorably that their version became nearly as well known and respected as the original. "Little Wing" proved an exception when Derek and the Dominos (led by Eric Clapton) put it on their 1970 *Layla* album, with Stevie Ray Vaughan's subsequent interpretation also garnering its share of admirers.

20. If Six Was Nine
First released on UK version of *Axis: Bold as Love*
1 December 1967; available on *Axis: Bold as Love* CD

"If Six Was Nine" was one of the first songs on which recording was started for *Axis: Bold as Love*, which might explain why it sounds more like something from *Are You Experienced?* than anything else on Hendrix's second LP. There's a crunching riff at the outset that immediately worms its way into your brain, an abundance of imaginatively varied, far-out guitar soloing and some radically subversive lyrics, Jimi embracing upside-down reality and an anti-authoritarian ethos with almost exhibitionistic relish when he pledges to wave his "freak flag high, high". Noel Redding's grunting bass and some of Mitch Mitchell's most adventurously boisterous, jazzy drumming are only too glad to join a party as raunchy as it is whimsical, although things threaten to get out of hand when the track disintegrates into near-noise at the end, Hendrix adding to the chaos by putting his two shillings in on a cheap Indian flute (which cost him precisely that sum to buy).

At a time when even the merest allusion to a certain sexual position was taboo, the title of "If Six Was Nine" couldn't help but bring a knowing wink to the eyes of those looking to find hidden (or not-so-hidden) meanings in the works of their psychedelic heroes. But it was just as, if not more likely that it reflected Hendrix's interest in numerology, Jimi being (like John Lennon) enamoured of the number nine in particular.

"If Six Was Nine", incidentally, very nearly didn't make it to record, at least in the form we now know and love. When Hendrix misplaced the master tapes for half the album shortly before it was due for completion, re-creating the original mix for this song in particular proved especially difficult. Fortunately Noel Redding had a rough mix at home, although Eddie Kramer had to physically iron out the tape's wrinkles before it could pass through the studio's equipment.

The Experience in their prime, 1968

21. Have You Ever Been (To Electric Ladyland)

First released on US version of *Electric Ladyland*
16 October 1968; available on *Electric Ladyland* CD

Hendrix's guitar playing often showed the influence of Curtis Mayfield, especially on his lower-key numbers. "Have You Ever Been (To Electric Ladyland)", however, shows Mayfield's influence extending to Jimi's singing and songwriting as well, while the vocal harmonies recall those of the group Mayfield led in the 1960s, The Impressions. Indeed, with the possible exception of a few psychedelic touches in the treatment of Hendrix's guitar and in the phasing on Mitchell's drums, it could have been recorded by many a soul vocal group in the late 1960s, though probably only the more adventurous ones would have taken a crack at it.

If the mood of the song is nothing out of the ordinary (if unusually lights-down romantic) for Hendrix, typically the words aren't exactly the kind that would be found in most soul songs of the era, even in the writing of innovative composers like Mayfield. In Jimi's worldview, the divisions between romance, music and fantasy were often fluid, and so it is here, with references to a magic carpet, "electric" women, making love as angels spread their wings, and good and evil "lying side by side while electric love penetrates the sky". Like many of Hendrix's visions, it was a scenario conspicuously removed from real life, Jimi's music being about as close as many of his fans (or Hendrix himself) could come to actually experiencing it.

The Music

The track marks a rare venture by Hendrix into falsetto vocals, on which he acquits himself surprisingly well. Supposedly it was this track that finally convinced Jimi that he really could sing, well over a year into his solo career. If so, it's a little surprising that he didn't use his upper vocal range more in the final two years of his life. It counts as one of many directions – and one of the least noted of such directions – that he might possibly have had more room to explore had he lived longer.

22. Crosstown Traffic
First released on US version of *Electric Ladyland*
16 October 1968; available on *Electric Ladyland* CD

The catchiest, poppiest item on *Electric Ladyland*, "Crosstown Traffic" marked something of a return – to those who had been paying attention to the somewhat more serious direction in which Hendrix's material was heading after *Are You Experienced?* – to Jimi's happiest, most exuberant side. Okay, the lyrics aren't among Hendrix's most profound and once again express the "don't cramp my style" attitude which might be among Jimi's less endearing attributes (at least insofar as it informed his relationships with women). The music, though, is irresistible, bursting with hooks that don't, refreshingly, rely on Hendrix's trademark hard-rock guitar riffs. Instead, the big attraction is an infectious chorus, along with chirping, downright giddy backing harmonies by Mitchell and Jimi's friend Dave Mason from Traffic.

"Crosstown Traffic" is also Hendrix's best fusion of soul and rock, and one of his best vocal performances of any sort, brimming with both humour and confidence. A macho confidence, perhaps, but from the viewpoint of pure pop craft, the mix of romantic and traffic metaphors is clever and essentially good-natured. So is the evocation of an actual traffic jam with the impatiently beeping interjections and stop-start beats, as is Hendrix's use of a kazoo to double his guitar line.

It remains something of a mystery as to why "Crosstown Traffic" wasn't a sizable hit single. It was issued as an American 45 right in the wake of the chart-topping *Electric Ladyland*, yet only managed to reach number 52 in the US listings, doing only a little better (peaking at number 37) when it came out in the UK a few months later. But it wasn't too long before it was about as popular as a genuine hit single anyway, and in mid-1969 it was included on the first American Hendrix best-of, *Smash Hits*.

23. 1983… (A Merman I Should Turn to Be)
First released on US version of *Electric Ladyland*
16 October 1968; available on *Electric Ladyland* CD

Of all the Hendrix songs (as opposed to live performances) that crash through the five-minute barrier – and if you throw out all the jams he recorded, there are fewer of them than is commonly thought – the thirteen-minute "1983… (A Merman I Should Turn to Be)" is the finest. This doesn't mean that it's without its self-indulgent aspects. But these are more than compensated for by the pure majesty of its principal riffs, especially the central anthemic one that sounds as though it's heralding some mixture of the Messiah and the Apocalypse. If Hendrix was ever able to make his guitar speak in a language that approximated the specificity and subtlety of actual words, this might be the closest he came to doing it.

Not all of "1983" is for everyone. From its opening mixture of gorgeous folk-rockish balladeering and martial drum patterns, the track soon melts into rather murky, swampy, eerie noise – like the soundtrack for a psychedelic journey to Atlantis – which, indeed, Jimi hears "full of cheer" by the end of the track. While the voyage has moments of beauty, it also taxes the listener's patience: the section dominated by Mitchell's free-jazz drumming in particular causes one's attention to drift, even as it increases Hendrix's standing among those who view him as something as a frustrated jazzman. For all its spaced-out sprawl, however, the song also has elements of earthiness, most notably in some passages which roughly approximate the sweet soul that Hendrix had been playing behind some singers just two or three years previously, albeit here with a somewhat otherworldly tilt. As for the occasionally near-indecipherable lyrics of "1983" – fifteen years into an unimaginable future when this was recorded in 1968 – these seem to be informed by Jimi's love of fantasy and science fiction, as well as by a certain idyllic romanticism that sees him and his lady reborn as a merman and mermaid respectively after escaping from a war-torn earth in a submarine-like ship for two.

Some might contend that "1983" should be judged as part of a suite with the much shorter cuts that bookend it, "Rainy Day, Dream Away" and "Moon, Turn the Tides... Gently Gently Away". But "1983" is listed as a separate track on the album, and is certainly the centrepiece of this trio of tunes, as well as being the most outstanding by a clear margin.

24. Still Raining, Still Dreaming

First released on US version of *Electric Ladyland*
16 October 1968; available on *Electric Ladyland* CD

Almost as if to jolt us back to earth, "Still Raining, Still Dreaming" is positioned as the cut right after the "1983"-dominated suite on *Electric Ladyland*. (The jolt's much more jarring on CD, where it follows after a gap of a mere second or two, than it was on the original double LP, where you had to flip the record over between the tracks.) This is actually the unofficial second part or continuation of "Rainy Day, Dream Away", yet hits a more solid groove than its prequel.

Again Hendrix makes effective use of the guitar as an extension of the human voice here, especially when his wah-wah comes close to emulating the kind of exclamations of surprise and delight you might hear from real live human beings. Session guest Mike Finnigan excels on jazz-blues organ, which in combination with Hendrix's futuristic guitar makes you feel like you're in a smoky bar that's somehow mutated into a spaceship, hurtling through the heavens as the patrons mix their drinks with particularly potent tabs of acid. It was a juke joint, however, missing two of its usual mainstays, this and "Rainy Day, Dream Away"

The Music

being the first Experience recordings in which neither Mitchell nor Redding participated.

It's a little unfortunate that Jimi didn't devote more attention to developing the lyrical side of "Still Raining, Still Dreaming". His jubilant singing at the track's outset is delightful, as is his unflappable why-worry attitude toward the rain, so often the signifier of sad and troubled times in popular music, yet celebrated here as something that should be allowed to "groove its own way". But as Chas Chandler noted on numerous occasions after Hendrix's death, this was a time when Jimi was less focused on standard songs and getting more into an improvisational groove. The jam that "Still Raining, Still Dreaming" develops into is certainly groovy enough, with more quasi-talking wah-wah and brotherly chants to keep the mood swinging. There's still the sense, however, that it could have been something more, or at least embellished with more thoughtful words.

25. All Along the Watchtower
(Bob Dylan)
First released on US version of *Electric Ladyland* 16 October 1968; available on *Electric Ladyland* CD

There have been a lot of good Bob Dylan covers over the last four decades or so, some of which can fairly be said to be both about as good as the originals and reworkings that bring a fresh perspective on the material. Very few, however, can be fairly said to absolutely slay the original in quality. One that does is Jimi Hendrix's "All Along the Watchtower", which immediately replaced Dylan's original

as the definitive rendition, even though it was issued less than a year later.

As one of the highlights on Dylan's *John Wesley Harding* album, "All Along the Watchtower" was acceptably urgent and apocalyptic, if a little bare-boned and muted. Hendrix, however, pulled no punches in making it into a hard-rock missive, starting with the burst of mournful power-chords – set to a steam-hammer rhythm not found anywhere in the original – that starts his version. Followed immediately by a hypnotic percussive rattle, the mood turns yet darker with some frenzied soloing before Jimi cools things down to sing the verse. But even in its quieter moments, Hendrix's "All Along the Watchtower" connects the song's almost biblical sense of impending catastrophe to the contemporary social turmoil of 1968, especially in the solo's creepy, weeping, swooping slides. Combined with Jimi's dependably heartfelt vocal, the song is transformed from a sentinel's warning into the desperate howl of a drowning man after the hurricane has descended, emitting shrieks of rage as the chaos engulfs him.

As with "Crosstown Traffic", the concise, hook-and-lyric-driven power of "All Along the Watchtower" was a little anomalous in the context of *Electric Ladyland*, which on the whole was considerably more experimental. But like "Crosstown Traffic", it was crucial to the record's balance, serving as a reminder that Hendrix could still deliver a focused rock classic in which the song and not the playing ruled supreme.

The Music

26. Voodoo Child (Slight Return)
First released on US version of *Electric Ladyland*
16 October 1968; available on *Electric Ladyland* CD

One of Hendrix's most noted excursions into blues-rock (albeit blues-rock of a highly futuristic and experimental sort), "Voodoo Child (Slight Return)" leads off with one of his most famous guitar manipulations. Somewhat in the same fashion as the wah-wah that starts "Still Raining, Still Dreaming", these have a talking quality. But here, instead of being mere expressions of surprise and delight, it's almost as though they're conversational. That relatively subdued intro dispensed with, he and the band then hurl themselves into a churning, gut-wrenching extended instrumental section with one of Jimi's most dead-on facsimiles of a bomb dropping from the sky – although he would outdo himself in this respect shortly afterward on "The Star Spangled Banner".

Yet once Hendrix starts singing, he reaches back in spirit to the 1950s electric blues that had been so crucial to launching his enthusiasm for listening to and playing music. Strip away the heavy guitars – *really* heavy, probably heavier than any previous Hendrix recording – and the volcanic rhythm section, and you'd have something that isn't too different from a vintage Muddy Waters classic like "Rollin' Stone". While Jimi's references to voodoo here and in other songs (including, of course, another cut on *Electric Ladyland*, "Voodoo Chile") could be seen as evidence of some kind of belief in supernatural powers, it should be remembered that voodoo was often referenced in blues and R&B before Hendrix came along, notably on another song popularized by Waters, "Got My Mojo Working". So here again, underneath all the bluster, Hendrix can be fairly viewed as continuing a long and venerable R&B tradition, though with far more heavy-metal thunder than any of his predecessors.

Some feel that "Voodoo Child (Slight Return)" can't be discussed in isolation from its companion cut of sorts, the roughly similar fifteen-minute "Voodoo Chile" (where the influence of Muddy Waters is even more apparent). But without underselling the appeal of the longer track's liquid grooves, "Voodoo Child (Slight Return)" is simply more focused and a far more powerful showcase for Hendrix's innovative guitar work, as recognized by a British public that sent it to number one when it was issued as a single shortly after Jimi's death.

27. The Star Spangled Banner
(Francis Scott Key and John Stafford Smith)
First released on *Woodstock* soundtrack June 1970;
available on *Live at Woodstock* CD

Jimi Hendrix performed "The Star Spangled Banner" live on numerous occasions, and even recorded a multi-track studio version with no instrumentation other than his guitar. By far his most famous rendition of the song, however, is the one he did at the Woodstock festival in August 1969, which became a cornerstone of both the *Woodstock* film and its bestselling soundtrack. As such, this must be considered his definitive performance of the US national

The Music

anthem, in spite (or perhaps because) of the fact that it was played under challenging, even dispiriting conditions which made the rest of his Woodstock set highly erratic.

The value of Hendrix's interpretation of "The Star Spangled Banner" certainly doesn't lie in its fidelity to the original, which has been sung (often quite badly) at so many official occasions as to test the patience of the most patriotic American. It's what Jimi does with it that matters. When he sticks to the main tune, he gives it a ringing sting that one imagines could have been heard for miles. And when he departs from the official melody – which is often – he summons up a maelstrom that skirts the border between heavy rock and white noise, re-creating bursting bombs and fireworks with industrial-strength volume. The chaotic violence of some of those passages, however, seemed not so much a celebration of American military glory as a condemnation of the random, meaningless havoc it wreaked, particularly on Vietnam.

For many years available primarily on the *Woodstock* soundtrack, "The Star Spangled Banner" can now be heard with most of the rest of Hendrix's set on the two-disc *Live at Woodstock* CD, or better still, in tandem with the visuals on the DVD of the same name.

28. Machine Gun
First released on US version of *Band of Gypsys*, 25 March 1970; available on *Band of Gypsys* CD

By far the most popular of the few songs Hendrix unveiled on the *Band of Gypsys* album, "Machine Gun" can be viewed as a continuation of the anti-war commentary he

had made, if only by inference, with "The Star Spangled Banner". Musically, however, it's more of a cousin to "Voodoo Child (Slight Return)", with a similar instrumental intro in which the guitar almost seems to be offering an amused spoken monologue. The body of the song is, again like "Voodoo Child (Slight Return)", surprisingly close to traditional blues in some ways, although this is blues for the post-modern era in its ear-splitting volume and twisted buzzing guitar riffs.

Yet the mood of "Machine Gun" is decidedly more malevolent than "Voodoo Child (Slight Return)", beginning with its disquieting rat-a-tat rhythms. And while "Voodoo Child (Slight Return)" is more or less a celebration of our hero's mystical powers, "Machine Gun" is despondent in its fatalism, if somewhat defiant in places. This doesn't just apply to the lyrics, which bewail evil forces shooting Jimi down repeatedly and tearing his "family" apart – perhaps a veiled reference to his African-American brothers, dying in Vietnam in numbers hugely disproportionate to their share of the US population. Much of the soloing depicts the carnage as vividly as any visuals could, with more rapid-fire machine-gun imitations and panoramic effects raining down like hails of bullets, though here (unlike on "The Star Spangled Banner") it's grounded by a real, if basic, Mitch Mitchell–Billy Cox rhythm section. But Jimi doesn't take the assault lying down, and when he announces "I pick up my axe and fight like a bomber", you can't help but think his "axe" is his guitar, now not a mere vehicle for entertainment but a lethal weapon.

"Machine Gun" is usually assumed to be a protest of sorts against the Vietnam War, an impression reinforced by Jimi's onstage dedications of the number to soldiers fighting in Vietnam. But Hendrix also seemed to intend the song as a protest against all pointless death, extending his dedications to soldiers fighting in all wars, as well as students protesting at universities. At a more personal, metaphorical level, his introduction to the song on the *Live at Berkeley* CD, recorded in May 1970, dedicates it "to other people who might be fighting wars within themselves".

29. Dolly Dagger

First released on *Rainbow Bridge* October 1971; available on *First Rays of the New Rising Sun* CD

"Dolly Dagger" was intended as Jimi Hendrix's next single at the time of his death, though as with many things over the last couple of years of his life, he might well have changed his mind or decided that it wasn't ready before the pressing plants actually got to work. Had he gone through with the plan, it's hard to say if it would have restored him to the upper reaches of the pop charts. It's certainly not as immediately compelling as "All Along the Watchtower", the last single in his lifetime to manage that feat.

But "Dolly Dagger" is undeniably catchier and more upbeat than almost anything else he had recorded since *Electric Ladyland*, and marks a return of his zest for fusing soul with relatively straightforward rock'n'roll. Some of the more mainstream Hendrix fans, if that's not a contradiction in terms, would have also welcomed the return of the biting blues-rock riffs that had characterized much of his earlier work. They would have also been pleased by the infectiously choppy rhythms, a memorable chorus and sweetly wailing background harmonies, supplied by Jimi's old friends Arthur and Albert Allen. Even the extended soloing is relatively economical and to-the-point by late-Hendrix standards, although the extended fade is too long, a sin plenty of other major rockers were guilty of in the early 1970s.

If some of Hendrix's songs can in retrospect be accused of having more than their share of macho braggadocio, here the tables seem to have turned. "Dolly Dagger" is no passive wallflower, her charms not so much seducing all who come her way as bulldozing them into submission. "This chick's gonna turn you to a block of ice", he warns. "Look out!" It's now well known that sometime-girlfriend Devon Wilson was the inspiration for the song, and there's a hint of malice in the references to her being a kind of vampiric witch. Yet the way Jimi sings the tune, oddly enough, conveys more good-natured admiration than fear or mistrust.

30. Angel

First released on US version of *The Cry of Love* 5 March 1971; available on *First Rays of the New Rising Sun* CD

"Angel" was not intended as a farewell statement, although the recording of the song with which most listeners are familiar was made just a couple of months before Hendrix's death. He had actually first started writing the tune quite a while before that, as the existence of an October 1967 demo confirms. Heard today, however, its ghostly, valedictory air seems like a grand farewell to earthly existence, and a hope for a better, less troubled one in the afterlife. From the soothing opening chords, it sounds as if Jimi is finally attaining some peace within himself, though we now know that artistic and business problems were raging just as hard as ever when he returned to the song in the summer of 1970.

The verses are on a par with "Little Wing" and "The Wind Cries Mary" as illustrations of Jimi's rather under-utilized talent for tuneful ballads. Where "Angel" really grabs you, however, is in the chorus. When he sings "fly on, my sweet angel, fly on through the sky", it's as anthemic a passage as anything Hendrix penned, but also as graceful as his more cel-ebrated rockers were hard-hitting. The eerie, heavenly ambiance is enhanced by the slight echo on Jimi's voice, as well as a fade-out that unexpectedly breaks into a gallop as the melody arches ever higher, as if Hendrix himself is ascending through the clouds, capped by a climactic wash of Mitch Mitchell cymbals.

Who is the benign angel that Jimi gently urges to fly on, and to come back for him tomorrow? Most speculation has identified her as his departed mother Lucille, with whom he seems to have felt a kinship despite her inadequacies as a parent. If it's based on any woman with whom he was romantically involved, there aren't any specific clues. Perhaps it's an ode to the woman he was looking for to quell his many demons, but seemed unable to find on this particular planet.

Part 3:
Hendrixology

Hendrix on Film

Just as hardly anyone suspected how much unissued music awaited release when Jimi Hendrix died in September 1970, few had any idea how much video footage of the musician would eventually become available. At the time of his death, the only real opportunities most of the world had had to see Hendrix on screen were his relatively brief appearances in the documentaries of the Monterey Pop and Woodstock festivals. Residents of the United Kingdom, and to a lesser extent some European countries, had been fortunate to see him perform on television occasionally from late 1966 on. In the United States, however, his TV appearances were limited to just a few spots on network programmes shortly before his death.

Fortunately, both lengthy concerts and shorter performances were being filmed and preserved almost all along. Had he lived just a little longer, in fact, Hendrix himself would probably have been involved in the making of concert films/documentaries for distribution in cinemas and other outlets – something being done by relatively few rock acts at the time, The Beatles' *Let It Be* being a notable exception. Back in February 1969, Hendrix's concerts at the Royal Albert Hall were filmed for that very purpose, although the movie that was planned didn't come out at the time (and still remains unseen). Footage of Hendrix performing in Maui, meanwhile, provided the centrepiece of the *Rainbow Bridge* movie in 1971, while in the same year his May 1970 concerts in Berkeley formed the basis for the first all-Jimi film, *Jimi Plays Berkeley*. The first Hendrix documentary followed two years later, in 1973.

Although it seems unlikely that anyone was thinking of it at the time, Hendrix's appearances at the Monterey, Woodstock and Isle of Wight festivals proved a godsend after his death, providing enough footage from the films of those events to eventually construct full-length DVDs based around Jimi's sets. And there was enough material from other sources to put together documentaries and other compilations of footage, or even films that combined the two formats. These not only preserve the music that Jimi played before the cameras, but also his flamboyant stage persona, astonishing technical guitar wizardry, gymnastic onstage athleticism and colourful psychedelic clothes, scarves and headbands of eye-bruising intensity. And since Hendrix died so young, he's forever preserved on celluloid as a young god at the peak of his physical powers – yet another factor in propagating his legend with undimmed brightness over the course of several decades.

Concert Films

The Jimi Hendrix Experience: Live at Monterey

D.A. Pennebaker and Chris Hegedus, 2007; MCA/
Experience Hendrix DVD

Considering Jimi Hendrix was virtually unknown in the United States when he played Monterey, it's fortunate that the documentary director D.A. Pennebaker and his crew had the presence of mind to keep the camera running during most of his set. Unfortunately, not quite all of the concert was captured, as technical difficulties evidently prevented "Can You See Me" from being recorded satisfactorily. The rest of it's here, though, and it's incredibly exciting in all visual and musical respects – not to mention the outrageous, psychedelically coloured finery, complete with ruffled shirts and pink feather boa, with which Hendrix took the stage. Some of his tongue wagging and guitar straddling here is just as outrageous in its sexual overtness, even for an event at which free love was the byword. And, most famously, you get to see Jimi set fire to his guitar for the finale, "Wild Thing" – an image, inevitably, selected for the cover of both the DVD and its CD counterpart.

This material was first issued for the home video market as *Jimi Plays Monterey* on VHS in the mid-1980s, with a frankly asinine introductory sequence in which someone does an action painting of Hendrix's image as the Monterey version of "Can You See Me" plays on the soundtrack. Better, though a bit puzzling in this context, is the addition of a performance of "Sgt. Pepper's Lonely Hearts Club Band" from an uncredited source (not the Monterey Pop festival) in the opening scenes. A Criterion Collection DVD issued in 2002 in conjunction with Otis Redding's Monterey set added a short interview about the festival with Pete Townshend and optional commentary from British music journalist Charles Shaar Murray, who makes much of Hendrix's adaptation of R&B/soul music and showmanship to his power-trio format. The disc is also available as part of a highly recommended three-DVD *Monterey Pop* box set, which also includes the original film, a whole DVD of outtakes from performances by other artists and various other extras.

That's not the end of the story, however, as the major addition to the Experience Hendrix catalogue in 2007 was *The Jimi Hendrix Experience: Live at Monterey*. This presents all the existing footage of the set in its original sequence, including "Purple Haze", missing from previous versions due to some technical imperfections; an interactive feature that lets you switch between multiple, previously unseen camera angles; documentary segments before and after the concert footage, including interview material with Hendrix, Mitch Mitchell and Noel Redding; a look at the festival itself with its co-founder, Lou Adler; and, not least, the earliest known live Experience footage – of "Like a Rolling

Hendrixology

Stone" and "Stone Free", in somewhat primitive, lo-fi black and white – from February 1967. Although the still available Criterion Collection version is hardly a disgrace, this fully restored and expanded edition has to be the top recommendation for both quality and quantity of content.

Live at Woodstock

MCA/Experience Hendrix DVD, 2005

As at Monterey, it turned out that most of Hendrix's Woodstock performance had been filmed for the documentary of the festival, although only a short section was used. This DVD puts all of the complete numbers that survive – which amount to the vast majority of the set – in their original performance sequence, adding up to well over an hour of brightly coloured footage, very skilfully shot and edited (although the film crew was almost running on empty by the time Hendrix went onstage and nearly missed "The Star Spangled Banner" when they reloaded their cameras). The DVD cover shot makes it plain that there was still a large crowd when Hendrix took the stage, even though many had left the festival by that time.

Although **The Star Spangled Banner** dwarfs everything else here, Hendrix was actually in pretty good, energetic form, not to mention very stylishly dressed in a fringed jacket, red headband and earring. The problems were more in the over-large, somewhat disorganized backing band, and it's a little surreal to watch the sextet and pretty much only be

able to hear Hendrix and Mitch Mitchell. Extraneous percussionist Jerry Velez leaps about and mugs quite distractedly, and there's some undisciplined jamming (especially on the lengthy instrumentals). But if you're stacking it up against the two DVDs featuring 1970 performances, it's more historic than *Jimi Plays Berkeley*

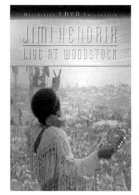

A stylish Jimi flashes the Woodstock crowd the peace sign on the cover of the *Live at Woodstock* DVD.

and not as much of an endurance test as *Live at the Isle of Wight*.

The 2005 DVD release is a two-disc set, the first of which presents the principal feature, with additional interview material with some of the participants providing some opening and closing context. The second disc features a black-and-white amateur videotape of much the same material, which is relatively inessential, but interesting for its different angles and the inclusion of one song, "Hear My Train A Comin'", that's not on the main programme. The second disc also has footage from a 3 September 1969 press conference in Harlem and interviews with Billy Cox, Larry Lee and engineer Eddie Kramer recorded specially for this package.

Hendrixology

Jimi Hendrix: The Dick Cavett Show

Bob Smeaton, 2002; MCA/Experience Hendrix DVD

Even with the addition of a 55-minute documentary produced especially for this DVD, this disc is kind of skimpy, coming close to being a "for-fans-only" release. Yes, it has the entirety of both of Hendrix's appearances on Dick Cavett's US network TV chat show (in July and September of 1969), but that only adds up to about half an hour, even counting Cavett's opening comic monologues (in which Hendrix didn't participate). Since much of that footage is repeated in the documentary (which intersperses snippets with latter-day interviews with Cavett, Billy Cox and Mitch Mitchell), it leaves the impression of something that's been padded pretty heavily to pass muster as a full-length production.

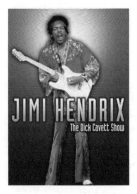

The colourful outfit Hendrix wears on the cover of *The Dick Cavett Show* was fairly typical for Jimi, but pretty shocking for a 1969 network TV chat-show guest.

Still, for the more serious Hendrix fan, it's a nice opportunity to look at two of his few major US television spots, in which he comes off as a wittily hip, if somewhat nervous and exhausted figure (especially in the September 1969 clip, where Cavett acknowledges that Jimi's left early after complaining about not feeling well). There's also some live music too, though Jimi's not at his best on the July performance of "Hear My Train A Comin'" (in which he's backed, incredibly, by the Cavett show's house band) and the September versions of "Izabella" and "Machine Gun" (backed by a slightly ragged unit of Mitchell, Cox and percussionist Juma Sultan). The florid shirt he wears in the shot used on the cover might seem like just another Jimi outfit, but was still a pretty strange sight for many of the Middle American viewers who tuned into the show without any warning as to what to expect.

Jimi Plays Berkeley

Peter Pilafian, 1971; MCA/Experience Hendrix DVD

The very first film to feature Jimi Hendrix as its principal subject, *Jimi Plays Berkeley*, shot at two concerts on 30 May 1970, is a bit of a disappointment these days. First, at 49 minutes, it's hardly a full-length production, which meant that after its release, it was sometimes shown on a double bill with *Rainbow Bridge*. In fact there was little choice but to issue it as such, since there wasn't enough film, or a large enough crew, to take all that much footage. So don't get your hopes up for an expanded edition adding new songs – if the raw material existed, it would almost certainly have come out by now.

Indeed, even to flesh it out to just under fifty minutes, the filmmakers resorted to cutting in some mildly distracting and largely irrelevant scenes of political protests at Berkeley, one of which shows a picket demonstrating against the outrageous ticket prices – $3.50, actually a pretty substantial sum in 1970 – for the then-new *Woodstock* movie. Why? Because *we* made it, insists a young woman in her belief that the counterculture is being exploited for profit, as though the filmmakers and performers at the event had relatively little to do with making the Woodstock movie a reality.

Despite performing on a rather dimly lit stage, however, Hendrix acquits himself pretty well, although he's not quite as animated as he had been in his slightly younger days. Certainly the charge through Chuck Berry's "Johnny B. Goode" is a highlight, both because Jimi rarely played it live and because his rendition is genuinely excellent. "I Don't Live Today", "Machine Gun" and "The Star Spangled Banner" are also fine, and nothing in the set's a turkey.

Note, however, that what you hear on the film soundtrack is *not* the same as the CD titled *Live at Berkeley*. The CD presents the second set of the night in its entirety, including some songs not in the film; the film mixes performances from both nights, and has some songs (including "Johnny B. Goode") not on the CD. The covers are even different, the DVD showing a moody Jimi dressed in blue from top to bottom, the CD sporting a poster of the gig. If you want it all in one place and have the equipment to hear it to full advantage, the DVD thoughtfully adds the recordings from *Live at Berkeley* as an audio-only bonus.

Rainbow Bridge

Chuck Wein, 1971; Rhino DVD

Jaw-droppingly awful in a stranger-than-fiction-like way, this incredibly disjointed, amateurishly acted/improvised scenario of hippies dropping out to get it together in Hawaii does nonetheless qualify as a Jimi Hendrix concert film by the barest of margins. For its one redeeming feature is the seventeen-minute segment in which Hendrix, Mitch Mitchell and Billy Cox play live before a few hundred free spirits in the windy Maui mountains. Well, almost live – Mitchell had to re-record many of his drum parts later because of technical problems. But Hendrix does manage a credibly energetic performance in spite of the chaos, highlighted by "Foxy Lady" and a clip in which a sluggish "Hear My Train

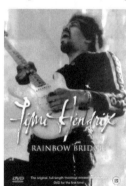

A Comin'" revs up into "Voodoo Child (Slight Return)". (Some entirely different Hendrix studio recordings are heard throughout the rest of the film on the soundtrack.)

Unfortunately you do have to sit through most of the movie before you get to that point, an ordeal prolonged by the 2000 DVD version, which restores the film to its

Not quite forgotten: the prominence of Hendrix in text and image in the cover design makes manifest the reason for *Rainbox Bridge*'s release on DVD.

Hendrix and his road manager Eric Barrett arrive at
Heathrow Airport en route to the Isle of Wight festival,
27 August 1970

original 125-minute length (and unsurprisingly has a picture of Hendrix caught in full flight on the cover). Jimi also has a small "acting" part in the film in which he "raps" with some of the local hippies. He's mediocre and incoherent in his role, but this is where the abject quality of the surrounding film turns out to be a blessing in disguise, as he doesn't so much stand out as an amateur as fit right in with the rest of the cast.

Blue Wild Angel: Jimi Hendrix Live at the Isle of Wight

Murray Lerner, 2002; MCA/Experience Hendrix DVD

Although an official live recording of Hendrix at the Isle of Wight festival on 31 August 1970 came out within a year of his death, it took until 1997 for Murray Lerner's film documentary of the event to be released. And it took another five years after that for this DVD of Jimi's performance to be issued, coinciding with a complete CD release of the audio portion.

Much has been made of Hendrix's tormented state of mind at this point, and certainly some of this comes across in his onstage manner throughout this almost exhaustively long disc. Part of it might have been down to impatience and annoyance at the sonic gremlins that afflicted the onstage equipment, most amusingly when security announcements somehow come through something-or-other during a marathon twenty-minute-

plus "Machine Gun". There are also some imperfections in the film itself, shot by a crew exhausted by the demands of the multi-day extravaganza.

But considering the less-than-ideal conditions, it's a fairly well-filmed, well-played document of the Hendrix-Mitchell-Cox line-up – the last such one ever made, though they did play a few more shows after this. Jimi does consciously seem to be cutting back on his showmanship much of the time – when he suddenly breaks into his usual routines for "Foxy Lady", it's almost as though he's pushed a "give the people what they want" button for a few obligatory minutes. (Check how he grins a sigh of relief after wandering behind the amps to make sure his trousers haven't split during this number.) Otherwise the camera catches him introducing new material like "Dolly Dagger" with a certain grim determination, and there are some really long solos throughout the programme that will test some less devoted viewers. His displeasure with the way things were going (though probably primarily with the sound problems) catch up with him at the end, when he mumbles "peace and happiness and all that other bullshit" before disgruntledly dropping his guitar onstage as he takes his leave.

Note that the DVD, long as it is, doesn't quite include the whole concert, omitting three songs that appear on the CD. It does, however, add some context-setting interview material with Mitchell, Cox and others in the introductory segment, as well as a bonus feature interview with Murray Lerner.

Documentaries

A Film About Jimi Hendrix

Joe Boyd, John Head and Gary Weis, 1973; Warner Home Video DVD

Simply titled *Jimi Hendrix* when it was first released in 1973, this nearly two-hour documentary has fielded its share of criticism for not probing deeply enough into the man's complexities, not having paid enough tribute to all his multi-dimensional talents, not being too slickly filmed or edited, and so on. Yet now that it's not the primary source of Hendrix on film either in terms of historical analysis or concert footage, it holds up as a valuable if flawed overview of his life and music. The cover of the DVD is as minimal as its title, showing Jimi playing the blues against a plain white backdrop.

Its chief strength is its wealth of **interviews**, not only with key associates like Mitch Mitchell, Billy Cox, Buddy Miles and Eddie Kramer, but also with important secondary figures in the Hendrix saga like Linda Keith, Fayne Pridgeon, Pete Townshend and a wildly entertaining Little Richard. If much more has been uncovered by subsequent biographers (and not

DELUXE EDITION

a film about JIMI HENDRIX

The cover of *A Film About Jimi Hendrix* is as minimal as its title, showing Jimi playing the blues against a plain white backdrop.

much is divulged by Monika Dannemann in her brief screen time), these have the advantages of being fresher recollections, filmed not long after Jimi's death. The musical footage is oddly disappointing – even with clips from Monterey and Woodstock, it doesn't come close to sampling the full scope of his work – but that's not such a problem now that so much more is available on other DVDs.

For its own DVD release, an additional hour-long film included previously unavailable 1972 interview footage with many of the talking heads featured in the original movie. Also tacked on were a performance of "Stone Free" from the 1970 Atlanta Pop festival and Eddie Kramer breaking down the mix of "Dolly Dagger".

Experience

Peter Neal, 2001; MCA/Experience Hendrix DVD

The most meagre of the major Hendrix DVDs currently on the market uses as its centrepiece a colour pseudo-documentary, *Experience*, apparently originally titled *See My Music Talking* and filmed for a TV programme around late 1967 (the packaging gives away nothing in terms of details). Running at a little under half an hour, it combines interview fragments (including some excruciatingly gimmicky bits where Redding and Mitchell ask Hendrix deliberately clichéd questions) and some very dated sequences where Experience studio recordings are used on the soundtrack to accompany vaguely psychedelic images of British life; "Foxy Lady", for example, is heard while a red-haired young woman flits around the streets.

What it does have, fortunately, is cinematically raw but acceptably exciting clips of the Experience playing "Purple Haze" and "Wild Thing" in Blackpool, as well as one of Hendrix playing an acoustic version of "Hear My Train a Comin'" solo against a white backdrop (this was later used in the *Jimi Hendrix* documentary discussed above).

Fortunately, the 2001 DVD release – using the murkiest cover art of any major Hendrix video product – adds more than forty minutes of bonus material which is unrelated to the *Experience* film, but puts some good live Experience clips into circulation. Among these are "The Wind Cries Mary" and "Purple Haze" in Stockholm in May 1967; "Wild Thing" in Paris in October of the same year; and – again in Stockholm – "Red House" and "Sunshine of Your Love" from January 1969, by which time there's a palpable decline of enthusiasm in the band. A 1997 video for "Dolly Dagger", however, is irrelevant.

Jimi Hendrix: Electric Ladyland

Roger Pomphrey, 1997; Eagle Rock Entertainment DVD

As part of the long-running "Classic Albums" video series, this is a fine, straight-ahead hour-long documentary on the making of *Electric Ladyland*. All of the most important surviving contributors to the LP were interviewed, including Noel Redding, Mitch Mitchell, Chas Chandler, Eddie Kramer and session guests Jack Casady, Dave Mason and Stevie Winwood. More surprisingly, and satisfyingly, some more obscure but interesting characters with a role in the story also get their say, including session organist Mike Finnigan and the photographer of the notorious UK "naked ladies" sleeve, David Montgomery, who tells the story of getting his subjects to bare all for a few extra pounds with rather seedy relish. (Unsurprisingly, the cover of the DVD itself chooses the image from the US sleeve, not the UK one.)

Also included are plenty of vintage performance/promo/interview clips, though none are very long. Audiophiles will particularly enjoy Eddie Kramer's isolation of certain parts of tracks as he explains how some individual contributions were recorded and refined, as well as the use of brief snippets of unreleased tapes from the sessions on the soundtrack. There are also lots of interesting, relatively fresh anecdotes, like Noel Redding's smirking revelation that he actually preferred Bob Dylan's version of "All Along the Watchtower", or Kramer's diplomatic recollection of how Brian Jones's piano part for that same classic track went unused. Not much is made of the tensions between Hendrix and Chandler, and Hendrix and Redding, which are known to have hindered the sessions. But overall this is an excellent, multifaceted review of what is indeed a classic album.

Hendrix: Band of Gypsys

Bob Smeaton, 1999; MCA/Experience Hendrix DVD

Like several of the DVDs listed in this section, *Hendrix: Band of Gypsys* has elements of both a documentary and a concert film, but is listed here as a documentary because that's the format used in the main section of this approximately two-hour disc. Here **Billy Cox and Buddy Miles** offer a lot of memories and opinions regarding the short-lived Band of Gypsys outfit, with others like Mitch Mitchell and Eddie Kramer pitching in as well. Actually, there wasn't much choice *but* to make a documentary, considering that the existing footage of the only Band of Gypsys concerts (the ones they did on the last day of 1969 and the first of 1970) is pretty ropey, technically speaking. Much of that footage is seen between the interview segments, which basically tell the Band of Gypsys story from several angles – usually positive, Afro-centric ones, although those who feel the band wasn't that workable or really

what Jimi wanted to do are allowed to give their two cents. (The cover, incidentally, uses the same shot as the one seen on the *Live at the Fillmore East* CD, but the DVD by no means includes all the music on the album.)

As a significant extra, the DVD also offers uninterrupted footage of eight songs, lasting nearly an hour, filmed at the Band of Gypsys concerts. Unfortunately this is in shaky black and white, but it does give you the only chance to see the short-lived group in extended action, with "Machine Gun" and "Foxy Lady" as the highlights. When all is said and done, the Band of Gypsys period wasn't the most significant or exciting chapter in Hendrix's history, but this disc covers it about as comprehensively as possible.

Hendrix the Guitarist

When Jimi Hendrix first burst on the scene, audiences and fellow musicians alike were literally open-mouthed in wonder as to how this guy was getting such unearthly sounds from his guitar. Some of the shock wore off, slightly, as he rose to worldwide fame: everyone got a little more used to his style and other rock musicians began to credibly simulate some of the same noises. But even at the end of his career and life, almost everyone was still basically at a loss to explain how Hendrix was coaxing what he got out of his instrument, as if he were some sorcerer casting spells to which only he held the key.

Now that we have the benefit of several decades of research – and the availability of more developed and affordable technology allowing even relatively amateur guitarists to imitate some of Jimi's signature riffs – much more is known about exactly how he created the sounds that he did. Much of that knowledge lies in the examination not only of his techniques, but also the equipment he used. Getting all the right hardware and studying all the playbooks still doesn't mean that Hendrix's guitar-work can be replicated, however. Above all else, the key ingredient was his imagination, and no one can quite re-create his tone and style no matter how hard they try.

There have been entire music instructional books and videos about these issues which, by necessity, have used much gearhead-muso terminology that most people will find as hard to digest as a calculus textbook. Because this book is for the general fan, not the musician (professional or otherwise), what follows in this section is more an overview of Hendrix the guitarist for the layperson, detailing the most important technical features of his art without using terms that require highly specialized knowledge. One should never let technospeak get in the way of enjoyment of the music, but on the other hand, knowing at least a little about this aspect of his genius enhances our appreciation of his legacy. Many elements went into making Jimi sound the way he did, the most important of which were his **guitars, techniques**, **amplifiers**, and **effects**.

The Hands

Even before Jimi Hendrix ever picked up an instrument, however, he had an asset that would become a massive advantage in his redefinition of the electric guitar: his **huge hands**. Although his body was only of average or slightly larger than average size overall, it's been reported that his hands were so big that the top joint of his thumb could press all six strings in a guitar fret down all by itself. Even if that's a slight exaggeration, his hands were definitely outsized in comparison to his other physical gifts, enabling him to grip his instrument hard, cover all manner of unorthodox and difficult positions, play both lead and rhythm simultaneously, and manipulate the strings in ways that forced them beyond their accepted limitations. Undoubtedly they also helped him to pull off some of his flashier onstage tricks, such as playing behind his back or producing a hellacious roar with just one hand.

As noted near the beginning of this book, although most would think of the left-handed Hendrix being forced to learn and play on restrung right-handed models as a stumbling block, it might have actually worked in his favour in the long run. Immediately it got Jimi used to playing in an unconventional way, which might have made him more open-minded to doing all sorts of things not listed in the rulebook. And by having to work so hard to simply master the instrument, everything else difficult he tried from that point on might have seemed just a little bit easier than it would have to most aspiring guitarists.

Even after he had the cash to buy any left-handed guitar he wanted, Hendrix stuck with the right-handed versions, and not just out of force of habit. There were simply far more right-handed guitars being manufactured than left-handed ones, and Jimi wouldn't have wanted anything to stand in the way of access to the widest possible range of options. As Chas Chandler told *Beat Instrumental* in

1967: "Funny thing about Jimi, he's a left-handed guitarist, but he just won't use a left-handed specially-built instrument. Says they can't be as good because there aren't so many made."

Playing upside down also gave Hendrix another secret weapon. Whether playing left-handed or right-handed, a guitar's tremolo arm, and volume and tone controls, are usually on the lower part of the instrument. The way Jimi played, they were on top – making it far less of a reach for him to grab them and rapidly change his guitar's tone and volume level, as he would often do with a magician-like sleight of hand.

The Guitars

When Hendrix was growing up, and for quite a while after he began playing professionally, the guitars he used were not his preferred models but whatever he could afford at the time. Coming from a poor family and dependent upon a father who didn't exactly encourage Jimi's budding musical abilities, his first electric guitars were some of the cheapest that were on the market, as was the Japanese one he used while in the army. If even half of the tales of Hendrix getting stranded on the road or hocking goods in pawnshops in the early-to-mid-1960s are true, it's likely that he had to at least sometimes borrow equipment belonging to someone else, or even do without a guitar altogether for brief stretches.

Jimi upgraded to a Fender Jazzmaster by the mid-1960s, but it really wasn't until he got his first **Fender Stratocaster** – probably in New York in 1966, with money from a girlfriend, Carol Shiroky – that he found his favourite model. Hendrix did occasionally use other brands, particularly when he wanted a certain tone for a specific track he was recording. But it was pretty much the Fender Strat that he stuck with for the rest of his life – even at the Isle of Wight festival a few weeks before his death, he can be seen playing a black one.

For several reasons, he went through quite a few Strats, the most notorious one being that he smashed a bunch of them onstage, or at least put them through such serious paces that they wore out sooner than usual. More prosaically, like most top professional guitarists, he simply loved collecting and playing different ones, especially after money became no object. Certainly many of them have since been auctioned for high sums, although there have been doubts as to whether all of these are authentic. But he may well have learned how to preserve his especially favoured axes intact as time went on, since the black one he played at the Isle of Wight had been used onstage for a good two years.

For someone as dedicated to exploring the maximum sonic range as Hendrix, the Stratocaster turned out to be the guitar that best suited his needs. "The Stratocaster is the best all-round guitar for the stuff we're doing", he explained in one of his earliest American interviews, for the *Los Angeles Free Press* in 1967. "You can get the very bright trebles and the deep bass sound. I tried Telecaster and it only has two sounds, good and bad, and a very weak tone variation. ... I tried one of the new Gibsons, but I literally couldn't play it at all, so I'll stick with Fender."

Incidentally, for about the last three years of his career, Hendrix played not in standard guitar tuning – tuned to the notes EADGBE – but in a different one that tuned each note down half a notch. This would have made the strings easier to bend, but actually Jimi did this primarily because playing in a slightly lower tuning made for a better, or at least easier, fit with his vocal range. Whichever tuning Hendrix used, however, his guitar often needed retuning during performances, such was the constant strain that his attack put on the strings.

The Techniques

Of course, lots of guitarists were playing Fender Stratocasters without making anything like the noises that Jimi was conjuring up. For that, Hendrix had to play the instrument with superhuman strength, operating its controls and attacking the strings in ways that would probably have made the designers and manufacturers cringe (although the upsurge in sales after it became widely known which model Jimi was playing probably provided ample compensation).

One of the most prominent techniques Hendrix used to create what might be called his waves of sound was his heavy – some might say extreme – use of the **tremolo arm** (sometimes called a vibrato arm) to vary the pitch of his notes and chords up and down, sometimes quite wildly. The tremolo had often been used in rock'n'roll prior to Jimi's emergence, nota-

Hendrixology

bly in surf music, but Hendrix took it to a new level of sheer tense power. Combined with the atomic volume at which he often played, the tremolo could create a pulsating sensation, much like a shaky camera suddenly going in and out of focus during an earthquake.

A related technique he employed was the **finger tremolo**, in which he would wiggle a string across the fret with a shaking hand to produce a rapidly wavering, quivering series of notes. Probably the most famous example of this – not just in Hendrix's repertoire, but in all of rock music – is the opening riff of "Foxy Lady", mimicking a stuttering supersonic bee-buzz. Again, it's a testament to the sheer strength of his large hands that he was able to make such a massive flutter just by pressing his finger to the fret board.

That strength also came in handy when he would tap various parts of his guitar to get miscellaneous weird and eerie effects, which has proved to be among the most difficult of Jimi's techniques to imitate. While most of these techniques did not involve altering the guitar itself, he would remove the plastic plate which covered the operating springs of the tremolo to make it easier for him to tap the springs themselves. When used in tandem with the tremolo arm, this came in especially handy when he was simulating the noise of diving bombs in some of his more aggressive tunes.

Hendrix's strength and outsize hands were also essential to him getting the most out of bending his strings in order to bend notes out of their customary shape. Bent notes, of course, had been used by innumerable guitarists before Hendrix, especially in the country blues and electric blues that he grew up listening to. Unlike almost any other guitarist, however, Hendrix could bend the first string on a bass all the way up to the top of the fret board – a feat almost impossible for most humans, let alone most musicians. Almost as if he was playing with three hands or two brains, he could also bend more than one string at once and in different directions, or even bend one string while playing another string conventionally.

As another virtuoso feat, he could also play chords and rhythm guitar at the same time as he played lead, often causing many listeners to believe that they were hearing two guitars at once. This wasn't mere gimmickry: as Jimi usually played as the leader of a trio after mid-1966, it was an essential part of fattening the Experience's sound.

But perhaps the best-known of the techniques Hendrix popularized was **feedback**, the ferociously loud, swelling sounds resulting from playing a guitar close to an amplifier or microphone. Jimi was not the first guitarist to use feedback on record or in live performance, and some of his more flamboyant flourishes, which were often assumed to be produced by feedback, were actually concocted by other means. He was undoubtedly a pioneer, however, in using it not just for cacophonous shock value – as Pete Townshend sometimes had in the early days of The Who – but to commandeer controlled, sustained siren-like tones. This couldn't have been done, of course, without amplifiers, which brings us to the next weapon in Hendrix's technical armoury.

White Stratocaster onstage, Olympia Theatre, Paris, February 1967

The Amplifiers

Until the mid-1960s, Jimi Hendrix was probably unable to put much of his resources into acquiring or experimenting with amplifiers for his guitar. Part of the reason, as with the guitars he bought, was financial – he simply didn't have the funds for high-end models, the main priority being to have an amplifier in the first place. He was probably often at the mercy of whatever amplifiers were used by the bands he was playing with or the clubs he was working at. And as a sideman, he would often have been

discouraged from playing too loudly or distinctly in the first place, or even turning up whatever amplifier was at his disposal too loudly.

This all changed when Hendrix started to lead his own bands in 1966, giving him the freedom to play as loudly and outlandishly as he wanted. Getting the right amps for him and the Experience soon became not only an aesthetic consideration, but a purely practical one. Although it might seem difficult to imagine in the twenty-first century, in 1966 and 1967, there had never been anything as loud as The Jimi Hendrix Experience before, in rock music

The Experience performing live onstage at the Marquee Club, London, 2 March 1967, filming the German TV show *Beat Club*, with Marshall amplifiers behind

or any other form of sound production outside the military-industrial complex. Even the sturdiest commercially available amps simply weren't set up to take that kind of aural pounding without blowing up or burning out.

Of probably greater concern to Hendrix was that standard amplifiers couldn't project the Experience's instruments with the volume and power he had in mind, also finding – as were some other early rock guitarists – that the amps of the era were simply too sonically clean for his tastes. Mitch Mitchell was on board with Hendrix in this respect from the start, remembering later that the group deliberately tried to break the relatively puny Burns amplifiers they had been given by Chas Chandler at their second rehearsal by throwing them down a flight of stairs.

In a remarkable coincidence, Mitchell's drum teacher as a teenager had been **Jim Marshall**, who had recently expanded his London drum shop to stock amplifiers and guitars. When young axemen of the new British rock generation told him they were searching for something harder and dirtier than the popular amps on the market, he began designing and manufacturing his own **Marshall amps**, which soon found favour with the likes of Pete Townshend and Eric Clapton. Instead of the two twelve-inch speakers that were the most that could be expected of other models, Marshall came up with cabinets with four twelve-inch speakers, taking things a step further by making it possible for two such cabinets to be stacked on top of each other.

This was the origin of the famous **Marshall stacks**, an innovation that Hendrix typically took to the limit by using as many as three 100-watt amps with six cabinets. This might sound like a mere light bulb several decades later, when stadium tours by big acts can end up using more wattage in a night than a village uses in a decade. At the time, however, little if anything like it had been heard in a rock concert, and in a very real sense, Hendrix's efforts paved the way for rock stadium concerts to be possible – or, at least audible – in the first place. Hendrix no doubt viewed it as a cosmically auspicious coincidence that his own middle name happened to be Marshall.

Although Hendrix did use amps and monitor systems made by other manufacturers on some occasions, for the most part he stuck with Marshall amps for the rest of his career. He became so well known for turning the controls up to the maximum (ten) level that it became known as "the Hendrix setting" – a possible inspiration for Spinal Tap's justly famous gag about an amp that goes up to eleven. Such was the stress that this put even on Jimi's preferred brand of speakers, roadie Eric Barrett told *Hit Parader* in 1969, that they had to be changed after every show. "If I tried to test his equipment, all I got was feedback", he noted in Harry Shapiro and Caesar Glebbeek's *Jimi Hendrix: Electric Gypsy*. "Jimi could control it all with his fingers, and I still don't understand to this day how he did it. It was all part of his genius."

The Effects

As much of a genius as he was at working his Stratocaster guitars and Marshall amps, Hendrix couldn't have sounded as exotic as he did without deploying a number of effects for which he needed additional equipment. These are probably the most colourful elements in Jimi's musical palette, and ones which had an appreciable effect on the musical-instrument manufacturing industry, as legions of both aspiring and veteran guitarists bought the same gizmos in search of the same sounds. Again, however, you needed more than the right device to duplicate Hendrix, and no one could use them in quite the same way.

In New York in the mid-1960s, even before the Experience formed, Hendrix was using a **fuzz box** built for him by Ken Pine, at that time guitarist in proto-punk satirical rock group The Fugs. By the time Jimi became a bandleader, fuzz guitar was widely used in rock, becoming a staple of US garage bands after Keith Richards used it to play the classic riff on The Rolling Stones' "(I Can't Get No) Satisfaction". Typically, however, Jimi wanted a sound that was even more distorted and overdriven. By early 1967 he had acquired a foot-switch-operated **Fuzz Face** with controls for both fuzz and volume, and quickly put it to use on the intro of "Purple Haze". With all the other techniques Hendrix was using to distort his tone, not everything that's fuzzy on his recordings is produced in full or part by a fuzz box by any means, but it's often present nonetheless.

A more celebrated signature Hendrix effect was the **wah-wah**, produced by a foot pedal and characterized by a tone that almost simulates a human voice saying the very words "wah-wah". Although he approximated a wah-wah on the studio recording of "I Don't Live Today" in early 1967, the Vox wah-wah pedal he used wasn't on the market in the UK at that point, and he probably didn't get his own pedal until his summer 1967 US tour, putting it to use almost immediately on "The Burning of the Midnight Lamp". The classic opening riff of "Voodoo Child (Slight Return)" remains Hendrix's most famous use of the wah-wah – indeed, it could well be the most famous wah-wah riff by anyone – but it also figures strongly in another of the highlights of *Electric Ladyland*, "Rainy Day, Dream Away".

Hendrix's friend **Roger Mayer** worked on specific modifications for Jimi's fuzz boxes and wah-wah units – another reason why those effects are simply impossible to replicate exactly by other guitarists or in other decades.

Mayer even invented a device specifically for Hendrix, the **Octavia**, so-named for its ability to simultaneously produce a tone an octave above the one being played. As he explained it in Sean Egan's *Jimi Hendrix and the Making of 'Are You Experienced'*: "It's a foot pedal with circuitry in it that doubles the frequency of the sound you put in, but in so doing – because a guitar string has many overtones – when you actually start doubling all the overtones, the guitar almost takes on like a flute sound." If that still doesn't quite give you the picture, just put on "Purple Haze" and listen to the searing high tones in the solo and outro.

To get something like a combination of an organ and guitar, Hendrix sometimes played through a Leslie speaker, whose rotating components produced a swirling effect. He did so on some of the *Axis: Bold as Love* sessions, most notably on "Little Wing". He wasn't the first or only guy who had thought of the idea: Chicago band The New Colony Six had made it a trademark on their mid-1960s recordings, and George Harrison used it on some of The Beatles' late-1960s recordings, especially from the *Let It Be* sessions.

As the Leslie was primarily intended for use with a Hammond organ, it was a heavy thing to drag around. In the last year or so of his performances, however, Hendrix was able to achieve much the same effect with the more portable foot-controlled **Uni-Vibe**, also designed for use with organs. The live version of "Machine Gun" on *Band of Gypsys* might be its most famous use on a Hendrix album, and it's also a Uni-Vibe that creates some of the galactic swirls on his Woodstock performance of "Star Spangled Banner". Though by no means the most famous of the devices Jimi employed, his use of it in that year alone was enough to make it strongly associated with him, so much so that Hendrix expert Caesar Glebbeek named his Hendrix fanzine *UniVibes*, later putting out some collector-oriented Hendrix releases on a label of the same name.

In the Studio

For the sake of clarity, it should be pointed out that the way Jimi Hendrix played guitar onstage and in the studio was often quite different, as was the equipment in each respective location. Now that there's so much live Hendrix available on disc, the distinctions between what he could and couldn't play in certain situations have become rather blurred, but he certainly came up with some effects and timbres that can't be easily replicated outside of the studio.

The most prominent of these is **phasing**, which sounds something like the rising and falling sounds of an airplane taking off and landing. In the psychedelic era, this was often used to add a bit of otherworldly fairy dust, notable examples being The Small Faces' great "Itchycoo Park" and Status Quo's kitsch-psychedelic classic "Pictures of Matchstick Men", although it had actually been used on disc as early as Toni Fisher's 1960 hit "Hurt". In the Hendrix catalogue, it's heard prominently on "If Six Was Nine" and "House Burning Down", for example.

Sunset-Highland Recording Studios, 20 October 1968, Hollywood, California

The technical ins and outs of phasing are a bit gearheadish, and as complicated as the following explanation (from Harry Shapiro and Caesar Glebbeek's *Jimi Hendrix: Electric Gypsy*) sounds, it doesn't get much simpler than this: "This 'jet sound' effect was produced by feeding a signal into two tape recorders and recording the combined outputs onto another machine. The effect produced a kind of swirling tonal sweep, achieved by varying the speed of one of the input tape recorders and altering the frequency response (EQ) of the audio signal to obtain the desired sound." Engineer **George Chkiantz** is most often credited as the key man behind constructing psychedelic phasing on "Itchycoo Park", and fortunately he was working on the *Axis: Bold as Love* sessions where the effect was introduced onto Hendrix's recordings.

Self-explanatory in comparison with phasing, **backwards tapes** were sometimes used on Jimi's more psychedelic tracks – a trick that was simply impossible to convincingly duplicate onstage at the time. Though now dismissed by some critics as something of a gimmick or a dated psychedelic relic, the use of backwards tapes on a 1960s rock record was still pretty cutting-edge, their eerie air-sucking ambience having been pioneered by The Beatles on 1966 tracks like "Rain" and "I'm Only Sleeping". The title track of *Are You Experienced?* is probably the most famous (and successful) example of its use on Jimi Hendrix's recordings.

Along the same lines, some of Hendrix's guitar lines were technologically cooked up by varying the speed of the tape. One example is "Burning of the Midnight Lamp", which made guitars sound like mandolins by playing licks deliberately slowly, and then speeding the tapes up to twice their normal rate. Varispeed was applied to voices, with less satisfying artistic success, on "EXP" (the opening track of *Axis: Bold as Love*) and the slushy Darth Vader-like murmurings of "Third Stone from the Sun". The stereo mixes of Hendrix's records – which

not everyone heard the first time around, stereo not being the universal standard on vinyl until near the end of his career – sometimes also used **panning** effects to simulate sounds and instruments careening from one speaker to another.

Learning the Licks

Learning how to play like Jimi Hendrix isn't nearly as difficult as it was between 1966 and 1970, when even top rivals would come away from the front rows of gigs mystified as to how he was pulling it off. In part this is because the equipment he was using – or at least equipment that can produce similar effects – has become both more common and more affordable. There are also a number of instruction books and recordings specifically devoted to his solos and techniques – which, for the vast majority of guitarists, make these much easier to figure out than they would be otherwise.

Music-book publisher **Hal Leonard** (online catalogue at *hallleonard.com*) has a particularly extensive line of volumes devoted to teaching guitarists how to play Hendrix. Admittedly knowledge of musical notation will help for many of these, but they include transcriptions and scores for several of his albums, including all three of his principal studio LPs (*Are You Experienced?*, *Axis: Bold as Love* and *Electric Ladyland*). For beginners, *Experience Hendrix Book One: Beginning Guitar Method* (which comes with a CD) is recommended. Those in need of a visual aid might want to check out *Learn to Play the*

Songs from 'Are You Experienced', hosted by Hendrix's friend Velvert Turner, which also includes some footage of Jimi himself playing the songs.

Even some collectors who don't play guitar might want to track down the five CDs in Hal Leonard's *Jimi Hendrix Reference Series* (issued 1989–1993), with volumes dedicated to *Fuzz, Feedback & Wah-Wah*; *Whammy Bar & Finger Grease*; *Octavia & Univibe*; *Rhythm*; and *Red House: Variations on a Theme*. For all contain otherwise unavailable Hendrix recordings, albeit – with the exception of the *Red House* instalment – in fragmentary solos and riffs. The *Red House* CD was devoted to six versions of "Red House" by Jimi (and one by John Lee Hooker), and thus the only one that seemed seriously intended for some crossover appeal to the general music market, though you would need to be a pretty specialized Hendrix freak to hear so much "Red House" at one sitting.

Diligent use of these and other study aids, of course, is no guarantee you'll sound like Hendrix. And unless you're planning on making a living as a Hendrix tribute act (as some do), mastery of these lessons is no guarantee that you'll get much notice or reward for your efforts, as credible simulation of Jimi's techniques and effects is much less eyebrow-raising in the twenty-first century than it would have been back in the 1970s.

Hendrix Locations

With a couple of notable exceptions, sites which mark vital landmarks of Jimi Hendrix's life aren't regularly visited by fans eager to pay tribute. In part this is due to Jimi's nomadic lifestyle; he seldom stayed in one place for long, and even when he became wealthy, he had few fixed points of residence, instead often staying in hotels even when he wasn't on the road. Some of the locations of his most significant achievements and experiences no longer exist; some are still in operation as commercial facilities, and not easily visitable; and only a few have signs indicating their connection with Hendrix.

There are still some surviving sites, however, which serious Hendrix fans might wish to check out should they be in the area. The bulk of them reside in the three cities in which Hendrix spent by far the most time: **Seattle**, **New York** and **London**.

Seattle

Born in King County Hospital in Seattle, Jimi Hendrix lived in so many places as a boy – shuffled as he was between relatives and relocating periodically as his father scuffled to support the family – that it seems a bit arbitrary to focus on any of them as his "boyhood home". The one that seems to have been chosen as the most significant is a small two-bedroom house in **Seattle's Central district**, in which he lived with his dad and brother Leon in the 1950s when he was between the ages of twelve and fifteen. In 2001, it was moved a few blocks from its original location to South Jackson Street, where it fell into weedy neglect, enclosed by a chain-link fence and attracting neighbourhood transients with drug problems.

The city of Seattle had been talking about demolishing the structure when real-estate investor Pete Sikov – treasurer of the Leon Hendrix-founded Jimi Hendrix Foundation (an entirely separate organization from the primary one administrating Jimi's estate, Experience Hendrix) – stepped in and bought it for $1.8 million. For another $30,000, it was moved in September 2005 to a mobile-home park opposite Greenwood Memorial Cemetery, where Jimi is buried. At the time, it was reported that the foundation was planning to remodel the house to re-create its appearance when Jimi and Leon lived there, as well as to use it as a music education centre (including studios) for children. Like some other ambitious programmes to honour Jimi's memory – including, right across the street, plans for a much more elaborate Jimi Hendrix Memorial near his gravestone – this has, at the time of writing, yet to be realized, although the foundation's website (*jimihendrixfoundation.com*) will probably announce any major developments in this direction.

The Central district itself – a little east of downtown Seattle, with Lake Washington a bit further east – remains home to much of the city's African-American population, though it's becoming more racially mixed and gentrified. Garfield High School, where Hendrix had a fairly desultory stint before failing to graduate, is still there at 400 23rd Avenue, albeit somewhat changed in appearance. Although there's a mural with images of Jimi in the school and a bronze bust of the legend in the library, there's still no specific landmark devoted to the guitarist in nearby Jimi Hendrix Park, a mile away in the Central district at 2400 S. Massachusetts Street. The park is still under construction and the only sign of anything to do with Hendrix so far is its name, but the recently opened Northwest African American Museum (2300 S. Massachusetts Street, *naamnw.org*; Wednesday and Friday 11am–4.30pm, Thursday 11am–7pm, Saturday 11am–4pm, Sunday noon–4pm; $6, students/seniors $4) on an adjacent property does present something of the historical/social context of the community in which Hendrix grew up. There's no Hendrix-specific content here either, though, with the exception of a wide-brimmed felt hat with a blue bandana that Jimi wore at a 1968 concert.

The best place to view actual relics of Jimi's career – his whole career, not just his Seattle

upbringing – is the **Experience Music Project**, in Seattle Center near the Space Needle, which devotes much (though by no means the majority) of its space to rotating Hendrix exhibitions. The one on display at the time of writing – the fifth, in fact, that the museum has mounted since it opened in 2000 – is titled "Jimi Hendrix: An Evolution in Sound", and will run until 11 April 2010. Divided into five different chronological phases of his musical trajectory, highlights include the "butterfly" costume he wore at the 1970 Isle of Wight festival; the Fender Stratocaster he played at Woodstock; pieces of the guitar he smashed at the Monterey Pop festival; the original artwork for the *Are You Experienced?* album; interactive displays illustrating how Hendrix used effects pedals and mixed studio recordings (including a feature which allows you to do your own mixes of four Hendrix songs); and rare Hendrix films and footage.

Unlike most of the other sites listed in this section, this attraction will cost you, especially if you're taking the family, with an admission price of $15 ($12 for seniors and under-eighteens). The museum does contain other rock history exhibits, however, and even if Hendrix is the main reason for your visit, you may well end up going again, as the 8000-plus items in the museum's collection – far more than can be displayed at any one time – are also exhibited in rotation. EMP, as it's usually called, is at 325 Fifth Avenue North (206-770-2700, *empsfm.org*), and open daily from 10am to 7pm.

EMP's Hendrix exhibit will probably remain by far the most visited Jimi-related site in

Hendrixology

Seattle, as the one that's arguably most meaningful to serious Hendrix worshippers is also the one that's hardest to get to. This does, however, ensure that your visit to his gravesite in **Greenwood Memorial Park Cemetery**, at 350 Monroe Avenue NE in suburban Renton, fifteen miles south of Seattle, will probably be undisturbed by crowds if you wish to pay serious tribute. Look for the marble stone inscribed with – in an unfortunate boo-boo, right-handed – guitar in the still-incomplete Jimi Hendrix Memorial; it should be easy to spot, but cemetery staff are usually pretty helpful in pointing it out if you need directions. A car makes the trek far easier, but if you're carless and patient enough to set aside a good chunk of the day, you can still reach the cemetery by bus from downtown Seattle: take the 101 or 106 and change to the 105 at the Renton Transit Center, then get off at the NE 4th & Monroe stop.

New York

Some of the New York clubs and studios that were instrumental to Jimi Hendrix's growth as an artist are gone or unrecognizably changed, and with development in early-twenty-first century Manhattan so rampant, it wouldn't be a surprise to see a few others befalling the same fate in the near future. But a few noteworthy ones are still around and, in a few cases, still surprisingly vibrant ongoing operations, though not always ones you can enter casually as a visitor.

When Jimi first came to New York around the beginning of 1964, one of the first boosts to his confidence came when he won a $25 first-place prize at the Wednesday amateur night at **Harlem's Apollo Theater**, although it would be another two years before he began to win respect as a featured solo attraction. The Apollo was for several decades perhaps the most famous venue for black popular music in the United States, featuring everyone from jazz divas Ella Fitzgerald, Billie Holiday and Sarah Vaughan to countless soul stars. James Brown in particular made the Apollo internationally famous by recording two of the greatest live soul albums of all time there in the 1960s. By the 1970s, it was in danger of falling into decline, neglect and even closure, but its survival was guaranteed when it was granted national, state and city landmark status in 1983, undergoing the most extensive renovation of any American theatre in recent years.

It's pretty doubtful that you'll see talent of the order of a young, undiscovered Jimi Hendrix on amateur nights, which still take place at the Apollo every Wednesday night at 7.30pm. You can, however, take an hour-long tour of the building (only available to groups of twenty or more, by appointment) at $16 per person; check *apollotheater.org/historic_tours.html* for tour times (offered daily, though schedules vary) and details for making arrangements. Admittedly, Hendrix's own role in the Apollo's venerable history was slight; he was just passing through. But checking out the theatre does give you some idea of the milieu in which he was operating before rising to fame, even if the Apollo would have been the most prestigious such venue he played on the chitlin' circuit.

When Jimi started leading his own bands in 1966, the Greenwich Village club he probably played more than any other was the **Cafe Wha?** Unbelievably, it's still there at 115 Macdougal Street, on the corner of Macdougal and Minetta Lane. Although Bob Dylan and Bruce Springsteen are among the other giants who played important early gigs here, these days you're not as likely to see such a diverse assortment of up-and-coming talent, the music now being supplied by several house bands encompassing various forms of R&B, rock and world music.

If you want to go in, there's no cover on Wednesdays and Sundays, though otherwise the price can vary from $5 to $20. There you can imagine what it would have been like to have been Chas Chandler, following a tip to check out an unknown guitarist in the summer of 1966, and finding something totally beyond his wildest expectations. And while other clubs in the area that Jimi played, like the Cafe Au Go Go (pre-fame), the Salvation (where he played a bunch of shows when he was just breaking in the US in summer 1967), and the Fillmore East (with the Band of Gypsys), are no longer around, just walking around the Village still gives you something of the anything-goes multicultural buzz he would have felt back in 1966, no matter how much more expensive the rents are these days.

Other venues at which Hendrix played key New York gigs – like the Scene, his favourite place to jam – are also gone. And while the **Madison Square Garden** (where he had his meltdown with the Band of Gypsys in early 1970) is still around, it's such an impersonal arena that even if you were at the original concert and paying a return visit, a wander round its premises isn't likely to give you a feeling of personal connection to Jimi.

While Hendrix played New York fairly often (if intermittently), the city was probably most significant to him as the place where he did more recording than any other. Sadly the Record Plant on 44th Street in midtown Manhattan, where Jimi cut many tracks in the late 1960s (including most of *Electric Ladyland*), shut down not long after being sold to George Martin in the late 1980s, although a studio of the same name still thrives in Hollywood. Also still thriving in the Village at 52 W. 8th Street is the facility at which Hendrix probably still would be recording had he lived to the present day, **Electric Lady Studios**. As it's on one of the busiest blocks of a neighbourhood where you're likely to spend a lot of time hanging out anyway if you're visiting New York, it's probably worth strolling past to pay homage, though no tours are on offer. To get inside, you'd probably have to record here – which, given the high rates and how often it's booked by top stars, might be a long shot even if you're a professional musician. But if you're so inclined, you can give it a try through their website, *electricladystudios.com*.

Hendrix bought so many guitars and so much associated gear in the last five years of his life that it's likely he patronized a few shops in Manhattan at one point or another (and many others in many other cities, if only to quickly replace items as they were damaged on tour). It's almost certain, however, that the one he frequented more than any other was **Manny's Music**, still going strong between Sixth and Seventh Avenues at 156 W. 48th Street. According to Manny's son Henry Goldrich, Jimi would buy several guitars and amps at once on a visit, as well as whatever other new gizmos caught his fancy; he was such a good customer, in fact, that the store would stay open after hours just to accommodate him.

Even if you're not a musician (or have no intention of buying anything), you might want to sneak in for a long look at the store's fabled **Wall of Fame**, crammed with signed photos of several decades' worth of famous customers. Or if you can't make it, you can look at lots of them in the book *The Wall of Fame: New York City's Legendary Manny's Music* (Hal Leonard, 2007), including one inscribed by all three members of the original Jimi Hendrix Experience. Jimi writes: "You told me to mention your FUZZ TONE ... thanks for everything, Be Groovy."

As all of the aforementioned New York locations are on streets that are busy and hectic even by Manhattan standards, for a much-needed breather you'd be well advised to head to the **Alice in Wonderland Statue** in Central Park (enter from East 74th Street and walk to the north side of the Conservatory water pond). This is where, in August 1968, The Jimi Hendrix Experience posed with some kids for photos intended for use on the cover of *Electric Ladyland*, taken by Linda Eastman (soon to be Linda McCartney, wife of Beatle Paul). To Jimi's displeasure, they weren't used on either the US or UK front sleeves – Hendrix becoming especially annoyed when the British version infamously substituted a group of naked ladies (see page 87) – but some of them were used on the inner gatefold of the American version. It was also in Central Park, on 5 July 1967, that the Experience gave one of their first major Stateside concerts, and if you're here in the summer, the SummerStage series still presents a wealth of outdoor shows in the park.

Finally, not in New York City proper, but only about a couple of hours away in New York State, is the site of the **1969 Woodstock festival** where Hendrix made his most famous appearance. Not in the town of Woodstock itself, but about sixty miles away in Bethel, many 1960s vets and their progeny still make the journey to the site, marvelling as to how half a million or so people could have possibly fitted into what's otherwise a pretty ordinary rolling, rural field. In June 2008, **Bethel Woods Center for the Arts** (at 200 Hurd Road, *bethelwoodscenter.org/museum.aspx*) opened a museum at the original site which, while not Hendrix-centred (though he's represented), has film and multimedia/interactive exhibits aiming to explore "the unique experience of the Woodstock festival, its significance as a culminating event of a decade of radical cultural transformation, and the legacy of the Sixties and Woodstock today". Admission is $13 (with discounts for seniors and under-eighteens), and it's open daily during the summer from 10am to 7pm; in other seasons, it's open 10am–5pm every day but Monday.

London

Even fewer of the major venues and studios in which Jimi Hendrix performed survive in London than in New York. Even the long-lived Marquee Club – where in any case the Experience played just a few times – moved from its hallowed Wardour Street location in the late 1980s, closing and reopening in several other spots over the past couple of decades. The Speakeasy, Bag O'Nails, 7½ Club, the Scotch of St. James – all now seem like legends from a long-off era where rock royalty once mingled before stadiums took over.

Yet London is also home to the one Jimi Hendrix landmark to receive official governmental recognition, in the form of a **blue plaque** affixed to one of his residences in the city by English Heritage. The plaque in question commemorates the building at **23 Brook Street** in the ritzy Mayfair district of central London, where Hendrix lived for a time in 1968 and 1969 with his on-off British girlfriend **Kathy Etchingham**, paying a then-expensive £30 a week when he moved in. It must have been a short time if measured by the hours in which Jimi was actually in the building, mind you, since he was out of the UK for most of that period. But it was enough to secure the honour for Hendrix, the location perhaps made yet more appealing by the presence of another blue plaque right next door for classical composer George Frederick Handel, who lived at 25 Brook Street from 1723 until his death in 1759.

Hendrix's former Brook Street flat is now used as offices, but is open for tours a couple of times a year, taking small groups through his bedrooms, kitchen, and studio, as well as showing a short film and rare black-and-white photographs. Hendrix and Etchingham weren't the only people to sleep here when Jimi was the tenant, as some of his rock-star friends, reportedly including George Harrison, would use the second bedroom after wild nights on the town left them in no condition to depart central London. For information on when the tours are given, it seems your best bet is to contact the Handel House Museum (*handelhouse.org*), which neither highlights nor shuns its Hendrix connection, having actually presented a special exhibition on Jimi in 2003 and 2004.

In all honesty, a flat of considerably more historic significance to both Jimi's career and his relationship with Etchingham is at **34 Montagu Square** in the nearby Marylebone district. This was where Jimi lived for a few months shortly after the Experience was formed, along with Kathy, co-manager Chas Chandler and Chas's girlfriend. Even by then Hendrix was on the road much of the time, but certainly he must have done some songwriting here and generally cooked up strategies with Chandler; "The Wind Cries Mary" was reportedly composed after a major row at the flat between Hendrix and Etchingham. Even apart from the Hendrix connection, the address has a secure place in rock'n'roll history, as Ringo Starr lived here for a few months with his first wife in 1965, and Paul McCartney used the basement as a home studio of sorts shortly afterward, writing "Eleanor Rigby" there. It was also here that John Lennon – temporarily house-less while in

Hendrixology

34 Montagu Square: the ultimate 1960s rockers' pad

the process of divorcing his first wife – posed with Yoko Ono for the nude photos adorning the *Two Virgins* LP cover, the pair also getting busted for marijuana here in late 1968.

If you're both a Hendrix and Beatles fan, you might be tempted to seek out not only the Montagu Square flat, but also the Brian Epstein-owned **Saville Theatre** at 135 Shaftesbury

Avenue in London's West End. This is where Jimi amazed and delighted Paul McCartney by playing the title track to *Sgt. Pepper's Lonely Hearts Club Band* in June 1967, just a few days after the LP had been released. Alas, the Saville was converted to a cinema shortly after Epstein's death, and though you can go there to see a film at the four-screen Odeon Covent Garden which now inhabits the building, it just won't be the same. The most venerated venue Jimi played in London, the **Royal Albert Hall**, is still around of course, though fans might feel a more Hendrixian connection with its premises if the film of his performances here in February 1969 is ever released.

One Jimi Hendrix landmark unlikely to make London rock tours is the **Samarkand Hotel**, in a quiet well-to-do Notting Hill neighbourhood at 21–22 Lansdowne Crescent, where he died in a basement flat on 18 September 1970. There's still a fair number of pilgrims to the building, which over the years has not announced itself to or encouraged visitors. Few if any have seemed to gain access to the flat itself or its garden, where Monika Dannemann took the last known pictures of Jimi, on the afternoon before his death.

Hendrix's Influences

Pinning down Jimi Hendrix's influences is in some ways an easy task, and in others exceedingly difficult. Unlike, say, The Beatles, The Rolling Stones, and even Bob Dylan, he didn't leave much in the way of cover versions on the official albums he released during his lifetime. Also, in some ways his style – particularly as a guitarist, but also as a singer and songwriter – was so unlike anything that had preceded it that it was hard to accuse him of pinching certain licks from certain songs. Certainly there was little if anything similar to, say, the opening riff of "Purple Haze" or the feedback of "Are You Experienced?" on prior records.

Yet dig a little beneath the surface of the four albums he put out before his death, and there are plenty of clues as to where he was getting much of his inspiration, though he rarely resorted to imitation. On the many live albums and BBC sessions that found official release after his death, there were quite a few cover songs, always done the Hendrix way, but nonetheless clues as to what he had listened to or was absorbing. Now that we know more about his pre-fame years, we have a much better picture of who he saw and played with on the chitlin' circuit. In interviews, he would occasionally cite some personal heroes, with his associates mentioning other names on the many occasions they talked to the media after Hendrix wasn't around to speak for himself. We even know quite a bit about which records he collected, although it will be impossible to ever compile a comprehensive list of these.

Indeed, Hendrix drew from so many musical sources that sometimes the problem is not so much finding the influences as sorting through all the people he is known to have admired and learned from. And while some critics have claimed he owed primary allegiance to one genre or another, an overriding feature of Jimi's music was eclecticism and open-mindedness, creating something new from the synthesis of his roots. As wide as those roots were, though, it seems undeniable that his single strongest core stylistic influence was the blues, followed in rough order by soul, British rock, Dylanesque-folk-rock, early rock'n'roll, jazz and bits and pieces from some pretty unpredictable directions. And even those categories don't encompass everything he lent an ear to: Nashville country-guitar virtuoso Chet Atkins and king of western swing Bob Wills are just a couple of the masters from other genres he admired.

Hendrixology

The Blues

At the back of the booklet that comes with the CD compilation *Jimi Hendrix: Blues*, there are pictures of no fewer than 33 outstanding blues musicians, as sort of a composite of greats from that tradition who influenced Jimi. There's some poetic licence in the inclusion of Curtis Mayfield, undoubtedly a heavy Hendrix influence but undoubtedly much more a soul star than a bluesman. Yet that still leaves 32 cats who emerged from the blues tradition, even if a couple of them, Ike Turner and Chuck Berry, went on (like Jimi himself) to make their primary mark in rock music. It might seem like an exaggeration to include so many faces in the pantheon, but if anything it under-represents the scope of blues musicians to whom Hendrix listened.

While blues wasn't the only music to which Jimi was exposed before he started playing guitar, it was probably the kind he heard the most, and the one to which he first formed a strong attachment. His father Al has remembered owning singles by the likes of B.B. King and Muddy Waters, and if it seems like perhaps he should have been spending more cash on shoes that fitted his young boys' feet than such indulgences, as a poor young man Jimi himself would similarly spend money on records before taking care of the basic necessities. He might have heard more gutbucket stuff from the 78s of a boarder the family took in for a while, Ernestine Benson, who given Al's wayward behaviour might have even been around the house more than his father was at the time.

Like many kids coming into adolescence in the 1950s, Hendrix turned his attention to rock'n'roll with the explosion of talents like Elvis Presley, Little Richard and Chuck Berry – all of whom owed much to the blues, but all of whom undeniably took it somewhere else. In the early-to-mid-1960s, however, Jimi seemed to drift back toward the blues, perhaps as a result of living for extended periods in the South for the first time. Though he wasn't playing sideman only to bluesmen at the time – more often, he was in early soul outfits – virtually all of those soul performers would have known much about the blues, as would their audiences.

A whole book could be written about which blues musicians specifically influenced Hendrix, and the 28-page booklet of liner notes that comes with the original 1994 edition of *Jimi Hendrix: Blues* is a useful place to learn more (though its speculation that Jimi learned many tricks from journeyman bluesman Eddie Kirkland in Georgia in 1956 seems highly improbable). A few of the more notable ones can be highlighted here, however. Certainly the fluid, expressive, stinging soloing of **B.B. King** is echoed in much of Hendrix's work, and Jimi of course honoured B.B. by covering King's "Rock Me Baby" live, at the Monterey Pop festival and elsewhere. Like King, Hendrix would sometimes do a sort of call and response between his vocal lines and solo guitar riffs (check out "Red House" for proof), though King did this because he couldn't play and sing at the same time, a feat that Hendrix never found difficult.

Albert King – a blues influence from Hendrix's chitlin' circuit days

Jimi also honoured Muddy with a number of cover versions in his stage performances, radio sessions and studio outtakes, including "Mannish Boy" and "(I'm Your) Hoochie Coochie Man". From Waters, whether consciously or unconsciously, it would have been a small step for Hendrix to check out other Chicago electric blues on the **Chess label**, and he certainly adopted one such number, Howlin' Wolf's "Killing Floor", to devastating effect, even using it to open his set at Monterey.

Several other Kings of the blues, in a quite literal sense, made their mark on Hendrix besides B.B. He had met **Albert King** on the chitlin' circuit, and would have been impressed not only by his burning guitar tone, but also by his ability to comfortably mix blues with funky soul – and play it left-handed. The Band of Gypsys would later record King's signature tune, "Born Under a Bad Sign", as a studio outtake. **Freddie King** had yet more crossover appeal between blues, soul, and white rock audiences with both vocal and instrumental numbers, and Jimi might have even digested his influence second-hand via Freddie's considerable stamp upon a young Eric Clapton, who played King's hit "Hideaway" on his monumental early blues-rock album as part of John Mayall's Bluesbreakers in 1966. Unpredictably, however, one of the only three covers the Experience put on their late-1960s studio releases was "Come On (Let the Good Times Roll)" by a far more obscure bluesman with the same last name, **Earl King**.

Bob Dylan is rightly usually cited as Hendrix's primary vocal influence, but it seems that Jimi took his share of attitude and phrasing from **Muddy Waters** as well, especially when he adopted a tone that was at once both playful and boasting. "Voodoo Child (Slight Return)" is the illustration most often trotted out, but you can hear traces even in some out-and-out psychedelic pieces like "If Six Was Nine".

As for some other things Hendrix would have soaked up, he would likely have learned about using the whammy bar to create blasts of reverberant sound from his short time in the band of **Ike Turner**, another musician blending blues with soul and rock'n'roll. From **Elmore James**, he might have derived the idea of producing slide-guitar-like effects – his swoops at the end of the verses of "Foxy Lady", for instance – though without using the conventional bottleneck techniques heard on James records like "Dust My Broom" and "The Sky Is Crying". From **Buddy Guy**, he might have picked up some ideas about hard, overdriven, sustained fuzzy tones, as well as – if he saw him live as well as heard him on record – some notions about crowd-pleasing showmanship. And whether in person or by word of mouth, he might have learned some other onstage gimmicks, as well as more conventional lessons about clean blues soloing, from **T-Bone Walker**, a big name in blues and R&B since the 1940s, and another guy noted for playing behind his back and executing athletic splits while playing his instrument.

Judging from what was divulged (in the April 1996 issue of *Guitar Player*) about the Hendrix record collection Kathy Etchingham auctioned to Sotheby's in 1991 for £2420 (now in the possession of the Experience Music Project), Jimi was quite a fan of **Lightnin' Hopkins**, a Texas bluesman comfortable with both country and electric styles. That collection – probably just a partial selection, it should be noted, of the discs Hendrix accumulated over the years – also included records by **John Lee Hooker**, **Jimmy Reed**, **Junior Wells** and both the first and second **Sonny Boy Williamson**, among other blues artists.

Additionally, Hendrix wasn't blind to work by top white bluesmen, owning several LPs by **John Mayall** (including ones on which **Eric Clapton**, future Fleetwood Mac founder **Peter Green**, and future Rolling Stone **Mick Taylor** took the position of Mayall's featured guitarist) and harmonica virtuoso **Charlie Musselwhite**; of course he'd briefly also played in the group of one white blues singer, **John Hammond**, who might have been more open to white rock'n'roll elements than other bandleaders. He also knew where the electric blues had come from, as he also had records by rural country blues greats **Robert Johnson**, **Blind Blake** and **Leadbelly**, even if Jimi would rarely play acoustically as those men had.

"People will argue with me, but I tell you, that guy was a bluesman", Etchingham told *Guitar Player*'s James Rotondi. "Anybody who tells me he would have become a jazz musician – well, balls to them". She went on to explain how Jimi would fit in with whoever he was playing with, whatever style they played – whether it was jazz or whether it was folk. But that, when it came down to it, blues was his touchstone.

Soul

As much as Hendrix liked blues, he didn't want to be a great bluesman so much as to pull its sensibility into a jet-age era with overpowering volume and innovative guitar effects. Plus he probably wouldn't have been satisfied with appealing mostly to a specialized blues audience, looking to cultivate crossover appeal to people who liked several different kinds of music. These weren't the only reasons he liked (and, before leading his own bands, often played) soul music, but they probably came into consideration. Blues was barely known to white audiences when Hendrix started playing guitar professionally; soul music was becoming the most popular music of choice for American blacks, as well as making far deeper incursions into the pop charts.

It's tempting to identify Hendrix's key soul influences as the acts he backed up in his days on the chitlin' circuit. The list usually reproduced by biographers is subject to incompleteness and inaccuracy as at least some of it seems based on speculation and hearsay, but it would include Hank Ballard, Solomon Burke, Jerry Butler, Sam Cooke, King Curtis, Chuck Jackson, The Marvelettes, Otis Redding, Carla Thomas, Tommy Tucker, Jackie Wilson and Bobby Womack. **The Isley Brothers** would have probably been bigger influences and mentors than most of them owing to Hendrix's longer, more involved stint in their band, though it seems to have been their raucous rock'n'soul rather than their gospel-derived harmonies that left any lasting imprint. Even **Curtis Knight**, as much of a mediocrity as he was, deserves some begrudging credit for giving Jimi some opportunities – albeit ones that ended up backfiring on Hendrix after the Experience became huge – to put a little modern rock into his brand of soul.

One soul legend, however, stands out above all others in regard to his effect on Jimi, as well as perhaps being the single most underrated influence on Hendrix: **Curtis Mayfield**. Many of Hendrix's less flashy, more melodic, more graceful and – dare we say it – tasteful riffs bear Mayfield's stamp, even if they sometimes took a relative back seat in Jimi's arrangements as transitional or responsive lines rather than solos. Similarly, although Hendrix's rhythm guitar work is pretty unheralded in comparison to his frenzied riffing, much of Mayfield's choked, choppy style of chording as leader of his 1960s group The Impressions also seems to have made an impression on Jimi. "Hey Joe", "The Wind Cries Mary" and "Little Wing" are some of the songs on which echoes of Mayfield's guitar style are apparent, and while Curtis's gorgeous upper-register vocals weren't as easy for Hendrix to emulate, the way Hendrix sings *Electric Ladyland*'s "Have You Ever Been (To Electric Ladyland)" seems like an obvious homage. Mayfield was also one of the earliest and best soul songwriters to branch out beyond the usual romantic R&B lyrics to incorporate social commentary urging brotherhood, and one imagines that this didn't pass unnoticed by Hendrix either.

As for Hendrix's other soul faves, it would be fair to say that he much preferred harder, grittier, more **Southern-flavoured soul** to the sweeter and poppier sound of Motown, lush Philadelphia harmony groups and New York "uptown" pop-soul. It's no accident that two such songs, "Land of a Thousand Dances" (probably modelled on the Wilson Pickett hit treatment of the song) and Don Covay's "Mercy, Mercy" (on which he had played as a session man), were part of the early Experience's repertoire in the absence of many or any Hendrix

Hendrixology

The Jimi Hendrix LP Collection: Odds and Sods

It came as little surprise to most Hendrix fans to learn that much of his LP collection was devoted to blues artists, with good-sized servings of contemporary rock groups and Bob Dylan, as well as a smattering of singer-songwriters and jazz. Less expected were some comedy, novelty, country and other miscellaneous vinyl which served as a reminder that, no matter how well you think you know someone, if their record collection's big enough, it will include some items for which you would never have suspected the owner had a taste.

Some of the more offbeat titles of the collection Kathy Etchingham eventually auctioned off would include Holst's *The Planets* and Handel's *Messiah*, the latter perhaps in tribute to the former occupant of the house next door. Another major classical composer was represented by *Bach on the Pedal Harpsichord*, performed by pipe organist E. Power Biggs, while contemporary avant-garde works were on hand via Pierre Henry's *Le Voyage* and John Lennon and Yoko Ono's famously unlistenable debut collaboration, *Two Virgins*.

There was also gospel singer Clara Ward's *Hang Your Tears Out to Dry*; Johnny Cash's *At Folsom Prison*, a very popular LP on both sides of the Atlantic in late 1968; The Bonzo Dog Band's fine comedy-rock piece *The Doughnut in Granny's Greenhouse*; Ravi Shankar's *Sounds of the Sitar*, given to Jimi by buddy Brian Jones; George Harrison's 1968 soundtrack *Wonderwall Music*, which one suspects might have been a personal gift from the artist; and crazed cult Texas psychedelia by The Red Crayola. Weirdest of all may have been The Zodiac's *Cosmic Sounds*, psychedelic ambient music with one song for each sign of the horoscope, featuring some of the first use of the Moog synthesizer (by Paul Beaver) on a popular music recording.

Naturally, mixed in with all these were discs by other non-blues artists that you'd kind of expect Hendrix to like, such as Otis Redding, James Brown, Dr John, The Spencer Davis Group (Stevie Winwood's first band) and Joe Cocker. So what was Jimi's favourite of the lot? According to Etchingham, it was the 1964 LP *I Started Out As a Child* by none other than Bill Cosby – not exactly the most hip and timeless of comedians, and yet another instance of Hendrix not just playing the unexpected on his guitar, but also playing the unexpected on his turntable.

originals. It's a good guess that the biting economy of the riffs by guitarist **Steve Cropper** in **Booker T. and the MGs** instrumentals like "Green Onions" found favour with Jimi, as did that band's overall simmering, organ-laced groove, traces of which can be heard in "Rainy Day, Dream Away" and "Still Raining, Still Dreaming". And whether or not Hendrix or anyone else involved in his early solo career gave it deliberate thought, the success of the MGs' interracial line-up set a heartening precedent for The Jimi Hendrix Experience.

Hendrix was probably a fan of many records Booker T. & the MGs played on at **Stax Records** in Memphis by the likes of **Wilson Pickett** and **Otis Redding**, which often used a beefy horn section as well. As odd as it might sound now, at both the beginning of the Experience's career and the end of his life, Jimi expressed a wish to play as part of a much bigger band with horns. It's hard to imagine how he could have integrated his very loud, very busy guitar work into such a setting, but it's one of several intriguing directions that he is rumoured to have considered pursuing without getting the chance to do so.

British Rock

Although some accounts have suggested that the **British Invasion groups** that stormed the US charts in the mid-1960s meant little or nothing to black American popular musicians, in fact many of them were taking notice and admiring the best of these groups, especially The Beatles. In one sense, they would have been irresponsible not to: The Beatles, Rolling Stones and other UK acts were selling so many records that at least checking out what the competition was up to was a necessity. There's no doubt that Hendrix himself was one of the more open-minded listeners to the new wave. "He bought all the popular records from people like the Stones, The Animals, some Beatles records, because he had a wide variety of taste", Curtis Knight told the Hendrix fanzine *Jimpress*. "He was always someone who spent a lot of money in a record store, always. I mean, almost every penny he got, he didn't spend it on a guitar, or an amplifier, he spent it on records."

Hendrix was probably particularly struck by those British bands that used a harder, more ferocious guitar sound than just about anything going on in the States at the time, and was more in line with what he was hear-ing as possibilities in his own head than what he was finding on even the wildest Chicago blues platters. The early **feedback, distortion** and **sustain** employed by **Jeff Beck** on **Yardbirds** hits like "Shapes of Things", "I'm a Man", "Over Under Sideways Down" and "Happenings Ten Years Time Ago" probably exerted the greatest influence, and while **The Who** were almost unknown in the US before 1967, it wouldn't be a surprise if he had been turned on to the primitive but earthshaking feedback used by **Pete Townshend** on "My Generation". Although he and **The Rolling Stones** (apart from Brian Jones) don't seem to have taken to each other particularly, the **fuzz tones** of Keith Richards on hits like "(I Can't Get No) Satisfaction" and "19th Nervous Breakdown" – sometimes thought by critics to be something of a substitute for actual Stax-like horns – might have impressed Jimi too. He also thought highly enough of **Them**'s classic raunchy rocker "Gloria", written and sung by Van Morrison, to make it one of the few white rock tunes he covered in the studio, though it wasn't released until after his death.

In the year and a half or so after he moved to London in September 1966, of course, Hendrix got to witness many of the British groups and guitarists first-hand. This had an impact not only upon his guitar work, but also his song-writing, which adeptly wedded pop hooks to his more R&B/blues-rooted foundation. Perhaps in part due to his friendship with **Eric Clapton**, Hendrix chose to honour **Cream** with one of the few British rock tunes he covered live, the proto-hard-rock, riff-laden "Sunshine of Your Love";

Hendrixology

he may also have been inspired to play **wah-wah guitar** after hearing Clapton's performance on the spring 1967 B-side "Tales of Brave Ulysses". (He didn't actually employ wah-wah on record, however, until he heard Frank Zappa use it at a New York concert that summer, overdubbing a wah-wah on "Burning of the Midnight Lamp" immediately afterwards.)

Like almost everyone else on the scene in the 1960s, Hendrix paid close attention to **The Beatles,** and it's no accident that the other two British rock songs he covered were "Sgt. Pepper's Lonely Hearts Club Band" and "Day Tripper". As someone heavily interested in expanding the use of the studio as a recording instrument in its own right, he would have listened especially intently to their records – not just *Sgt. Pepper*, but also *Magical Mystery Tour* from late 1967, another item in his collection – as they got more sophisticated from the production end. It's known that he kept on listening at least up to the end of the 1960s, since *Abbey Road* was also one of the LPs he owned.

It comes as a surprise to many fans to learn that Hendrix also had a sweet spot for fey British pop-rock that made the Beatles sound as brutal as, well, Hendrix in comparison. One of the LPs on his shelf was **The Bee Gees'** 1967 LP *First*, which he and Etchingham, she told *Guitar Player*, used to listen to "quite a lot. Jimi thought their harmonies were really great." Yet more surprising was his fondness for the 1967 single "I See the Rain" by the Scottish group **Marmalade,** a mildly psychedelic pop-rock flop with Beatlesque harmonies.

Bob Dylan and Folk-rock

Bob Dylan's influence on Hendrix loomed so large that it's covered at length in the main text of this book. It's known that Jimi virtually wore out some of his Dylan LPs from repeated plays, especially *Highway 61 Revisited* and *Blonde on Blonde*. It wouldn't have been the guitar work on Dylan's records that impressed Hendrix (though Mike Bloomfield had some penetrating blues-rock leads on *Highway 61*) so much as the lyrics, vocal delivery and attitude (and, on the cover of *Blonde on Blonde*, semi-Afro hairstyle). Dylan also probably gave Jimi much-needed courage to sing in a style that favoured personality over conventionally pretty vocalizing, and the licence to be poetic in his wordplay. **"All Along the Watchtower"** became a hit in Jimi's hands, and he also covered Dylan's "Like a Rolling Stone", "Can You Please Crawl Out Your Window?" and "Drifter's Escape". Etchingham told *Guitar Player* that Hendrix also considered covering "I Dreamed I Saw St Augustine", but thought it was "too personal".

Hendrix's love of Dylan, however, didn't seem to extend to the many talented folk-rock singer-songwriters who followed in Bob's wake, at least to the point of letting them audibly influence his music. No covers of, say, Leonard Cohen, Donovan, Tim Hardin or Joni Mitchell songs cropped up in his repertoire, although it's known that he met Mitchell and much liked her music when he heard her in

Dylan in his Mayfair hotel room, London, 3 May 1966

most Dylan interpreters, **The Byrds**. It's likely, though, that he got The Byrds' *Fifth Dimension* – which, unlike many of their LPs, didn't have a single Dylan song – at least as much because of Roger McGuinn's Indian-jazz-tinged psychedelic twelve-string guitar work (as heard on the record's most famous song, "Eight Miles High") as because of an affection for the group's jangly folk-rock.

Rock'n'roll

Because Jimi Hendrix's psychedelic rock seemed so far removed from rock's beginnings, it might also surprise some devotees that he would also count classic 1950s rockers as primal influences. True, this might have been as much due to their role in firing his personal ambitions as love of the music, and also a product of a time when so many more of his teenaged peers would have been into Buddy Holly than Muddy Waters. But there's no question that he was a genuine fan of **Elvis Presley, Chuck Berry** and **Little Richard**, though his enthusiasm for the last of these legends dimmed considerably after having to work under his thumb as a mid-1960s sideman. **Duane Eddy** was an early guitar hero for his use of thick echoing twang, as was **Eddie Cochran**, who pioneered power chording and self-studio-overdubbing (and some of whose LPs Hendrix still owned in the late 1960s).

Canada in March 1968. He did, however, keep the odd singer-songwriter/folk-rock LP around the flat, with albums by Tim Buckley, Richie Havens and Roy Harper turning up in his collection. And of course, "Hey Joe" was at its root a folk song by Billy Roberts, with the folk-rock cover by Tim Rose probably influencing Hendrix's arrangement.

Interestingly, Jimi also had all-Dylan cover albums by Joan Baez and The Hollies in his collection, as well as a couple by the fore-

While Hendrix's rock'n'roll roots can seem submerged under his galactic sonic stew, he would unveil them from time to time. He paid tribute to Elvis in a BBC version of **"Hound**

Dog" – originally an R&B hit for Big Mama Thornton, true, but it's obvious from the track that Jimi modelled his performance on Presley's version. Berry's **"Johnny B. Goode"** made for a great performance (subsequently issued on both LP and CD) at Hendrix's May 1970 gig in Berkeley, at the soundcheck for which he ran through **"Blue Suede Shoes"**, the Carl Perkins rockabilly classic which also became identified with Elvis. And while he might have clashed with Little Richard over who had the right to wear pretty threads and hairstyles, it's likely that Hendrix picked up some of his outrageous fashion sense – the loudly coloured ruffled shirts and head scarves, for instance – from his time backing the Georgia Peach, though Jimi stopped short of wearing the lipstick and mascara also favoured by his one-time boss.

Jazz

Although Kathy Etchingham forcefully denied that jazz was a big influence on Hendrix, Jimi did have a few jazz records in the flat they shared, including a collaboration between guitarist Wes Montgomery and organist Jimmy Smith, a couple by pianist Jaki Byard and one by Charles Lloyd. Basically, though, Etchingham seems on sound ground in her assertion that jazz simply wasn't one of Hendrix's main bags, although certainly some of his solos and rhythm work (check the opening chords of "Third Stone from the Sun") have a jazzy tinge. He is known to have liked **Roland Kirk**, whose simultaneous multi-instrumentalism would have appealed to Jimi's sense of nervy rule-breaking, and probably took in some **Miles Davis**, if only in preparation for the mooted collaborations that never came to pass.

It would be going too far to say that Hendrix was pushed into jazz on some of the late-1960s jams – with jazzmen like Larry Young and John McLaughlin as occasional participants – which form some of the most ill-lit corners of his official and unofficial discography. But it's likewise going too far to say that this was certainly the path he would have taken if hard-hearted suits hadn't stood in his way. Some jams have been held up as indications of a new jazzy direction, but as Peter Doggett wrote in *Jimi Hendrix: The Complete Guide to His Music* of Alan Douglas's claim that Jimi was moving into jazz in his final years, "more accurate would be the acknowledgement that Hendrix loved to jam".

Rarities and Oddities

As extensive as the Jimi Hendrix official discography is, the story doesn't quite end there, especially if you're determined to track down every last track that's leaked out through official and semi-official means. Hundreds of hours of additional material circulate on bootlegs and unauthorized releases in the form of live concerts, studio outtakes, and even some home recordings. Hendrix also found time, even after he achieved stardom, to play on some records by other artists as a guest or session musician, as well as to make a few modest forays into producing acts other than himself. There are also a few nifty official oddities that even some devout fans might have missed, so low is their visibility.

This chapter isn't a complete listing of all such Hendrix oddities and rarities – just to give basic details on the bootlegs alone would require an entire book. Instead, it's a look at selected highlights of what's available in this area, all of which illuminate some aspects of his artistry that aren't always evident in his standard discography.

Book/CD

Jimi By Himself: The Home Recordings (available as CD bound into *Voodoo Child: The Illustrated Legend of Jimi Hendrix*)
Berkshire Studio Productions, November 1995

Not quite part of his official legacy on record, yet certainly available through legitimate means, was the 26-minute CD *Jimi By Himself: The Home Recordings*. Offered as a bonus with a graphic novel telling Jimi's life story via comic-book illustrations/narrative, it's not quite Hendrix unplugged, as he's actually playing a very lightly amplified electric guitar. But it is Hendrix accompanied by nothing other than his own guitar and voice, working out some songs on his own in a Manhattan apartment in spring 1968 (though the book in which this is packaged doesn't reveal this, or indeed any other useful details about the tapes).

Though brief and somewhat rambling, capturing Jimi running through incomplete compositions and fragments that don't seem to have yet cohered into a whole, these recordings – with very good, clear sound quality – have considerable charm. For they show Hendrix at his most personal and gentle, and frankly, after you've heard dozens of higher-profile releases which almost unceasingly highlight his scorching loud leads, the low-volume intimacy of the setting is a mighty refreshing change of pace. The apparently works-in-progress tunes are quite good as well, including "1983... (A Merman I Should Turn to Be)", "Angel" (an obviously major composition he took surprisingly long to get around to seriously working on in the studio), and "Gypsy Eyes". "Voodoo Chile" isn't in a highly developed state at this point, and "Hear My Train A Comin'" and "Cherokee Jam" are likewise something of improvisational throwaways, but not without their appeal, both for the informality of the performances and as insights into Jimi's creative process.

As for the accompanying book, it laid out the essentials of Hendrix's life in floridly illustrated panels that were reasonably faithful to the events, though some poetic licence was inevitably taken in dialogue reconstruction, and the mystical overtones of the artwork and narration might seem over the top to earthier readers. The CD was the big attraction for more serious Hendrix fans, although a fair number of them already knew that you could find plenty of such extra-official material – if not that many other home recordings – on bootlegs. Which brings us to our next section...

Bootlegs/Unauthorized Releases

When rock bootlegging took off at the very end of the 1960s with the appearance of Bob Dylan's 1967 *Basement Tapes* with The Band, outtakes from The Beatles' January 1969 sessions for what was then titled the *Get Back* LP (and re-titled *Let It Be* when some were

compiled for an official 1970 album), and live performances from The Rolling Stones' late-1969 US tour, it was only natural that superstars such as Jimi Hendrix would be next in line. Certainly, **Hendrix bootlegs** were appearing on vinyl as early as 1970, when some jams (including Juma Sultan and Jerry Velez, who played in the short-lived ensemble that accompanied him at Woodstock) circulated on an LP titled *This Flyer*. Other bootlegs – of live concerts and even BBC radio sessions – soon followed, and the stream has continued unabated in the CD era.

The early 1970s also saw the appearance of a number of **unauthorized releases,** which – despite their being available, unlike the aforementioned bootlegs, in mainstream record shops – were certainly not approved by Hendrix (or, after his death, by whoever was controlling his estate at the time). In a sense, the very first such LP appeared back in 1967, when some of his pre-Experience recordings were packaged, with his name prominently billed, as *Get That Feeling*; even if it was on a major label (Capitol), however, Jimi and his managers certainly hadn't authorized it. And although two LPs (*Experience* and *More Experience*) taken from the soundtrack of the film made of Jimi's Royal Albert Hall show on 24 February 1969 appeared on the UK Ember label in 1971 and 1972 respectively, the legality of the recordings is still disputed by Experience Hendrix, which obtained a summary judgment against *The Sunday Times* for giving away a CD of material from the concert with its 10 September 2006 edition. Other such unauthorized releases have made their way into official commercial retail outlets from the 1970s to the present day.

It's impossible to say exactly how many Hendrix bootlegs and unauthorized releases have appeared, especially since similar material is often reissued under different titles. The situation has become murkier still in recent years, now that so much unreleased material – by Hendrix and countless other artists – is exchanged and downloaded over the Internet, by methods whose legality is still in doubt. A survey of some of the more comprehensive websites and books in which various Hendrix bootlegs and unauthorized discs are listed, however, indicates that at least five hundred have been pressed at one point or another. And now that file-sharing is so prevalent, it seems unlikely that this material will ever be out of circulation, as much as official bodies try to put a stop to it, and even though CDs have declined in popularity as the vehicle for distributing it.

Now that so much previously unissued live and studio Hendrix has been made officially available, however, whether on standard MCA/Experience Hendrix CDs or Experience Hendrix's collector-targeted Dagger imprint, there's frankly much less need for even ardent fans to investigate this underworld. As is the case with many bootlegs (and some relatively easy-to-find unauthorized discs), much of this material is of low fidelity with substandard packaging; even some of the good-sounding, good-looking ones offer little in the way of variation from the other versions of the same

songs on official releases. So the question becomes: is there *anything* of note only available through such channels?

The answer is a qualified yes – the qualification being that you need to appreciate this material for the insights it offers into Hendrix's musical development, rather than as something comparable to the Hendrix albums that have been packaged for mass consumption. As for Jimi's studio recordings, quite a few outtakes have recently appeared on CDs on the Reclamation label, complete with pretty official-looking artwork, bar codes, and a note indicating that they've been manufactured under licence from the estate of Jimi's former manager, Michael Jeffery. This isn't, needless to say, the same organization as the Experience Hendrix outfit that administers Jimi's own estate, and these are certainly not authorized by Experience Hendrix, though you can get them from some quite high-profile outlets.

No matter what your view on the morality of its availability, however, virtually every Hendrix fan would have to concede that Reclamation's ten-CD box set **In the Studio Volumes 1–10** contains an enormous repository of studio outtakes from throughout his career, usually in very good sound quality. Even taken a volume at a time, however, this will wear out the patience of the average listener, much of it being devoted to marginally different alternate versions/mixes, rambling jams and halting works-in-progress. Unlike, say, Bob Dylan, Hendrix didn't record an appreciable number (barely any, actually) of complete and interesting unreleased songs; and unlike, say,

Hendrixology

The Beatles, he didn't even record a handful of songs in versions with significantly different and worthwhile arrangements.

If you've got the stamina, though, the Reclamation recordings will give you a fly-on-the-wall picture of Jimi trying out and perfecting ideas in the studio, as well as the odd curiosity that's interesting in its own right, such as a February 1969 version of "Sunshine of Your Love" and nine minutes of work on the backing track for "Can You See Me". Weirdest of all is an instrumental backing track for the French pop tune "La Poupée Qui Fait Non", cut during sessions for *Are You Experienced?*, though it's anyone's guess as to how it could have fitted onto that LP. Especially valuable is an entire 64-minute disc of low-volume home recordings from early 1968, seemingly taken from the same source – or at least performances taped around the same time in very similar circumstances – as the ones used on the much shorter *Jimi By Himself* CD distributed with the *Voodoo Child* book.

Also of significant value in completing the picture of Hendrix's work in the studio – though likewise, not offering the greatest entertainment value for the average Hendrix fan – is Reclamation's **Message to the Universe**. This is in fact an expanded version of sorts of the 1980 LP *Nine to the Universe*, which though an official release has never been issued on CD. It's the record that's cited more than any other as an example of Jimi's appetite and facility for studio jamming, as well as – particularly the "Young/Hendrix" jam, with jazz organist Larry Young – an illustration of some of the jazz directions into which he might have been heading. In fact, however, it's more for students of Jimi's playing than anything else, since the five instrumental jams on the original LP don't have anything in the way of conventional tunes, though "Easy Blues" has a nice, loping, cool jazz-blues groove. The Reclamation CD version presents unedited versions of the songs from *Nine to the Universe* and adds five other similar jams (with occasional vocals) from the same era which seem even less fully baked. Indeed, for all its lesser fidelity, if you're looking for inspired Jimi soloing in a jam setting, you might be better off with the 17 March 1968 New York live recording *Cafe Au Go-Go Jam Session*, where he really lets rip on "Jamming Wing" (which melodically resembles "Little Wing" in some respects).

With so much live Hendrix in print in his official catalogue, the many concert bootlegs floating around will only be of interest to hardcore fans. This is especially true when you consider that there really isn't much in the way of atypical shows in which Jimi played songs rarely heard elsewhere, or in a style or context in which he seldom played in other circumstances. Among the gigs that Dagger Records somehow hasn't made available yet, however, one standout is **Stockholm Concert**, an approximately two-hour double-CD set issued by Purple Haze in 2004. Recorded in very good sound on 9 January 1969 (a couple of songs from the same date can be seen on the official *Experience* DVD), it captures the late-period original Experience in a somewhat more jammy and sombre mood than usual, including a few songs ("Killing Floor", "I Don't Live Today", "Spanish Castle Magic", "Sunshine of Your Love") not heard over and over again on other Hendrix live recordings. Experience Hendrix certainly didn't approve of its release, however, successfully challenging Purple Haze's right to distribute it shortly after it came out.

As to whether yet more unreleased Hendrix of fine-to-dubious sound quality will find its way into circulation, there seems little doubt that there's more being hoarded somewhere. For details on what's floating around and what's known/speculated to exist, see Steven Roby's book *Black Gold: The Lost Archives of Jimi Hendrix*.

Hendrix as Producer

Hendrix undoubtedly had both the artistic acumen and technical expertise to make him a good producer. Both officially and unofficially, indeed, he produced many of his own recordings, especially in the later part of his career, but only acted infrequently in this capacity for other artists. In part this was probably because he directed so much energy into his own music, both inside and outside the studio. When one considers how much difficulty Jimi was having in completing his own studio projects in 1969 and 1970, however, one wonders whether he would have been the best candidate for other musicians in need of some direction.

The two LPs that Hendrix had a hand in producing for other artists were curiously unlike the music released under his own name, and Jimi probably wouldn't have been given the role

if all three hadn't shared Mike Jeffery as manager. The production of **Cat Mother and the All Night Newsboys'** *The Street Giveth and the Street Taketh Away* is co-credited to Hendrix and the band. Distinctive for its frequent use of multi-instrumentalist Larry Packer's violin, it's otherwise pretty run-of-the-mill if versatile late-1960s rock, with nods to funky good-time roots sounds and wistful light psychedelia with harmony vocals, though it did produce a medium-sized US hit single in 1969 with a medley of 1950s rock oldies titled "Good Old Rock'nRoll". Better is the Irish band **Eire Apparent**'s *Sunrise*, from the same year, in part because Hendrix plays on some tracks, though it's rather pleasantly middling late 1960s psychedelia with far more of a pop flavour than the Experience. (To be strictly accurate, Jimi produced most, not all, of *Sunrise*, being credited as producer for all but two tracks.)

Hendrix's production of half of **Buddy Miles'** *Electric Church* in 1969 was less of a surprise, as Miles played with him in the Band of Gypsys and as a sideman on assorted studio recordings. It's actually a not half-bad soul-rock LP, Miles's singing and songwriting holding up much better when he doesn't have to suffer direct comparison with Hendrix's abilities in these departments, as he did on *Band of Gypsys*. As a not inconsiderable bonus, Jimi himself adds tasty wah-wah guitar to the instrumental "69 Freedom Special", as well as more straightforward R&B licks to "Miss Lady". Hendrix also produced a session for **Noel Redding** in August 1968, which resulted in an early version of a song later included on the first album by Redding's band Fat Mattress, though tensions between the pair were such that it's not surprising they failed to collaborate again in this manner.

Because he had so much invested in Electric Lady Studios both financially and artistically, one imagines that if Hendrix had lived, he would probably have tried his hand at producing some of the artists using the facilities. It's yet another road he didn't take, and one can only guess as to where it might have led him.

Hendrix as Session Man

For someone who was seemingly up for jamming with almost anyone, anytime, Hendrix made surprisingly few appearances as a **session man** on other artists' records after 1966. Part of the problem might have been contractual: it's hard to imagine Mike Jeffery being too happy about his prize client's talents being lent out to anyone else. Another factor might have been reservations on the part of other artists: as much as they might have admired Jimi's guitar playing, they might not have wanted it dominating their own records, and doubted whether it would be easy to persuade him to tone himself down in the service of the song at hand. Or perhaps Hendrix himself had had enough of doing sessions after his unrewarding work as a sideman in his pre-Experience days. (For an overview of the best such pre-1967 sessions Jimi played on, see the box in the second chapter of this book.)

The only really popular album on which Hendrix made a guest appearance was **Stephen Stills**' self-titled 1970 solo debut LP – a rather good and underrated singer-songwriter folk-rock effort, though not too similar to Jimi's own music – to which Hendrix contributes an admirably tense extended solo on "Old Times Good Times". In March that same year, he teamed up with his old buddy **Arthur Lee** at a recording session in London for Lee's group **Love**. But "The Everlasting First", the one track to be issued from the session – on the aptly titled *False Start* – was pretty unmemorable hard rock, Lee having passed his peak as a songwriter and Love having gone downhill after the break-up of its mid-1960s line-ups left Arthur as the only original member. It's been reported that Hendrix recorded a fair amount of other material with both Love and Stills, though none of it has yet gained official release.

Much more offbeat was a one-off 1969 collaboration (unissued until 1984) with **Lightnin' Rod** of the Alan Douglas-produced group **The Last Poets**, "Doriella Du Fontaine", on which Hendrix played guitar and Buddy Miles handled drums and organ. The instrumental track is a relatively workmanlike soul-jazz groove, though Lightnin' Rod's rapping – replete with urban sex'n'drugs references – anticipates hip-hop by a decade. Yet by far the weirdest of any project in which Hendrix was involved (with the possible exception of a mid-1960s Jayne Mansfield single – see page 23) was another Douglas production which featured **Timothy Leary**, the self-styled "high priest" of LSD. Jimi plays bass on one cut, "Live and Let Live", on Leary's 1970 spoken-word album *You Can Be Anyone This Time Around*, which matched his pseudo-hip aphorisms to a very basic – indeed, rather dull – blues-rock-psychedelic jam with Stephen Stills, Buddy Miles and ex-Lovin' Spoonful leader John Sebastian.

One of Hendrix's best moments as a session man was also one of his most obscure. In January 1968, he and Noel Redding played on three tracks recorded by **McGough and McGear**, namely Roger McGough and Mike McGear (a.k.a. Mike McCartney, brother of Paul) of the British comedy group **The Scaffold**. One song, "Oh to Be a Child", later surfaced on a Scaffold album, but is only notable for the fact that it features Jimi, not on guitar, but on toy drum. The other two appeared on the duo's 1968 *McGough and McGear* LP, a fine slice of period comedy-pop-rock that would have appealed to Hendrix, who gained a solid appreciation of British humour in his relatively short time as a UK resident. Of that pair, "So Much" is a good power-poppish number, and "Ex-Art Student" a terrific satirical psychedelic pop-rocker with sunny high Beatlesque harmonies, given an extra push by Hendrix's wah-wah guitar in the lengthy instrumental break.

What might have made for the most interesting Hendrix session appearance of all never actually took place. In 1968, when **Donovan** wrote his classic psychedelic song "Hurdy Gurdy Man", his original hope was for Jimi himself to record it. When producer Mickie Most convinced the folk-rocker that he should make it his next single instead, Donovan still hoped to get Hendrix to at least play on the track. By this time, however, Jimi was understandably too busy to make it, although the smoking guitar solo on the hit that resulted – variously attributed to Jimmy Page, Alan Parker and Allan Holdsworth – ensured that nobody missed him all that much.

Hendrixology

Books and Websites

Books on Hendrix

Just as Jimi Hendrix's catalogue of recordings is amazingly large considering he spent just four years cutting music under his own name (and only managed to get four albums out during that time), so the literature about him is quite extensive for someone whose career was so short and who died at the age of 27. Several dozen books have been written about Hendrix – including but not limited to biographies, memoirs and music guides – and no doubt more will be written in the future.

For all the depth in which he's been documented, however, much mystery continues to surround Hendrix. It's not just because the years preceding his move to London in September 1966 – which actually constitute the overwhelming majority of his life, including more than half of his time as a professional musician – remain cloudy in terms of exactly what he was doing when and where. It's also because the man himself remains an enigma in many respects when it comes to determining what drove him; where his extraordinary creativity came from; why he showed so much confidence in so many areas, yet failed to assert himself in so many others; and where he would have gone next had he survived. Of course,

these very qualities are the ones that drive biographers to keep examining what might have made him tick, even if the ultimate answers are unknowable.

This overview of books about Hendrix does not pretend to be comprehensive – to do so would almost take a book in itself. Instead, it focuses on the best and most useful volumes that have been published, which together form about as well-rounded a picture of Jimi and his music as is available at the time of writing.

Hendrix Biographies

**John McDermott with Eddie Kramer:
Hendrix: Setting the Record Straight**
Warner Books, 1992

Although it might be more weighted toward the music than the man (in part because of the participation of Eddie Kramer), this remains, more than fifteen years after its publication, the best place to start for a general overview of Jimi Hendrix's life and career. Highly readable

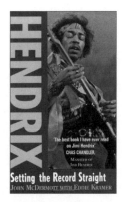

and extremely detailed, it has the best balance between coverage of his recordings, his prowess as a concert performer, his technological and studio innovations, his business difficulties, and his personal strengths and failings. Though Kramer was an insider in Hendrix's circle as his favoured recording engineer, the book isn't blind to Jimi's weaknesses, and takes a lot of angles into account when examining his triumphs and failures. Inevitably, a lot of additional information has been unearthed since the book's publication in 1992, but much of it has been uncovered by McDermott and Kramer themselves in the course of their research for numerous Experience Hendrix CD/DVD/book projects, and is included in the text for these.

Janie L. Hendrix and John McDermott:
Jimi Hendrix: An Illustrated Experience
Simon & Schuster, 2007

While the basic bio forming the text of this 64-page coffee table book is a serviceable overview of Jimi Hendrix's life, the real attractions are the photos and, above all, some inserts of scrapbook-like memorabilia. These include reproductions of childhood drawings; letters and postcards to his father; gig posters; the handwritten lyric to "Purple Haze"; and his handwritten instructions for the *Electric Ladyland* cover artwork. As you'd expect from a book co-written by Jimi's stepsister and copyrighted to Experience Hendrix, it's not too critical of the late musician, and even with all the perks it's overpriced. Fans will like the rare mementos, though, and the

inclusion of a bound-in CD with more than seventy minutes of interviews and rare music – mostly recorded at a March 1968 concert, although there's also a long November 1969 Hendrix–Buddy Miles studio jam – helps to ease the financial pain.

Harry Shapiro and Caesar Glebbeek:
Jimi Hendrix: Electric Gypsy
St Martin's Press, 1995

While there's inevitably some overlap with the later (and usually better written) books in this section, and some of its findings – like those of McDermott and Kramer's bio – have been superseded by subsequent research, *Electric Gypsy* remains a highly worthwhile Hendrix biography. Like *Setting the Record Straight*, it's more recommended to fans of Hendrix the musician than to those looking for insights into Hendrix the human being, although these aren't lacking. At about 750 pages, it's certainly comprehensive, and if some of the more technical information might not be for everyone, it's valuable to have. The inclusion of unusual photos and some handwritten letters/lyrics are good bonuses.

Charles R. Cross: Room Full of Mirrors:
A Biography of Jimi Hendrix
Hyperion, 2005

For those who want more on Hendrix the man, this recent biography gives much more attention to Jimi's inner conflicts, contradictory behaviour and personal relationships. As a long-time Seattle-based rock journalist, Cross was especially well positioned to

Hendrixology

research Hendrix's boyhood, and this volume has by far the most in-depth coverage of his pre-army years, drawing upon first-hand interviews with many friends, relatives, and neighbours. It also gives the most detailed run-down of his 1961–66 struggles to establish himself as a professional musician, and if only the critiques of his music and creative evolution after moving to London were as thorough, this would indisputably be the best Hendrix biography. There's still much to learn from the sections on Hendrix the star, Cross steering clear of both harsh judgment and forgiving idolatry in his assessment of Jimi's character and achievements.

Hendrix Recordings

Steven Roby: Black Gold: The Lost Archives of Jimi Hendrix
Billboard, 2002

A guide to the vast hoard of unreleased Jimi Hendrix recordings – studio and live – that's known to exist, or even speculated to exist, going all the way back to his teenage years in the late 1950s. Like *Jimi Hendrix Sessions* (see below), this has more to offer the Hendrix fan than the less obsessed listener might guess, providing not only details of what exists and where and when it was recorded, but also analysis offering insights into Hendrix's music which might not be available through standard sources. It's true that, unless you're a serious devotee, you probably wouldn't want to hear all the jam sessions Roby describes. But it's certainly interesting to read about all the people Jimi played with at one time or another, as well as the numerous odd/ambitious projects that were unfinished, such as the *Black Gold* concept album of sorts which gives this book its name.

Sean Egan: Jimi Hendrix and the Making of "Are You Experienced"
A Cappella, 2002

An excellent, passionate 200-page volume on the genesis and realization of what's ultimately – though many fans might hotly dispute it – Hendrix's best and most influential album. Egan interviewed plenty of people, both central and peripheral, for fresh insights, including Noel Redding, engineer George Chkiantz, musical device-maker Roger Mayer, girlfriend Kathy Etchingham, early Hendrix champion Linda Keith, Monkee Micky Dolenz and even Philip Jose Farmer, who wrote the science-fiction story that helped to inspire "Purple Haze". Egan not only covers the recording of the album itself, but also the formation of the Experience and the sto-

ries behind the songs, also offering opinionated track-by-track analysis (of all the cuts from both the US and UK versions) that isn't afraid to go against conventional critical wisdom. One wishes there were similar volumes for *Axis: Bold as Love* and *Electric Ladyland*, and there is indeed a much smaller one on the latter (as part of Continuum's 33^1/$_3$ series of mini-books on classic rock albums) by John Perry, though it's more oriented toward aesthetic criticism than historical research.

John McDermott with Billy Cox and Eddie Kramer: Jimi Hendrix Sessions: The Complete Studio Recording Sessions
Little, Brown & Co., 1995

Written by the leading Jimi Hendrix authority (McDermott) with two people (Cox and Kramer) who were often there at the time, this day-by-day guide to Hendrix's recording sessions is a necessary volume for anyone seriously interested in his music. It's not just a reference as to what was done when, though much of that information is here: it's written to be *read*, with many comments from musicians and technicians involved in cutting the tracks, as well as entertaining anecdotes and commentary on the music itself, giving an insight into Jimi's creative processes. The only substantial criticism is one that can't be held against the authors – some of the information about, and session tapes of, the recordings seem to have been unavailable for scrutiny. An updated edition planned for publication in 2009 will also include descriptions of all Hendrix's concerts between 1963 and 1970.

Peter Doggett: Jimi Hendrix: The Complete Guide to His Music
Omnibus Press, 2004

While this compact-size volume is on the slim side (160 pages), it's an extremely handy guide through the jungle of Hendrix's discography, especially if you're overwhelmed by its sheer size and just want a handle on where to find what. Veteran British rock historian Doggett offers succinct rundowns not just on the main studio and live albums, but also the mass of reissues, compilations and posthumously released material that's flooded the market. Includes not only the high-profile releases, but also some "grey area" unauthorized discs and off-the-wall limited-edition collector-oriented productions, taking care to note differences between various editions of the same album. Refreshingly, it's not a dull facts'n'figures book either, Doggett making quite sharp and witty critiques which aren't afraid to take labels to task for not doing things right.

Hendrix the Musician

Keith Shadwick: Jimi Hendrix Musician
Backbeat, 2003

What better title, indeed, for a book focusing on Jimi Hendrix the musician? Actually it's a superb, nearly coffee-table-sized, 250-page examination of Hendrix's artistic evolution in all departments, though particularly as an instrumentalist and recording artist. There's a lot of off-the-beaten track information here, especially on the pre-fame years and his formative influences, with a good third of the text devoted to the period pre-dating his move to London. While this might be a little more musician-oriented than most other Hendrix books, it's by no means exclusively for players or gearheads. It's clearly and accessibly written so that anyone interested in Jimi will get a lot out of it, with plenty of stories you might not have come across elsewhere. Lots of fine photos and excellent layout/design, too.

Hendrix the Songwriter

David Stubbs: Voodoo Child: Jimi Hendrix: The Stories Behind Every Song
Carlton, 2003

While this doesn't quite feature every song Hendrix recorded (even if you're only looking at major official releases), it does cover most tracks most listeners would consider to be a significant part of his canon, including all of his originals (and covers) from the discs he released under his own name during his lifetime. Stubbs doesn't just cover the specific circumstances which motivated/inspired Jimi to write his tunes, although plenty of these are noted; he also delves into vivid descriptions of the tracks themselves, as well as how the themes reflected events in both Hendrix's life and the overall times and society in which he lived. His style won't always be to everyone's liking, occasionally lapsing into smugness, and he's not afraid to aim some stinging putdowns at tracks some fans might hold dear, calling (for instance) the opening riff of "Highway Chile" "horribly prescient of Deep Purple at their most weedily portentous". Still, it's a well-done guide to Jimi's songwriting – an essential aspect of his craft sometimes overlooked by those who focus on his amazing guitar work and wild image – covering the tracks from not only the major three studio albums and *Band of Gypsys*, but also most of the major posthumous releases.

Hendrix Memoirs

Noel Redding and Carol Appleby: Are You Experienced: The Inside Story of the Jimi Hendrix Experience
Da Capo Press, 1996

While Noel Redding's autobiography is more detailed and more of a standard tome than Mitchell's (see below), it's frankly much more of a slog, if not without its redeeming qualities. The first half of the book is the better part, and if the detailed remembrances (aided by Redding's diary) might be a little on the dry side for some readers, at least his meticulousness ensured more accuracy when retelling the events years later. Even during the Experience, however, Noel seemed by far the most prone of the three to dissatisfaction, particularly with management and money matters. After he left, those frustrations multiplied, and the last sections of the book get quite exasperating as Redding dives deeper and deeper into the legal side of the many ways he got screwed financially by the music business. Many of those complaints are justified, but it doesn't make them any less exhausting to read, ultimately rendering it a chore to finish the volume.

Mitch Mitchell with John Platt: Jimi Hendrix: Inside the Experience
Harmony, 1990

Some readers might have wished for something more comprehensive, and perhaps more controversial, in Mitchell's account of his Experience days. Presented in close to coffee-table format, it linked extended Mitchell quotes with text outlining the basic progression of the Experience, embellished by numerous pictures and poster reproductions. Yet on the whole it's quite entertaining, with lots of good road stories and some studio recollections, and not a few insights into the musical dynamic of the Experience (with both Noel Redding and Billy Cox). It's also quite even-tempered, upbeat and balanced in its views of the Experience's ups and downs and its members' personalities – and, as such, quite a contrast to Redding's own memoir detailing largely the same journey.

Miscellaneous Hendrix Books

Chris Potash (ed.): The Jimi Hendrix Companion: Three Decades of Commentary
Schirmer, 1996

Just over two hundred pages of articles written about Hendrix from 1966 to the mid-1990s, encompassing record reviews, concert reviews, interviews, essays on specific aspects of his craft and more. The sheer scope of this anthology ensures that very few people will enjoy everything here, but also guarantees that everyone will find at least a few pieces that interest them.

Johnny Black: Jimi Hendrix: The Ultimate Experience
Thunder's Mouth Press, 1999

A sort of day-by-day guide to the life of Jimi Hendrix, detailing the major events of his career in chronological order, though most of this 250-page book covers the four years immediately preceding his death. Not a mere list of dates and occurrences, it's punctuated by tons of direct quotes from many of his associates and acquaintances, quite a few of which are hard to find elsewhere. For that reason, it actually makes far better conventional sit-down reading than you'd think, packed with lots of interesting stories. It's marred, however, by its failure to give the specific sources of many of the quotes, lots of which are taken from interviews other than those conducted by the author.

Hendrix Websites

EarlyHendrix.com
Ⓦ earlyhendrix.com

This site's mission is "to collect information about the pre-fame career of Jimi Hendrix, i.e. the years he spent as a backing musician before the formation of The Jimi Hendrix Experience in October 1966." There's still a long way to go before this period is fully documented (if it ever is), but there's a lot of information or at least informed speculation here, including a discography of records on which Jimi's "confirmed" to have played; a discography of discs on which his appearance has been rumoured but is, in the view of this site, "unconfirmed"; and a timeline overview of his activities during the era.

Hendrixology

The Jimi Hendrix Record Guide
Ⓦ pagesperso-orange.fr/hendrix.guide/hendrix2.htm

Extensive details on Hendrix's official and unofficial albums, as well as pre-fame appearances, side projects, home recordings, singles, interview discs and so on. The descriptions are more passionate than polished, but there's a lot of interesting trivia here if you have the patience, as well as some rarely seen record covers.

JimPress
Ⓦ jimpress.co.uk

One of the two major Hendrix fanzines, published twice a year. Subscriptions and many back issues, as well as larger specialized publications on Jimi's recordings and video footage produced by the same organization, can be ordered through this site.

Just Ask the Axis
Ⓦ digitalhighway.co.uk/axis/index.asp

Searchable database of information on Hendrix's live shows, and evaluations of the sound quality of recordings made at the same.

The Official Jimi Hendrix Website
Ⓦ jimi-hendrix.com

As this site is administered by Experience Hendrix and geared toward the merchandising of his catalogue, you shouldn't expect too much in the way of unflattering or esoteric information. Still, it does have a lot of useful info about his DVDs and CDs, including mail-order-only releases on the Dagger label designed for the Hendrix collector; various news items

regarding Hendrix archive projects and exhibits; back issues of the long-discontinued Experience Hendrix magazine; and some recordings available as webcasts and streaming audio exclusively through the site. Although the front page looks very good, some aspects of the design and functionality were at the time of writing surprisingly awkward the deeper you dig, and some of the content is incomplete or doesn't seem to have been updated for years.

Plug Your Ears
Ⓦ osiris.cs.kun.nl/~tvdw/pye/index.html
"A comprehensive guide to the audio and video recordings of Jimi Hendrix", with lots of nuts-and-bolts details about what was captured on tape and film where, though little in the way of additional commentary.

UniVibes
Ⓦ univibes.com
The website of one of the most respected Hendrix fanzines doesn't actually offer a lot in the way of content, though it does have a few interviews, reviews and miscellaneous info of interest to the Jimi obsessive. It's through this site, however, that you can subscribe to and order many back issues, which are filled with in-depth specialized info.

www.hendrix-links.de
Ⓦ hendrix-fans.de/index2.html

A roundup of links to sites with some Hendrix content, useful for finding pages with a very narrow Hendrix-related focus.

Index

Index

Index

Index